LIVE WELL BETWEEN YOUR EARS

110 WAYS TO THINK LIKE A PSYCHOLOGIST, WHY IT MAKES A DIFFERENCE, AND THE RESEARCH TO BACK IT UP

Doug Spencer, Ph.D.

Produced by:

FriesenPress

Suite 300 – 852 Fort Street
Victoria, BC, Canada V8W 1H8

www.friesenpress.com

Distributed to the trade by The Ingram Book Company

TABLE OF CONTENTS

For Charlie, Jocelyn, Kiley, Sophia, and Tully.
From your Grandpa who was too far away.

Acknowledgments

Thanks to the editors and designers at friesen press. to the editors for their careful reading and useful suggestions, and to the designers for creating a clean look from front to back. Thanks to my account manager, Ceilidh Marlow, for her cheerful and prompt answers to all my calls for help. Special thanks to Darlene Roney for the hours she spent on the phone listening to me read many of these columns. Her common sense and insight led to the addition, deletion, or change of many words and sentences.

INTRODUCTION

MOST PSYCHOLOGICAL THOUGHTS AND ADVICE COMES TO US FROM day-time talk shows, poorly referenced self-help books, or something on a bumper sticker. This book is different. In language anyone can understand, it offers the scientific research behind the bumper sticker advice.

Understanding of the language, concepts, and science of psychology can help us deal more effectively with negative feelings such as stress, depression, anxiety, and anger. Alternatively, it can help us find and maintain happiness, contentment, courage, patience, and self-esteem.

The 110 short chapters in this book were originally published as newspaper columns between mid-2011 and mid-2013. They are organized into six broad themes that address: motivation, psychological health, education and science, happiness, relationships, and change and technology. Each one ends with my wish that you live well between your ears, a phrase meant to describe the good feeling that comes with a content life, free of mental and emotional turmoil. I hope that wish comes true.

I
MOTIVATION

WHY DO WE DO WHAT WE DO, THINK WHAT WE THINK, AND FEEL WHAT we feel? Why do we love, argue, kill, and hate? We've wanted answers to these questions since we've been on the planet. Psychologists began addressing these questions in the late 1800's and they've made considerable progress.

For the most part, we can't do much about the genetic and electro-chemical factors that play a role in motivation, other than live a healthy life style, and chose to eat for fuel rather than for taste. Similarly, we can't change anything about our past—good or bad. But, by understanding personality characteristics such as field dependency, self-esteem, internal or external locus of control, and many others, we can change our interpretation of past events and our reaction to them.

The chapters in this section focus on why and how we are motivated, and why some people achieve so much and others so little. What role is played by our many personality characteristics, our values, our courage, our ability to make decisions, and our time management skills? The way we manage stress, how effectively we talk to ourselves, the expectations we have, and our need to achieve balance between what we think, feel, and do are only some of the factors used to understand many of the these questions.

WHY KNOWLEDGE OF
PSYCHOLOGY HELPS

"When we are no longer able to change a situation,
we are challenged to change ourselves."

– Viktor E. Frankl, *Man's Search for Meaning*

REALLY! YOU'VE GOT TO BE KIDDING! I CAN HARDLY BELIEVE MY EYES
when my TV describes some disease I've never heard of and the medicine needed to "cure" it. The medicine is worse than the disease! The TV
guy says the side effects can include Lord knows what: dizziness, vomiting, back pain, itchiness, and sudden bowel movement. I can handle
itchy—but a sudden bowel movement? I don't think so.

To make matters worse, the diseases are described so generally we
believe we have them. Then what? Convinced to take the medicine, we
risk the forewarned, but unexpected bowel mishap, and as you stand
panic stricken in the checkout line, your worst nightmare runs down
your leg.

What's the point? The point is when you get sucked into the TV
diagnosis and buy the new medicine to control what you think are your
"symptoms", you could, actually and metaphorically, end up filling your

pants. Living well between your ears is about trying to prevent that, not so much at the physical level, but at the psychological level.

For example, if you learned the language and customs before you visited a foreign country, you would feel safe and would be able to navigate stress-free. Similarly, when you know the language and concepts of psychology, you are better equipped to conquer life's challenges and the self-doubt that comes with them. It's when your mind is focused, not racing from thought to thought and doubt to doubt.

Knowing the language helps you live well between your ears. Not plagued by fear and anxiety, you are confident and unafraid. You know where you are going and you have a plan to get there. The plans will change, they always do, but it won't matter because you trust yourself to always adapt and move forward. In short, it's about maintaining a good feeling in your head, between your ears.

An example of a psychological concept that eliminates confusion and helps us understand everyday events first originated with Witkin and Asch (1948b).They researched two types of cognitive style: field-dependency and field-independency. It's a concept that remains current in psychological research. Field-dependent people rely more on outside cues from the environment to make decisions, while field-independent people rely more on bodily sensations or internal cues.

For example, field-dependent people are more likely to lose their balance when skiing in whiteout conditions. It's because they rely on external, visual cues such as the angle of descent, the trees, and the bumps, to help them navigate down the mountain, and those cues are made invisible by the whiteout.

For the same reason, don't let the field-dependent guy drive in a blinding blizzard. He relies on road signs and highway lines, but they aren't visible in a snow storm. Conversely, the field-independent guy is more attuned to internal cues, such as wind gusts sensed through the steering wheel and bodily sensations of moving left or right. Consequently, he has a better chance of staying out of the ditch.

More recently, Larsen and Buss (2005) reported that each type has their own strengths. Field-independent people are able to analyze complex situations more effectively because they can ignore distractions, and field-dependent folks have stronger social skills because they are more attentive to context. Both of these cognitive styles are present in all of us to varying degrees, but one or the other will be dominant. Neither is better than the other, and they aren't a disease or something to worry about.

But what if you didn't know about this difference in cognitive style? After discovering that your buddy never fell when skiing in a snowstorm while you couldn't ski ten feet without falling, you might conclude there was something wrong with you—maybe a neurological disorder! Isn't it better to know it is normal and not a disorder? You certainly don't need medicine or its trouser-filling side effects.

The conclusion: knowledge of the language and concepts of psychology may explain the symptoms you think you have. Inform yourself before you swallow the latest medicine, and live well between your ears.

TALK TO YOURSELF

"Your self-talk is the channel of behavior change"

– Gino Norris, author of *Stress Diary*

TALKING TO OUR SELF IS SOMETHING MOST OF US DON'T WANT TO BE caught doing. We believe it occurs in children to facilitate language and cognitive development in their immature minds. In adults it is a sign of feeblemindedness due to advanced age or illness. Since we prefer to appear adult-like, and in full control of our faculties, we don't talk to ourselves—at least not out loud.

But all of us talk to ourselves sub-vocally; we think the thoughts or say them inaudibly. For example, after doing something dumb you may mumble, "That was stupid." If you say it aloud it will draw puzzled looks. And, if we talk out loud to ourselves often, at least in the presence of others, our goofiness score will definitely rise. Friends and family will think we are child-like, getting feeble, going crazy, or perhaps all three. But this column encourages you to talk out loud; to yourself, by yourself, and about yourself, without fear of being immature, old, or crazy. Talking out loud versus just thinking the thoughts has much greater impact (Spencer, 1978). In fact, done in a positive, constructive fashion, it may be one of the most helpful things you can do to live well between your ears.

Most commonly we engage in negative self-talk. It becomes a habit we don't realize we're doing. It's when we make statements like, "I have no will power" or "I'm always tired" or "I can't get it right". When we say such things we hear them, and over time, they have a negative impact on how we act and feel.

Suppose, as a kid, your parents always said that you were slow? It would shape your attitudes and behaviour. It's no different when you say it to yourself. What we say to our self is heard, registers in our little noggin, and eventually becomes part of who we are; it's a self-fulfilling prophecy. While damaging, negative self-talk is common; constructive, positive self-talk is rare.

Hhmm, you say, I'll be damned if I'm going to walk around talking to myself. The point is you already do, but it's mostly negative and it's mostly just thoughts or sub-vocal speech. The suggestion here is that you make it positive and do it out loud—but by yourself. When you are troubled, worried, confused, upset, indecisive, lonely, or feeling down, you may be surprised at how quickly you start to feel better when you have a little heart to heart chat with yourself. There is scientific evidence and bucketsful of anecdotal support for the usefulness of self-talk.

Joseph Jordania (2009) even suggests that talking to oneself has evolutionary significance. Since our warring ancestors interpreted silence as a sign of impending danger, it became stressful to remain silent. People who experience long periods of silence become stressed and anxious due to this evolutionary connection, and talking out loud is one way to relieve the stress. Of course, you could also turn on the TV or listen to your iPhone, but it isn't the same. Actual self-talk has received support from a variety of sources.

In a 2007 Sports Medicine journal, Gibson and Foster reported that task specific self-talk had a beneficial effect on physical performance. They also found corresponding neural activity associated with self-talk in the left frontal cortex and left temporal regions of the brain. Sports psychologists have found strong evidence for the importance of self-talk on enhanced performance. As far back as the seventies, psychologist Sandra Bem recognized the significance of self-talk to help shape gender identity and self-concept.

The relationship between what we think, what we say, what we do, and what we become, has been studied extensively. When thoughts and words come from our own mind and mouth they have just as much impact as they do when spoken by a significant other.

India's 20th century leader and philosopher, Mahatma Ghandi, articulated the mechanics of the process best when he said: "Keep your thoughts positive because your thoughts become your words. Keep your words positive because your words become your behaviours. Keep your behaviours positive because your behaviours become your habits. Keep your habits positive because your habits become your values. Keep your values positive because your values become your identity." It's a description of how thoughts and words create who we are, and it is a strong endorsement for the value of constructive conversations you have with yourself.

When we are troubled and confused our mind becomes thought soup. Our attention flits from one worrisome thing to the next so that focus on any single thought or idea is impossible. If it persists it becomes inca-pacitating, creates anxiety, and you get nothing done. You can fix this by talking to yourself—constructively and out loud.

As you carry on this conversation—asking and answering your own questions—the issues become clearer and your mind becomes more peaceful. You must be honest. Ask the tough questions, and answer those questions the way your inner wisdom says you should. Lying will do no good. You may not solve all the issues, but you will clarify them. Having this type of discussion with yourself reduces the soupiness of your thoughts. Continue the conversation with yourself for twenty minutes or less. Any longer, and I find I'm ready to stop to let things solidify.

Both sides of your personal conversation may go something like this: "Alright, settle down. Why don't I feel better? What's bothering me? Well…..you're worried that you haven't heard from your son for a while. Exactly how long has it been? Three weeks. Have you said or done any-thing to upset him? No, I haven't—at least I don't think so. His life is busy. I know I will talk to him soon. I will phone him tonight."

Making a commitment out loud to take action (I will phone him tonight) helps solidify what you need to do and it enables you to move forward with the conversation.

The self-talk may continue:

"What else is bothering me?"

"I feel like my spouse may be drifting away from me. Or, am I drifting away from her?"

"Yes, I think I am."

"How can I tell?"

"Well, I talk to her less frequently and I don't feel as loving toward her."

"Is she maybe drifting away from me too?"

"Yes, maybe."

"Do I want to improve the relationship?"

"Yes, I do. Does she?"

"Yes, I think so."

"So what needs to happen for the relationship to improve?"

"As always, I guess we need to have some communication about it."

"What, exactly, has she said or done that makes me think she is distancing herself from me?"

"What exactly will I say to her when we talk?"

You get the idea. Be sure you ask yourself what you really want to have happen. Ask tough questions; not watered down wishy-washy questions. What are your goals regarding the issues you want to address?

Your conversation will focus around troubling situations in your life. The only thing your self-talk will have in common with the examples above is honest questions and answers. Just imagine you are two people: one seeking answers, the other supplying them. Ask the difficult questions and be brutally honest with your answers. Most times we know what a wise person would tell us if we asked them a tough personal question. Be that wise person.

So when you're feeling anxious, depressed, indecisive, or less content than you like, talk to yourself—out loud. Ask questions to get to the bottom of your feelings. In the beginning you'll feel self-conscious. Do it anyway. It will help, and you'll have a laugh or two. Let your honest questions and answers provide clarity, and live well between your ears.

DRUMMING IN FIJI:
CAN THOUGHTS BECOME REALITY?

"All that we are is a result of what we have thought."

– Buddha (563 BCE-483 BCE)

I RETIRED AND MOVED BACK TO SASKATCHEWAN AFTER 28 BUSY YEARS in Colorado and California. I live in a little house in a little town, play my drums, write a column for some newspapers, and life now is plain. The one thing I'd still like to do is be a drummer in an old guys' rock band somewhere in the South Pacific. I've thought of being able to kick back, write during the day, and play four nights a week. But they're just idle thoughts, so life goes on. However—there's this nagging thread of discontent—I'm not really doing what I like.

A while ago, I saw a movie called *The Secret*. It was adapted from Rhonda Byrne's (2006) book by the same name. It said things I'd read before about the power of thought to transform my life. The movie made me think. I realized that most major decisions I'd thought long and hard about ultimately happened: good and bad.

The movie urged me identify my greatest passion, focus on it, visualize it, put up pictures, and write out statements or affirmations to describe the life I want, as though I lived it right now. So, what the hell, I drum up some statements and find some pictures. The statements were: I write in the afternoon and drum at night. I play my drums four nights a week in an old guys' rock band. Life in Fiji is warm, interesting, and filled with music. And the pictures: drums, clear blue ocean, even a palm-thatched stage with a band playing—middle aged guys and girl singer. Perfect.

I started out strong. Pictures went up and statements were spoken, but in a month I looked back and realized I hadn't paid attention to the pictures, I quit saying my statements, I couldn't remember visualizing anything, and I lost track of the passion. But, the nagging little thread was still there.

I went back to the drawing board and dug out information to rediscover important pieces of the puzzle that had been under my nose all along. It was exactly what I needed to explain why thoughts could create my reality.

The explanation lies at the heart of Leon Festinger's (1954) idea of Cognitive Dissonance, a theory of motivation that has stood the test of time. It simply states that it is impossible to hold two conflicting thoughts in your mind without doing something about changing one of them. It creates an uneasiness called dissonance.

In my case, one set of thoughts about an exotic life drumming in Fiji was radically dissonant with the other set of thoughts of who I am today—a boring guy doing boring things. Those two thoughts don't go together. I was lying to myself. To achieve consistency, my exciting Fiji thoughts had given way to less exciting thoughts about staying at home and doing—well—nothing much. Staying home and doing nothing had become consistent with being a boring guy doing boring things, and I was back in my comfortable rut.

The theory also says that when you have thoughts that are in conflict, the ones you give up first are the ones that take the least effort to change—most often the newest ones—because they are aren't as firmly entrenched.

With that new information it was easy to see that my thoughts of being a regular guy in a regular town doing regular things were more firmly established than my thoughts of drumming in Fiji, cavorting in the warm ocean, and sitting on my thatched porch enjoying a rum and coke.

But, the nagging little thread, why is it still there? It's there because I'm still not doing what I want. In addition, I know for a fact there are ordinary people who do extraordinary things. I've seen interviews with successful people who, when asked about their turning point, say, "I just decided I had to do it." Or, "I've always been focused on this." Or, "I got tired of not following my passion, so I quit my job and jumped in." And, I think to myself, I didn't quit anything, didn't jump anywhere, and I lost my focus. So I try again.

Up go the pictures, out come the drums, the South Pacific map gets tacked to the wall, and I start my affirmations. But this time I say them often throughout the day since I don't want to lose my focus again. I persist because I was reminded that it's impossible to hold two conflicting ideas for long. I also know that the thoughts and behaviors that I've held the longest are going to be the most difficult to change. So I constantly tell myself to stick to my goals to assure that my new thoughts—my Fiji thoughts—become the strongest. In a nutshell, I become passionate about playing in the South Pacific.

And, sure enough, the uncomfortable feeling of dissonance and living a lie started to melt away. I began checking on the cost of living and air fares to Fiji. I shared my plan with my friend. She knows someone who knows a bass player in Fiji. I heard from another friend who knows someone in the south pacific. I emailed them both and asked questions about bars with bands, opportunities, and musicians. The pieces of my new jig saw puzzle of life magically began to fall into place.

All this is happened because I immersed myself in my passion. I stayed with it until my stubborn thoughts of being a boring guy, doing boring things, were replaced by more frequent thoughts of playing in Fiji and being an adventurous guy, doing exciting things.

For me, while I'm not yet living, writing, and drumming in Fiji, the message is clear: Persist. Understand how the power of affirmations is rooted in the notion that actions will become consistent with strongly held thoughts. Hold on—relentlessly—to the thoughts that reflect your desired outcome, and live well between your ears.

STRAIGHT TALK ABOUT
SELF-ESTEEM

"Believe in yourself! Have faith in your abilities! Without a humble but reasonable confidence in your own powers you cannot be successful or happy."

– Norman Vincent Peale

ARE YOU FRUSTRATED WHEN YOU HEAR TALK SHOW HOSTS, CELEBRITY guests, and other modern-day gurus talk about the importance of self-esteem, but then leave you in the dark about what it is, how it develops, or how to improve it? This column may shed some light on those omissions.

What is self-esteem? Simply defined, it is our sense of self-worth. It stems from how we evaluate ourselves. It is relatively stable, but fluctuates throughout life, depending on our current satisfaction with our skills and characteristics. Such satisfaction, or dissatisfaction, depends on three broad outcomes: (1) positive or negative feedback from others, (2) whether we fail or succeed to meet expectations, and (3) how well we measure up when we compare our skills and characteristics with those of others.

Commonly thought of as confidence, an inadequate level of self-esteem makes us less competent, less daring, more anxious, less in control, more stressed, less successful, unhappy, less content, more insecure in our relationships, and sicker with more physical ailments. It's a nasty list.

If the volume written about it is any indication, it's a big deal. According to the American Psychological Association, more than four thousand articles on self-esteem appeared in psychology journals between 2005 and 2010. Google provides over 58 million results and Amazon has over 92,000 items with self-esteem in the description. Apparently, it's a popular topic. Although high self-esteem is a good thing, we don't worry about it unless it's in the tank.

So, how do we know whether our self-esteem is high, low, or in the middle? It's done with tests or questionnaires which ask us if we agree with statements such as, "at times I feel worthless". The problem is most of these tests provide no indication how to improve self-esteem because they focus on general feelings instead of specific attributes.

Many years ago, when I was working on my Ph.D., I developed a test to measure self-esteem: the VIP Self-Esteem Scale. I obtained responses from 453 people who listed over 100 different personal skills and characteristics that they believed influenced their self-worth. Further analysis reduced this number to 27 which were common to both men and women, occurred most frequently, and were judged by more than 400 people to be most important. The test is based on how we rate our satisfaction with these 27 items. It provides four scores: one for your verbal, interpersonal, physical, and over-all self-esteem. More importantly, it shows which of these contribute most or least to feelings of self-worth.

The research indicated that verbal self-esteem stems from our satisfaction with 6 skills: our ability to express ourselves, our intelligence, our power of concentration, and our comprehension, thinking, and listening abilities.

Reading more non-fiction, and discussing what you've read with others, is one way to enhance these verbal skills. Reading adds knowledge; discussion with others forces you to concentrate, listen carefully, clarify your thoughts, and express them well, all of which promote high self-esteem.

Interpersonal self-esteem grows out of satisfaction with 12 characteristics: our helpfulness, friendliness, sense of humour, facial appearance, openness, honesty, degree of tenseness and nervousness, complexion, temper, shyness, level of vanity, and confidence in our movements.

The list itself provides clues for increasing interpersonal self-esteem. For example, we can learn to control our temper, overcome shyness, or be less self-centered. Research also tells us that people with high self-esteem smile more often, are more open about their feelings, initiate conversation, and develop stronger social bonds with others.

You might wonder, as I did before I examined the data, why facial appearance and complexion affect interpersonal rather than physical self-esteem. It's because we lead with our face. We don't worry about facial appearance until we're in front of people; it's more an interpersonal rather than a physical factor.

Physical self-esteem is a function of our satisfaction with 9 characteristics: our health, agility, athletic ability, neatness, walk, shape, posture, weight, coordination, and clothes.

Getting plenty of exercise, working all your muscle groups, developing new skills, choosing food for nutritional value rather than for taste, and doing whatever it takes to improve these characteristics, increases physical self-esteem.

The bottom line is that self-esteem grows out of satisfaction with specific verbal, interpersonal, and physical abilities and characteristics. Dissatisfaction with any of these characteristics is more devastating to our self-esteem when we are in the presence of others than when we are by ourselves (Lyttle, Spencer & Perry, 1976). Anything you can do to improve these factors, for you and the people you care about, will increase self-esteem for everyone and help them live well between their ears. The complete scale and how to score it is at www.livewellbetweenyourears.com.

ARE YOU LIVING A LIE?

"Never try to do anything that is outside of who you are.
A forced smile is a sign of what feels wrong in your heart,
so recognize it when it happens.
Living a lie will reduce you to one."

– Ashly Lorenzana, author

THE OLD GUY VOMITS IN HIS FOOD. THE NURSE CLEANS IT UP WITH A
smile and says, "It's okay, just a little accident", but you head for the exit.
The crazed druggie screams and kicks to get out of the patrol car. The cop
is out there dealing with it, while you roll over and go to sleep.

Spend some time with a dying person or a doper waving a gun and see
how you like it. At the very least it's exhausting. At worst it's terrifying.
Try it for a month. What if it was your job? Most of us prefer to avoid
sadness, disgust, fear, and revulsion. But if you're a cop or a critical care
nurse you can't; they're a regular part of your job. You're in up to your
eyeballs, calmly trying to make things less tense. But there's a problem.
Feeling upset, but concealing those feelings and acting normal, creates
emotional dissonance—the topic for today.

In 2006, Bakker and Hueven studied stress and job burnout among
police officers and nurses, and guess what they found? Their jobs are

stressful and cause exhaustion, cynicism, depersonalization, impaired job performance, and eventually, job abandonment or burnout. They also reported that when we try to hide negative emotions that eat at us daily, physical problems and illness begin to surface, including high blood pressure and cancer.

The critical part of this is not the vomit or the druggie. It's living a lie that's the problem; feeling negative but portraying positive. It's called emotional dissonance, a term rooted in cognitive dissonance, a concept first introduced by psychologist Leon Festinger in1954. It's when your actions contradict your beliefs and you feel conflicted. For example, you gorge on chocolate when you know it's bad for you; or you doubt God exists, but pray anyway. But, with emotional dissonance, it's not conflict between *beliefs* and behaviour that is the problem. It's the conflict between *feelings* and behaviour that causes stress.

Your insides scream danger, but you have to act like everything is fine. A steady diet of this contradiction eventually leads to debilitating stress and perhaps illness. If you're the cop or the nurse you have two choices: convince yourself not to feel that way, or quit your job. The first choice is not an option. It's difficult, if not impossible, to deny the feelings because of how we're wired. Faced with dangerous or negative situations, our automatic hormonal responses produce fear and sadness whether we like it or not. Quitting, the second choice, is ruled out too, assuming the cop and nurse need a pay cheque. But there is help.

According to Bakker and Hueven, relief comes when you talk about it and get it off your chest. When the police and nurses developed supportive resources and created opportunities to vent, discuss, take breaks, and compare notes, rather than keep the emotions bottled inside, the negative effects were lessened.

Is any of this relevant for those of us who aren't cops or nurses? Yes. Emotional dissonance doesn't care if you are a cop or a nurse. It can happen in relationships. It shows up when you experience prolonged dissatisfaction, anger, or fear which you never express because to do so creates too much hassle. When you feel the negative emotions but have to put on a happy face to smooth things over, the stress of emotional dissonance goes to work.

If emotional dissonance is part of your life, believe the research and don't keep it bottled inside. Find a way to vent those feelings or remove yourself from the situation. If nothing else, realize that dissonance-produced stress is normal, that you don't have to live a lie, and choose to live well between your ears.

HARNESS THE POWER
OF YOUR MIND

"Man's mind once stretched by a new idea,
never regains its original dimension."

– Oliver Wendell Holmes

MOST OF MY LIFE I'VE HAD THIS STUBBORN BELIEF THAT I SHOULD BE more than I am. I don't know how to take advantage of the capacity that I think is there—in my head—somewhere between my ears. No, I don't believe I've been especially blessed with any surplus of skill, intelligence, or alien influence. We all have greater capacity for achievement and personal fulfillment, but most of us don't quite know how to get there.

There are processes that take place in our unconscious mind that—if we knew how to harness them—would enable us to live a better life and achieve our wildest dreams. I frequently hunt for relevant scientific articles to better understand these processes. Sometimes I find bits and pieces.

Many years ago, and again a few nights ago, I read Napoleon Hill's book, *Think and Grow Rich*. First published in 1937, it references the lives of 50 famous and successful people—Andrew Carnegie, Henry Ford, Theodore Roosevelt, Woodrow Wilson, Thomas Edison, Alexander

Graham Bell, F.W. Woolworth, and John D. Rockefeller, to name a few—all of whom claimed to benefit from the principles found in the book.

In 1918, mega-millionaire, Andrew Carnegie, commissioned Hill to interview hundreds of successful people and write a book to reveal what he refers to as the "secret". It helped him build US Steel Corporation, create wealth, and remain positive. It turns out that the secret is a belief system fueled by a relentless desire to achieve, coupled with conscious and unconscious mental processes. By their admission, the key to the success of Carnegie and the men interviewed by Napoleon Hill was their fervent belief in the powerful role of the mind; it made their lofty dreams a reality.

A few quotes from the book help clarify what he meant when he referred to the powerful role of the mind. The most famous is, "Whatever the mind of man can conceive and believe it can achieve." Another of his statements that describes the power of the mind is, "Our brains become magnetized with the dominating thoughts which we hold in our minds, and, by means with which no man is familiar, these 'magnets' attract to us the forces, the people, and the circumstances of life which harmonize with the nature of our dominating thoughts." A quote that relates to how the mind can manifest physical reality is, "All thoughts that have been emotionalized (given feeling) and mixed with faith begin immediately to translate themselves into their physical equivalent." The book is loaded with testaments to the power of mind.

Rhonda Byrne's 2006 book, *The Secret*, could have been written by Napoleon Hill. She wrote almost a century later, but the language and concepts they use to describe the role of the conscious and unconscious mind are uncannily similar. Both focus on how our mental processes create our reality. Both assign a prominent role to our unconscious mind, and both have a large number of successful people who subscribe to their views.

While compelling, these two authors, and their famous endorsers, only reinforced something I already believed: the power of the mind, most notably the unconscious mind, can create our reality. I wanted scientific proof.

At least partial proof arrived courtesy of John A. Bargh's recent brain research. I was excited because it offered a scientific basis for the claims of

Hill and Byrne about how our unconscious mind influences perception, evaluation, and behaviour. Hill's and Byrne's treatment of the subject, while compelling, is not convincing because it lacks research support. Bargh's scientific evidence added a new level of believability.

He and his colleagues at Yale University have conducted many studies to better understand the effects of unconscious processes. One of the world's foremost brain researchers, he uses functional magnetic resonance imagery, electroencephalograms, and advanced research design to investigate what's going on in the nether reaches of our brain and how it affects us. The focus of his work is illustrated in a quote from a 2010 article published in the Psychological Bulletin that he co-authored with E. Morsella: "spontaneous conscious thoughts, even if they appear to be arbitrary, irrelevant, unwanted, or intrusive, may still play an adaptive role in life-relevant problem solving and learning. We know that spontaneous ideation goes on during all of our waking hours, during dreams, and even in slow wave sleep. It is unlikely that such a great allocation of mental resources has no useful adaptive function."

His research on cognitive priming shows that when stimuli (words, pictures, numbers etc.) are presented to his research subjects for extremely short durations—in the 10 to 30 thousandths of a second range—the subject has no awareness of the image or word, but none-the-less, it influences or "primes" subsequent attitudes and behaviour.

For example, in one of Bargh's studies, two groups of subjects were asked to describe the personality of a man they saw on video. The clip showed the man interacting with a salesman and later returning a product for a refund. Both groups were exposed to undetectable words, flashed well below the threshold for visual awareness. The group exposed to words like tough, mean or angry, later described the man in the video as more hostile than did the group who were exposed to neutral words such as table or chair. The real surprise is that the first group judged the man as hostile without really knowing why!

Bargh placed his priming messages (positive or negative flashed words) in the unconscious mind using images projected below his subjects' threshold of perception. For Hill and Byrne their primers are the affirmations that instill ideas and desires in the unconscious mind. The point isn't so much what the primers are, or how they get there. Rather, it's that these wishes, desires, or thoughts—the primers—somehow register in our unconscious and, despite the fact that we are unaware of them, they influence our behaviour!

Bargh's work has shown only mild priming effects; nothing as dramatic as Hill and Byrne's notion of changing your entire life. But, let's not forget, Bargh gets these effects with an unperceived stimulus that only lasts a few fractions of a second, and they are not repeated day after day. Hill and Byrne, on the other hand, aren't talking about a few seconds. They recommend daily affirmations and constant reminders of your goals, with the hope that, somehow, they get permanently planted in your unconscious and generate larger effects—for life. The magnitude of either the primer or the effect isn't the exciting part; the exciting part is that millions of readers who want to believe in the principles of *The Secret* and *Think and Grow Rich*, now have some convincing scientific support for their beliefs.

I recommend you read (or re-read) both books. This time read them with the knowledge that science has offered a reasonable explanation — some would call it proof — that things implanted in our unconscious mind influence our attitudes and behaviour. In the meantime, try to harness the power that resides in the deep recesses of your mind, and live well between your ears.

Locus of Control: Internal, External, or a Bit of Both?

"I have learned that I really do have discipline, self-control, and patience. But they were given to me as a seed, and it's up to me to choose to develop them."

– Joyce Meyer, author.

IF YOU READ THIS COLUMN, YOU KNOW THE TOPIC OF INTERNAL AND external locus of control has come up a few times. Each time it's been pushed to another day. Today's the day. Psychologist, Julian Rotter, introduced the concept in 1966 and it still appears regularly in the research literature.

The APA Dictionary states, in part, that people with an external locus of control tend to behave according to external circumstances. They perceive life outcomes as arising from factors out of their control. People with an internal locus of control tend to behave in response to personal states and intentions. They perceive their life outcomes as arising from their own behaviour and will.

Does it make a difference if we're more internal or external? Externals believe their behaviour is guided by fate, luck, circumstances, or a Higher Power. Internals believe their behaviour is guided by personal decision and effort. So yes, it is one of the many things that make a difference in how we live our lives. For example, externals are more likely to attribute their success to being at the right place at the right time, whereas internals take credit for the success, believing that is was due to their good choices and persistence.

What does the research tell us? Internals tend to enjoy better health after age 65. But if you are 25 to 64 it doesn't make much difference to health (Infurna, Gerstorf & Steven, 2011). Preparing for retirement and planning for the future is more common among internals (Noone, Stephens & Alpass, 2010). Internals are more satisfied with their jobs and life in general (Wang, Bowling & Eschelman, 2010). When discriminated against, externals become more depressed than internals (Jang, Chiriboga, Kim & Rhew, 2010). And there's more.

Job performance for both leaders and team members is better among internals than externals (Ozer, 2008). According to Meier and colleagues (2008), job stress is handled better by internals than externals. Internal locus of control has also been associated with greater knowledge about disease (Seaman and Evans, 1962), ability to stop smoking (Coan,1973), ability to lose weight (Balch & Ross, 1975), more effective practice of birth control, and regular dental visits, all of which suggests that internals take better care of themselves.

Damn! The internals seem to have the edge. But, if you think you might be an external, there is some good news. The evidence suggests we develop either an internal or external locus of control depending upon what we learn from our parents, teachers, and others. For example, if we're told that stuff happens because it's "just how life is" or "God's will" or "the luck of the draw", we learn to be externals. But if we learn that the same things are due to personal decision, choice, and our own behaviour, we become more internally controlled.

Research by Seligman (1975), Bandura (1977), and Hans (2000) supports the view that we learn to be predominantly internal or external. According to Seligman, if we don't connect the dots between what we do and what happens to us, we begin to believe our actions don't make a difference. When that happens, we actually learn to be helpless, and we become more external than internal. Bandura echoed a similar point, saying our sense of self-efficacy is reduced. Hans reported that people who participated in an outward bound program, and had the connection between behaviour and outcomes pointed out to them, developed a greater sense of internal control.

But, you say, "what about me? How can I learn to be more internal?" Pay attention to the connections. The extra 60 pounds of fat comes from poor choices, not God. You're an A student because you work at it. Practice, not luck, makes you a scratch golfer. Do your best to get rid of the "it's just the way things are" mentality. Remember that each choice has a consequence, and live well between your ears.

ACHIEVING EXCELLENCE

"The quality of a person's life is in direct proportion to their commitment to excellence, regardless of their chosen field of endeavor."

– Vince Lombardi

WHAT IS EXCELLENCE? THE DICTIONARY DEFINES IT AS THE QUALITY of being outstanding or extremely good. Adjectives such as exceptional, terrific, and first class come to mind.

How do we achieve excellence? Is it practice, talent, or something else? Who do you think has achieved excellence? How does it happen? Is it even possible for you?

What about Mother Theresa? Surely she would qualify as someone who achieved excellence. How about Ghandi, Albert Einstein, hockey-great Wayne Gretzky, or basketball's phenome, Lebron James? You can think of many who achieved a level of excellence in their field. You may not agree with or like them, but do they measure up to the definition?

For at least a century, psychologists have studied many dimensions along which people differ. We are extraverted or introverted, confident or doubtful, aggressive or timid, or any combination of dozens more.

Are there basic characteristics common to those who achieve greatness? What about these three things?

Love in the broadest possible sense seems an obvious factor. Extraordinary people talk about feeling great passion or love for what they do. If you listen to or read about them, you find they are lovers of humanity, their community, or country. People refer to them as tolerant, forgiving, kind, and understanding.

A second critical factor is giving. Giving or offering help to others is revered in all cultures. Givers are not concerned with what's in it for them. They are motivated to make things better for their family, team, community, or the world. They make sacrifices to further the cause.

A third quality required for excellence must be the consistent ability to take action. People who achieve greatness are not bogged down by indecision, procrastination, or apathy. Doers get things done and lead by example.

If loving, giving, and doing lead to excellence, do their opposites—hating, taking, and wishing—lead to mediocrity or worse? How would you rate Mother Theresa on these three dimensions? She loved humanity, gave tirelessly, and rolled up her sleeves and took action.

What about you? Grab a pen and paper and rate yourself on these three dimensions, and then connect the dots.

Love… … … … … … … …..Hate
Take… … … … … … … …. .Give
Do… … … … … … … … … Wish

If you rate yourself closest to the 'love', 'give', and 'do' ends, the connected dots are shaped like a cone pointed to the right. Use the shape as a reminder that, as we move forward, these characteristics help deflect life's problems, and excellence becomes attainable.

If you rate yourself closer to the 'hate', 'take', and 'wish' ends, the connected dots look like a cone with the wide end to the right. This shape reminds us that, as we move forward, these characteristics trap life's problems like fish in a net and any hope for excellence is a tall order.

The majority of us rate ourselves somewhere in the middle, doing our best—so we say—but never really knocking the ball out of the park.

Check your ratings. Are you an aerodynamic cone, a trap, or somewhere in between?

Whether it's your birthday, Christmas, or some other special time, give yourself the gift of excellence. Chose to love, give, and do more than you hate, take, and wish, and live well between your ears.

TODDLERS, TIARAS, AND SELF-ESTEEM

"Self-esteem is as necessary to the spirit as food is to the body."

– Maxwell Maltz

RECENTLY A GOOD FRIEND OF MINE—A MOTHER AND GRAND-mother—came totally and uncharacteristically unglued when she told me about a Toddlers and Tiaras (T&T) program she saw on TV. Her anger, directed at the mothers, was brutal. "They feed their kids sugar cubes to keep them pumped up, spend thousands of dollars on inappropriate, over-the-top outfits, and seem oblivious to the damage done to their kids' self-esteem." My question was how do you know it hurt their self-esteem?

Any conversation about kids, placed in serious competition by their parents, elicits emotional debate about the pros and cons of winning, failure, and effects on self-esteem. Until we get more specific about what self-esteem is and what it stems from, these conversations will always cast more heat than light on the subject.

For the few who don't know, Toddlers and Tiaras is a reality TV beauty pageant for young girls and their parents. It cranks up the intensity of the critics' response because it tends to sexualize little girls with thousands of dollars-worth of costumes, make-up, and hair-do's more appropriate for someone in their twenties than for five and six year-olds.

The goal today is to show that the effects of such competitions are better understood if we look at their impact on the individual characteristics that make up self-esteem rather than considering their impact on self-esteem as a whole.

Early in my academic career, I developed a scale to measure self-esteem. My research identified 27 abilities and characteristics that contribute to verbal, interpersonal, and physical self-esteem. Together, they form an objective system to assess whether competitions such as T&T are beneficial or harmful to a child's self-esteem.

Does the T&T experience do anything to increase verbal self-esteem? Verbal self-esteem increases when a person is satisfied, more than dissatisfied, with the following six characteristics: ability to express yourself, intelligence, power of concentration, comprehension ability, thinking ability, and listening ability. The question to ask is which of these attributes are enhanced or diminished by what these little girls go through?

What about interpersonal self-esteem? High interpersonal self-esteem is reflected in satisfaction with twelve abilities and characteristics: friendliness, helpfulness, humour, facial appearance, confidence in your ability to move easily and gracefully, openness and honesty, amount of tenseness and nervousness, ability to be relaxed with others, complexion, temper, shyness, and amount of conceit and vanity.

A good thing about T&T is that the girls learn to handle the pressure of performance which results in confidence in movements, less nervousness, and less shyness, all of which increase self-esteem. However, there are some negatives. For example, the judges place heavy emphasis on facial appearance and complexion, so despite how pretty they are, many little girls will feel their face and complexion don't measure up, leading to lower interpersonal self-esteem.

As for the other interpersonal characteristics, there is no expectation that the girls be particularly friendly, helpful, humorous, or modest, so those factors would not contribute to high self-esteem. However, the T&T experience could make them overly vain and dishonest. The whole costume and make-up routine is designed to do one thing: to portray them as something they are not, which would lower self-esteem.

Finally, high physical self-esteem is a product of satisfaction with nine characteristics and abilities including: health, agility and athletic ability, neatness and cleanliness, walk, body-shape, posture, weight, coordination, and clothes. T&T has little to do with health. However, it has plenty to do with agility, walk, body-shape, posture, clothes, coordination, and weight. If they do not measure up on those characteristics, and only the winners do, their self-esteem comes under serious attack and it is difficult to see a silver lining in that cloud.

So, when embroiled in a discussion about whether something is good or bad for a kid's self-esteem, ask if it enhances or diminishes how they feel about these 27 characteristics, draw your conclusion from that, and live well between your ears.

ALMOST

"The greater danger for most of us lies not in setting our aim too high and falling short; but in setting our aim too low, and achieving our mark."

– Michelangelo

IT'S THREE IN THE MORNING, AND I'M ALMOST READY FOR BED. MY little green router lights are flickering. I love the night. I love the quiet. It's so secure, peaceful, and full of promise. Greatness is here I just cannot get my arms around it. I feel it, I sense the potential. I just haven't yet committed myself to the work that is required.

Maybe big accomplishment is beyond me. Maybe I just don't have the ability or know how to do something really good. But I want to. Apparently, I don't want to badly enough, or I'd do it. Even as a kid I thought greatness was out there, just beyond my reach. I think we all harbour such private thoughts.

But the single word that sums me up best is: almost—almost but not quite a lot of things. I was almost a good enough drummer, almost a noteworthy academic, and I almost had a successful agriculture business. Later, I moved to the United States where I was almost successful in the murky world of international business. I sold a lot of what I was supposed to sell, but the real glory would have been the other stuff.

I almost sold 2,000 used cars to Indonesia from Australia to serve as taxis. I almost brokered diamonds from South Africa, oil from Nigeria, and other more dangerous stuff. I got in so far over my head I was almost a joke. I even talked my way into a numbered account in Switzerland in preparation for my almost millions. But the absence of planned-for-riches and the presence of high service fees dried up my account. From the late 80's to 2008, I was almost very successful in financial services, and now, I'm almost a decent writer. I'm not complaining; life has been great so far. It's this almost thing that bugs me.

Then there were my stupid days when, but for dumb luck, I was almost dead. In Zimbabwe, against the best advice of the locals, I took Easter weekend to drive from Bulawayo to Victoria Falls, alone, on the Matabeleland Road. I wound up looking down the business end of a nasty machine gun more than once when some rag-tag soldiers wondered what a guy like me was doing at their check points. I wondered the same thing.

And, if that wasn't enough, when I got to Victoria Falls, I decided to take a trail along the Zambezi River. A badly faded sign with a symbol I didn't recognize warned not to get out of the car. I thought it meant wild animals in the area. Tempted by the red African sunset I stopped, checked carefully for any animals, as if I could see them in the bush or out run them, walked fifty yards, and sat by the river. I later learned the sign warned of unexploded land mines. Almost a goner.

Another careless episode found me at seventy feet, without a buddy, in the Aegean Sea, with the wrong equipment. As I struggled to not drown, the words of the Dive Master who trained me registered in my tiny brain, "never dive without a buddy." Almost terminally careless.

I gave all these things months, sometimes years, but apparently I missed the final steps. I came close but either got scared off, ran out of opportunity, ran out of money, or got distracted by the glitter of something else. I never quite did anything as much as I might have. Never took anything as far as I could. Like I said: almost. Doug-Almost-Spencer. I even kept most of the documentation for all this stuff as a reminder of how close I almost was. But then again, it's not getting there that's important, it's the journey that matters most.

So I better get on with it. I'll be one pissed off puppy if I end up lying in some home, almost dead, with the same thoughts. I've always said, "don't die wishin." And if I don't get my act together I will die wishin'. I need to pay attention, get serious, stick with it, and live well between my ears.

Trying to Decide

"There is no more miserable human being than one
in whom nothing is habitual but indecision."

– William James, father of modern psychology.

IT'S TIME TO FISH OR CUT BAIT. IT MEANS IT'S TIME TO MAKE A DECI-
sion. It isn't always easy. As I wrote this, I identified four methods that
help when you are stumped or immobilized by indecision: Ben Franklin's
method; follow your principles method; flip a coin method; and the
listen to your gut method.

For starters, you need facts to make a decision. Benjamin was not able
to evaluate all the choices and facts in his head at the same time so, on a
sheet of paper, he made two columns: pro and con. He allowed himself
two or three days to accumulate all the positives and negatives, and then
he weighted them in importance. If the plus of one pro roughly equalled
the minus of one con, he would stroke both off his list. If one pro equalled
two cons or vise-versa he stroked out all three and so forth. When he was
all done, the column with reasons left in it was the choice he favoured. It's
the most rational way to make a decision.

A second method is to base your decision on principle. It makes some
decisions easy. If a guiding principle for you is to do no harm and value

life, then deciding whether to kill momma cat's kittens or find a home for them is a no-brainer. But principles aren't always involved. When the dilemma is whether to take your vacation in Puerto Rico or Jamaica, principles don't make much difference unless, of course, you discover that one country promotes child labour and the other doesn't. Then, principle might play a role.

A third option, favoured by many, is the coin toss. It comes after we've assessed the pros and cons and still can't make up our mind. But—and it's an important but—if you are unhappy with the flip, it may mean the coin was wrong.

An example illustrates the point. Suppose, after all your analysis, you still can't decide whether to travel cross country to visit your relatives, so you decide to flip a coin: "heads" you'll stay, and "tails", you'll go. Assume it's "heads". If it felt wrong the instant you saw "heads" then you may want to disregard the coin toss and conclude there is another reason—one not immediately apparent—for you to visit your relatives.

When the rational process of comparing pros and cons leaves you stuck on the horns of a dilemma, it means something else is at work. That something else is your gut. For decades psychologists have known that when thoughts, feelings, and behaviour are not in agreement, there is often a problem. In this case the problem is indecision which leads to the fourth way to make decisions: listen to your gut.

We rely on two types of information: logical and emotional. J. Bargh and E. Morsella, in their 2010 review article, state that the unconscious mind influences our perception, evaluation, and motivation like a huge data processor. Our unconscious operates non-stop (24/7) to organize and seek meaning from all we are exposed to, even though we are unaware of it. It stores an enormous amount of information from both the environment and our past history. We sense this information as a gut feeling, and the authors argue convincingly that we should pay attention to it. The problem is that when we can't decide we can't act decisively either, and life just pushes us along. When we do nothing, we're like a ship without a rudder or without a Captain.

Theodore Roosevelt said, "In any moment of decision the best thing you can do is the right thing, the next best thing is the wrong thing, and the worst thing you can do is nothing." No matter how we strive to make good decisions, perfection will elude us. All we can do is weigh the pros and cons, rely on our principles, flip the odd coin, and listen to our gut to make decisions that help us live well between our ears.

Courage

"I learned that courage was not the absence of fear, but the triumph over it. The brave man is not he who does not feel afraid, but he who conquers that fear."

– Nelson Mandela

"Courage is what it takes to stand up and speak; courage is also what it takes to sit down and listen."

– Winston Churchill

IN A 2012 ISSUE OF *THE MINDFUL EXPRESS*, MELANIE GREENBERG LISTS six attributes of courage: (1) feel the fear yet choose to act, (2) follow your heart, (3) persevere in the face of adversity, (4) stand up for what is right, (5) let go of what is familiar and expand your horizons, (6) face suffering with dignity or faith.

When it comes to these six attributes are you courageous? Do you confront threats or retreat? Can you follow your heart to pursue your goal when your friends and family think you're crazy? Have you fought through lack of funds, lack of experience or scorn and ridicule to start something new? Do you stand up for a person when you know they are right? Can you let go of needy, sticky parents to feel free enough to leave and pursue your dream? Are you able to face pain or death with dignity and resolve? Each of these attributes requires courage, the lack of which limits our lives and guarantees mediocrity.

According to a growing number of psychologists, courage isn't only about saving people, fighting wars, and doing heroic feats. Courage occurs daily when we make decisions we know are right. It helps us maintain our moral compass and live life to the fullest. Philosophers agree that the root of cowardice is fear, and the key to courage is to face and conquer your fear.

How can you display courage? You can take a stand on global warming, poverty, corporate greed, environmental sustainability, false advertising, or other issues you feel strongly about. At the personal level, you can follow your heart and do what is right for you and your family regardless of whether it is the easiest route. But, can we make ourselves more courageous? Robert Biswas-Diener's (2012) book entitled *The Courage Quotient: How science can make you brave*, suggests that we can.

Biswas-Diener lists four things we can do to become more courageous. Most importantly, we can reduce uncertainty by obtaining facts. Second, courage comes from a place of clarity, so he recommends that we learn to relax our mind, meditate, breathe deeply, and practice relaxation techniques to avoid being overwhelmed. Such techniques also lower heart rate, blood pressure, and muscle tension which reduces stress and fear. Third, he suggests that we develop a courageous mindset, which includes constructive anger that you direct against the "ways in which your most precious values are being trampled." Finally, he says we must avoid the "bystander effect".

The "bystander effect" was first investigated by Latané and Darley (1970) to understand why 38 law-abiding and responsible New Yorkers stood by for half an hour, without raising a finger to help, while Kitty Genovese was repeatedly stabbed to death. Only one person called the police, but not until after Ms. Genovese was dead. The incident has since been discussed as one where the bystanders lacked courage to take action.

Latané and Darley concluded that diffusion of responsibility was the biggest culprit. It is when we wrongly assume that someone else will do something about it, so we back off and avoid involvement. For example, we assume someone has already called the fire department, or they're already working on cleaning up the river, or surely the bus driver has already reported the bullying kid. Another possible, but much less admirable reason for inaction, is when we believe that a victim probably deserves their plight, so we remain uninvolved.

Biswas-Diener says we are more likely to reduce the bystander effect and display courage when we pay attention and notice problems, realize that the situation is urgent, assume personal responsibility, know how to help, and decide to help. So, step up and make a difference in yours or someone else's life. Speak out on important issues, be willing to get outside the box, act courageously, and live well between your ears.

Violence: When our need
for self-esteem is harmful

"Life is largely a matter of expectation."

– Horace, Roman poet of the first century BC

We usually associate high self-esteem with good behaviour. But a weak moral compass and the absence of self-esteem drove Jordan, an 18 year old, to open fire in the direction of houses, penetrating the hip of an innocent child. He did it to earn membership in a gang. Such occurrences are rare, but increasing. A 2006 *Feature Focus* report by the RCMP that dealt with youth and guns confirmed that there is a significant increase in violence, particularly gun violence, on the part of males and females between their late teens and age thirty.

Psychologists have known for years that self-esteem increases when we receive positive feedback, meet expectations, and compare favourably with our peers. It increases due to improvement in three broad skill sets: our verbal skills, interpersonal skills, and physical skills and characteristics. But troubled teens are often dissatisfied with their skills and abilities. They may not express themselves well, they may listen and comprehend poorly, they may have trouble concentrating, or any combination of the three.

They may also feel socially isolated and dissatisfied with their ability to make friends. It gets even worse if they are unhappy with their appearance and physical abilities. Low self-esteem, created by such dissatisfaction, leads to a festering psychological mess and drives the sufferer to extremes in order to fix it. Membership in a gang, with its upside-down standards of what it takes to be a hero, makes it simple: all it takes is a gun to gain respect from his peers, and the self-esteem that comes with it.

For Jordan, one pointless, gang-related act increased his verbal self-esteem. He became less dependent on words to express who he was; his violent acts spoke for him. Those actions also increased his interpersonal and physical self-esteem. The shooting brought respect from gang members and he no longer felt isolated or inadequate. He didn't have to be physically strong or good looking. Instead, the violence made him powerful and attractive in the eyes of his peers. His willingness to pull the trigger increased his self-esteem quickly, compared to the time it would have taken to improve his academic and social skills.

Why are violent incidents like this so frequent? The need for self-esteem is a powerful motivator, especially for underachieving young adults. In this example, Jordan's limited ability to read, listen, understand, and express himself earned him ridicule, not praise. In addition, perhaps due to family or personal problems, his social skills were not well developed and he had no friends. Physically, he was not particularly strong or attractive. He struck out on every count.

Without such attributes, he received less positive feedback at home and at school, did not meet expectations that were placed upon him, and did not feel as though he compared favourably to his peers. Absence of any one of these factors causes low self-esteem; absence of all three is devastating.

The cure is not to pamper the Jordans of the world to guarantee they don't feel inadequate. The cure is the opposite. We need to expect more from our kids, provide clear standards for them to attain, and hold them accountable when they fall short. Cops and teachers have had a belly full of do-gooders saying that we can't be strict, that we can't discipline, and that we can't let anyone fail.

What we can't do is deny them success, but that is exactly what we do when we set low standards or fail to enforce the ones we have. When we continually allow kids to underachieve, they slip further behind, gravitate to the bottom, and miss out on the joy of success and high self-esteem that comes with achievement.

The need for self-esteem is powerful. To foster it, families and schools need to push for superior skills, hold kids responsible for developing them, and cheer when they succeed. We have to expect and foster more—not less—from our kids. They have to successfully meet standards that are higher—not lower—in order to live well between their ears.

Take it up a notch

"Strive not to be a success, but rather to be of value."

– Albert Einstein

"Status quo or grow: You are in control of your future."

– Mary Mihalic, *Made to Make It*

How often have you felt overwhelmed, like your world is falling apart, when the demands on your time, ability, patience, and damn near everything, has you immobilized? When this column was syndicated, the pressure to produce a quality column each week for three years snuck up and hit me like a brick. Since retirement, I had prided myself on being committed to nothing, but now, with a three year contract, commitment and I are as tight as two coats of paint. If it weren't for that tightness, I might not have been able to do what I did today.

Pressure to produce to a deadline can be overwhelming. There are many examples: you delete a month's worth of data and have to reconstruct it in a week, or it has rained non-stop, the forecast is for more, and you have 3,000 acres yet to seed. In my case, I wasn't sure I could produce a column each week for three years. All three examples have the same characteristics: doing it is your only good choice, you're pushed for time, and panic only makes the situation worse.

You understand all the issues, but you just don't know if you have it in you. You're tempted to say screw it and bail on the responsibility, but you can't. That's the point of today's column. You have to figure out a way to rise to the occasion, find a solution, and let your light shine.

When I need solutions I walk in circles, counter clockwise, usually around the kitchen table, talking to myself. Every so often I stop at the fridge, open the door and peer in. I don't know what I'm expecting to find: an idea, a treat to eat—something to fuel my brain. It's more than a little goofy and it was no different today; no treats, and nothing came to my head, so I veered off course.

I broke from my circling and headed out to get the mail to give myself a distraction. As my hand reached the door knob a solution popped out of my mouth, "Damn, Dougie, just take it up a notch."

It hit me. Exactly! This is a universal problem; something worth writing about. Everyone has been totally overwhelmed but knows that somehow they have to rise to the occasion—to be better than they've been—and really nail it.

Psychologist John Eliot's 2011 book, *"Overachievement: Behind What It Takes to Be Successful"*, proposes some radical ideas about taking it up a notch. His counterintuitive suggestions make sense. Don't get hung up on goals; go beyond them. Don't work hard at your job; play at it, and pursue the "heart-pounding, really big, difference-making ideas."

He says to put all your eggs in one basket. I agree. If you really want to win the race you can only ride one horse. He's worked with great performers in many fields, and he says they only focus on what they know they can control. They operate from a "trust mindset", which means they trust their abilities and experience and they go for it.

Much of the rationale underlying Eliot's off-centre beliefs is sound science. Our sympathetic nervous system is designed to maximize our potential under stressful times. Trying to relax when we have to perform is a mistake because it engages our parasympathetic nervous system which helps our body look after the maintenance tasks such as breathing, digestion, and getting rest. Instead, we need to be out of our comfort zone and activate our sympathetic nervous system so our "fight or flight" response takes over.

We might feel we need rest but it is not the way to meet the challenge. Let "fight or flight" kick in and don't try to squelch it with a snooze, booze, or other avoidance behaviour. Get neck-deep in the pressure, quit over-thinking, put your mind in drive, and hit the gas.

You've conquered challenges before; do it again, only bigger, better, and with pizzazz. I'm going to re-read Eliot's little book and take it up a notch. Try it yourself. The next time you feel overwhelmed, seek out his book or retrieve this column, and live well between your ears.

Keys to time management: Clear goals and balance

"The game has its ups and downs, but you can never lose
focus of your individual goals and you can't let yourself
be beat because of lack of effort."

– Michael Jordan

When it comes to time management, most of us fit into one of
three categories: we have clear goals and manage our time well, have clear
goals and manage our time poorly, or have poorly defined goals and are
like Yogi Berra described, "Lost, but making good time." According to
statistics, pundits, and local scuttlebutt, most of us are in Yogi's category.

It is true, we are lost without goals and it becomes more difficult to
manage our time because it raises the question: "manage my time to do
what?" An old saying, "most people aim at nothing in life and hit it with
amazing accuracy," speaks to this issue. I found reference to a survey in
Time magazine that supports the saying. The survey claimed that only
three percent of people had written goals. Ninety-seven percent had never
written their goals and rarely thought about them. The three percent
were more successful. Even the thought of time management is goofy if

we don't have goals. After all, goals are destinations, and if we don't have any, it's impossible to know where we're going or how to get there.

Research on goals confirms their importance. Without them our sense of well-being is diminished. Lapierre, Dubé, Bouffard, & Alain, (2007) found that when they offered a personal goal intervention program to early retirees aged 50 to 65 it increased their subjective well-being, and raised their levels of hope, serenity, and flexibility, providing a positive attitude about retirement. Their levels of depression and psychological distress also decreased significantly and were maintained at least six months later.

In 2010, Morisano and colleagues, working at McGill University and the University of Toronto, investigated the effect of a goal setting program for struggling students at McGill. It improved their academic performance significantly. These researchers cited other evidence of the positive effects of goals. People with clear goals possess increased enthusiasm and persistence; it makes them less susceptible to the undermining effects of anxiety, disappointment, and frustration. Many studies also indicate that individuals with clear goals are able to direct their attention to goal-relevant activities. This last finding has a direct bearing on good time management.

A few years ago, I developed a brief test to measure time management. It is simple to take and is free on my website: *www.livewellbetweenyourears.com*. It is based on goals and how much time you spend on goal-relevant activities. The test tells you if the amount of time you spend on your activities is out of whack with the value you place on them. It isn't perfect, but it provides a good starting point for determining how to better manage time. It graphically illustrates which activities you need to increase or decrease in order to manage time more effectively.

Too much time spent on things that do not contribute to goals is time wasted and creates a sense of uselessness. Too little time spent on goal-relevant activities blocks achievement of our goals and contributes to frustration and anger. In either case, poor time management is the result and it drives us crazy. For example, if book-work is determined to be fifty percent of your job, and you only have ten percent of your time devoted to it, you're going to feel under attack, pushed for time, and frustrated with the imbalance. That's when you need help with time management.

In almost all fields, expectations are being ratcheted up, and we are forced to do more with less—less time, less money, and less help. Better time management will help. Take the time to develop crystal clear goals and prioritize your goal-relevant activities. Seek a comfortable balance between the time spent and the importance placed on those activities, and live well between your ears.

CHECK YOUR EXPECTATIONS.

"If you paint in your mind a picture of bright and happy expectations, you put yourself into a condition conducive to your goal."

– Norman Vincent Peale

SUPPOSE YOU WERE TOLD THAT A ROUTINE GENETIC SCREENING AT birth revealed that, on her 17th chromosome, your daughter possessed the Quati 47 gene, known to be responsible for creativity. Might you have raised her differently than if you had not been told? Certainly, it would have created a set of expectations you would not otherwise have had.

If your friend tells you that your child's new teacher is aloof, curt, and has criticized parents for helping their kids with homework, it establishes expectations in your mind about the nature of the teacher. Will that information affect how you approach your first parent-teacher interview? You will likely be more nervous when you first meet so that your voice, body language, and choice of words will indicate caution and a less relaxed approach.

Upon meeting, the teacher will pick up on your behavioural cues and may think you are cold or don't like her. She may even interpret your coolness as disinterest, creating the expectation that you don't care about your kid's progress in school. As you can see, negative expectations can get matters off to a bad start.

Conversely, positive expectations can enhance everything. For example, in 1968 psychologist Robert Rosenthal conducted what became a classic study of expectations. In his research he led teachers to believe that some of their students had been identified as "academic bloomers" who would probably make remarkable gains in the coming academic year. In fact, the students had been selected randomly. There was no difference in intelligence between the group identified as "bloomers" and the other students.

But, by year end, thirty percent of the students, whom the teachers were led to believe would excel, had actually shown an increase of over twenty-two points as measured by an objective intelligence test. Almost all of them gained at least ten IQ points. What explains the dramatic effects?

The teachers' expectations, formed by the bogus information fed to them by the researchers, caused them to interact with the bloomers differently than they interacted with the other kids. According to Rosenthal (1974), they were friendlier towards the bloomers, paid closer attention to their performance, and placed greater demands on them because they "knew" those kids had greater potential and could do the work.

This study illustrates the powerful role of expectations. At the beginning of the year the two groups of kids did not differ significantly on any measure. The increase in IQ was due to one thing only: teacher expectations and the resultant differences in the interaction between the teachers and the so-called "academic bloomers".

The truth is, there is no Quati 47 gene on the 17th chromosome, but if you believed your daughter had such a creativity gene, you would expose her to more creative opportunities, pay more attention to her creative efforts, expect greater creativity from her, and—you guessed it—she'd become more creative. It would not happen because she actually was more creative. It would happen because you *thought* she was more creative. You would act, and she would react, in accordance with the expectations and the cycle would continue.

This effect has been demonstrated hundreds of times. Holding expectations—positive or negative—influences how we treat others, how they react to us, how they see themselves, and how we see ourselves. Expectations rule. When positive, they create complex feedback loops that perpetuate and enhance performance and similarly, when the expectations are negative they create feedback loops that perpetuate undesirable behaviour.

Do expectations affect every aspect of our behaviour? It seems they do. Decades of research tell us that if you expect less from yourself or others, you will get less. It starts when parents, teachers, and significant others expect nothing exceptional from you, and for the most part, if that's how they treat you, that's how you'll act. If you expect to be non-exceptional there is a greater likelihood you'll continue on that path unless you reject those notions—a difficult thing to do—and decide to break out of your ordinary mold and re-cast your life with higher expectations.

The bottom line: check your expectations. Bump them up for yourself, your loved ones, and those you care about, and live well between your ears.

WHO WILL YOU BE THIS
HALLOWEEN?

"If human beings had genuine courage, they'd wear their costumes every day of the year, not just on Halloween."

– Douglas Coupland

IT'S TIME FOR SOME MAKE-BELIEVE. SUPPOSE YOU'RE GOING TO THE Halloween party and you can be Mother Theresa or a Vegas Showgirl. If you're a guy, you can be Peter Rabbit or Superman. Who will you be? If you said Mother Theresa or Peter Rabbit, I'm not sure I believe you.

October 31 is the only time we are allowed—even encouraged—to take on a different identity. It's special for the kids because this spooky night gives them power. Dressed as adults or action heroes, they go door to door and threaten grown strangers with, "trick or treat." In 1976, psychologists Diener, Fraser, Beaman, & Kelem, studied kids' behaviour at Halloween and found they were more likely to steal candy when their identity was unknown than if they were recognizable. Similarly, if a kid is at your door with a crowd of kids, he is more likely to pull a prank than if he is there by himself. Not surprisingly, kids who could be identified were less inclined to misbehave.

Psychologists have known for years that anonymity weakens our inhibitions, causing us to do things we would not ordinarily do. For example, people are more daring in groups, and anonymous suggestions dropped in the suggestion box may be a bit crazier than those where the writer's identity is known. Similarly, a mask makes you bolder and we know that the private you is more risqué than the public you. When privacy or anonymity is guaranteed, we are less inhibited; social convention flies out the window; guilt, fear, and shame exert less control over our behaviour, and we become more daring. Why is that?

Freud would say that anonymity reduces the control function of your superego which allows your animalistic desires to come bubbling to the surface. Psychologists say anonymity contributes to de-individuation, and we become less self-aware, less accountable, and less concerned about what others think.

Is it possible that the secret you—the Superman you—can find the courage to flex your muscles this Halloween? Similarly, if you are female, might your secret inner woman throw caution to the wind and emerge as the sexy and provocative version of who you are?

Or are you wound so tight you can't imagine doing something so wild? "It's just not me," you say. Of course it isn't you—at least not the everyday you—but it might be the once-in-a-while you; that person you'd like to set free at least once.

What attracts kids and adults alike to Halloween? It's because the opportunity to take on a different identity is rare, and short of going through a maze of paperwork to legally change who you are, Halloween is the only time you can do it for a night—no paperwork or court appearance required. It's a time when, without being judged, you can be sexy, scary, an animal, a celebrity, a super hero, or a cartoon character. You can scare the crap out of somebody. The office manager can be a little slutty, or the boss can don his favourite cowboy hat, chaps, and man-thong—a scary thought all by itself.

So, does your costume reveal an inner you? As kids, the boys can be masculine and tough—something they secretly wish for—while the girls can become fairy princesses or grown women. As for the adults, you have to believe that if a man steps out as Dopey (Snow White's third dwarf) it sends a different message than if he's out there as a red devil with horns. Likewise, Cat Woman brings out a whole new you.

In any case, have some fun this Halloween. Pay attention to the costumes of the trick-or-treaters at your door, and if you're brave, unleash your own secret character for a few hours. You may not be a Vegas showgirl or Superman, but if you look hard enough you'll find someone inside your head. Slip into that different character, play it to the hilt, and live well between your ears.

CREATE CONTENTMENT WITH LESS

"Be content with what you have; rejoice in the way things are.
When you realize there is nothing lacking, the whole world
belongs to you."

– Lao Tzu

THIS TAOIST SAYING FROM TWO AND A HALF THOUSAND YEARS AGO
reflects the belief that contentment comes from within and not from
something or someone else. Do you really think your life improves with
the new iPhone, a fancier car, or this fall's newest fashion? We've had it
drilled into us that if we have more, accomplish more, and make more
money, we will have a greater sense of well-being. But the connection
between more stuff and contentment is not supported by data.

Despite the fact that wealth has increased, we are not more
content. Studies by the Organization for Economic Cooperation and
Development (OECD) and others have found that our sense of well-
being has declined over the past half century, despite greater wealth,
more possessions, and an increase in GDP. Similarly, a 2005 British study
found that since 1957 we've seen a three-fold increase in wealth and
gadgets, but a sixteen percent decline in happiness.

Webster's dictionary defines contentment as satisfaction with and acceptance of the way things are, which is similar to the Taoist proverb. The proverb and the definition suggest that, whether we have many possessions or none, we will be content as long as we are satisfied and accepting of our lot. Hmm, that sounds too good to be true. How can having a lot or having nothing both lead to contentment?

The flaw in the argument is that nothing lasts forever. The more we have, the more that can go wrong. Ultimately possessions wear out or break, so owning less—less with which to become dissatisfied—is preferable when contentment is the objective. We know that objects break causing discontentment, but what about situations and relationships? They change too, usually for the worse. Often we don't accept it, and we try to change both the situation and the people involved, rather than change ourselves.

The conclusion seems to be that having less produces more satisfaction, acceptance, and contentment. It is a decidedly un-Western thought. Popular culture says that contentment comes with a more perfect relationship and more possessions, even though most religions advise against consumerism, materialism, and dependency on another person for contentment. But how can we learn to accept people and situations that upset us and to be satisfied with less instead of more? It may have to do with balance.

For years, psychological research has suggested that we are content when our behaviour, thoughts, and feelings are in balance. As long as we are psychologically healthy we can control our behaviour and thoughts, and consequently, have control over our emotions. For example, if you think or behave positively about others, yourself, or anything else, you become content. But how can we behave and think positively more of the time?

In 2002, a study by the Fetzer Foundation confirmed that with focused awareness and contemplative meditation we can learn to get positive behaviour, thoughts, and feelings in balance and thus feel more content. They developed a training program of integrated lectures, discussions, and meditation, combined with classes and exercises to increase awareness and understanding of emotional experience.

The study found that participants in this training reported reduction in negative mood due to an increase in their ability to stay calm in the face of adversity. Participants also reported an increase in awareness of their emotions, their thoughts, and their reactions to others that allowed them to respond in unique and constructive ways. They also experienced a significant decline in depression, anxiety, and hostility, and were better able to tolerate stress. In short, they became more content.

The psychological balance theories predict what the Fetzer Foundation discovered: when behaviour and thoughts are positive, your feelings will be also. If you work on it, you can control your behaviour and thoughts, and through them create your feelings. If this is true—and the research suggests it is—you can create contentment and live well between your ears.

NIGHT LOVERS

"Darkness is sweet, night-time is king. Become who you want
without risking a thing. Alone in the blackness,
my palm on my head,
I love it so much I have nothing to dread.

The silence is soft, the darkness secure.
Greatness starts here, if not for the light.
As night turns to day, wisdom fades too. Oh, night-time
don't leave me, I'm better with you. I see it all coming, my
critics asleep. I make it all happen and then fall asleep."

I WROTE THOSE WORDS WHEN I LIVED ON MY BOAT ON THE
Sacramento River Delta. Anchored to the starboard side, I slept in a
queen bed tucked in the stern of my twenty-eight foot cruiser. No place
was more peaceful or holds sweeter memories. Tiny 12 volt swivel lights
cast shadows across the cabin, to be replaced by a flickering candle when
I conserved my batteries, or no shadows at all when my candle burnt out.

My quarters were tight; every space familiar. If need be, I could slip off
my reclining position in the bow, and, in total darkness, make my way to
any half-eaten cookie, half smoked cigarette, half drank rum and coke, or
anything else in that boat.

Damp, foggy, November nights on the delta were pitch black, inside and out. It was quiet as a tomb except for the soft rippling of the current against the hull. I felt secure for three reasons: It was night, I was in the middle of nowhere with my anchor light on, and I was never more than two to five steps from the gun in my bed. There were stories of piracy on the river. Some of them were true. But the kachik-kachik as I pumped a shell into the chamber of my Model 870, Remington Wing Master, 12 gauge shotgun was an ominous sound for the uninvited if they ever put weight on my swim platform.

I am a night person—through and through. Researching this column, I've concluded that two reasons weigh heavily on whether you are a day or a night person. The first, and most common, is our genetically determined circadian rhythm. Beyond that, at least for me, there are psychological reasons for loving the night that are far stronger than any biological factor. I can't speak for those who don't love the night—I simply don't understand you. It's not that I dislike the day. I just love the night.

The research on circadian rhythms indicates that morning people are governed more by social values, are less open to change, more agreeable, and more conscientious (Vollmer and Randler, 2012), while evening people are more individualistic, open to change, and slightly neurotic. In 1999, Roberts and Kyllonen reported that night people have higher intelligence scores, and Chelminski and his colleagues (1999) discovered night owls were also more likely to be depressed.

In 2009, D. Collins and his students at the University of Alberta found that the physical strength of morning people stayed level throughout the day but declined in the evening, while evening people became physically stronger throughout the day indicating that, "the early bird may get the worm but the night owl has more stamina." Similar results demonstrated that after 10.5 hours of wakefulness, night owls are able to concentrate more effectively than early birds.

The extent to which a few of us love the night is tied to more than just circadian rhythms. Over our lives we have learned we are safe at night. By sundown, the phone quits ringing, no one needs us, no one is in our face, and expectations of the daily grind end. Night is when freedom and contentment permeate the night lover's being. Public turns to private, busy to calm, stressed to relaxed, and restraint becomes loose, so that night owls can live well between their ears, especially on their boat.

WOMAN IN THE WOODS

"Life has no pause buttons; dreams have no expiry date; time has no holiday, so don't miss a single moment in your life."

– Ritu Ghatourey
"Getting what you want isn't the problem; deciding what you want is the hard part."

RECENTLY, I SPOKE WITH A REMARKABLE WOMAN IN HER MID-SIXTIES. Married at fifteen with a ninth grade education, she's been very successful. When we spoke, she was at peace in the woods, in her cabin, on her lake. She has worked in finance, made millions, and is a prospector with forty claims. She is also a poet, photographer, and who knows what else. I don't know her well, but her story made me think.

Most of us, if we admit it, are stuck. We adopt beliefs that limit us and hold us back. The woman I spoke with is not stuck and knows nothing of limits. Left in an orphanage at birth, she was soon adopted by a loving couple and led a sheltered life until she married. Her beliefs were always that she 'could', never that she 'couldn't'.

In the 1970's, in her twenties, while she lived in a motel, she started a finance company with three hundred dollars in her purse. Had it been me, I would have thought it impossible—out of my league—and I would have given up without trying. Not her. She had worked as a loan officer, knew how to put loan proposals together, and decided she would do it for others—for the big dogs—and take a small percentage of the loan amount as a fee. It worked.

I asked her, "How did you achieve so much, coming from so little?"

Her response, straight out of some naïve, Mary-Poppins-like movie was, "I didn't do it for the money; I did it to make a living. I've always tried to do the right thing—just like in the Bible. My foster parents actually insisted that I read it when I was very young."

Her explanation didn't satisfy me. She, like others who describe their success, blithered on about her values, how much she cared, and day-to-day details. More importantly, I wanted to know how she motivated herself to do such big things in the first place. We all think big thoughts but we rarely follow through, not because we don't care or don't have the knowledge, but rather, we simply never start. She had received no help from a famous name or bundles of cash. She started as nobody with nothing. I wanted to know the origin of her drive to tackle the really big stuff.

Most of us spend our life in a rut. We fall into what we do and give it little thought. Granted, some ruts are more interesting than others, but none-the-less we are stuck. It's not like we procrastinate, which occurs when we know what we want to do, but just don't do it. No, I mean stuck in the sense that we can't decide what we want. Of course, we all want a good life, a decent income, a good job, a happy home life, and all those platitudinous things, but we can't decide what we really want—specifically. Our sought-after goals are too general and not crystalized in our mind. Oh sure, we move forward, but only because the engine's running, the thing is in gear, and the ruts keep us on the road. Beyond that, we don't actually do what is necessary to get us out of the rut. It becomes a rut of sameness and mediocrity, and it's how we live.

The lady I'm talking about is rut-free. She's repeatedly been able to achieve the first miracle—decide what she wants—and then go straight ahead and achieve the second: execute successfully without fear or excuse.

The simplicity of her explanation for always moving forward stunned me. "I never made excuses," she said. "When other people said 'too many people are doing it,' or, 'if the idea had merit, someone would have already done it', I just did it."

It seemed too simplistic but I believed her. Most of us dream, but never act; squat, but never leap. She'd been able to do the hard part—to make a decision and act on it. So, decide what you want, accept no limits, follow the advice of the woman in the woods, and live well between your ears.

ARE YOU A BIG PICTURE
OR A DETAIL PERSON?

"A man sooner or later discovers that he is the
master-gardener of his soul, the director of his life."

– James Allen

ARE YOU HARD WIRED TO SEE THE FOREST OR THE TREES; A BIG
picture or detail person; someone with a holistic view of the world,
or one who enjoys analyzing the component parts? The big picture,
holistic types are probably field-dependent. The others, those who
don't allow themselves to be influenced or distracted by the messy
reality of life, who get straight to the nitty-gritty and analyze things, are
likely field-independent.

In 1948, Herman Witkin coined the terms field-dependence and field-
independence to reflect two different cognitive styles. You are predominantly one or the other, and whichever it is, it has a significant impact on
your life. In a review article, Terry Musser (1996) claimed it is the most
researched variable in psychology—but what difference does it make?

Field-independent people have a bucketful of characteristics that are
highly regarded in our society. After 30 years of studying this personality characteristic, Witkin reported that they tend to be mathematicians,

scientists, and engineers. Hanson (1980) found that these detail-oriented, field-independent folks were more analytical, more precise, and more readily learned a new language. They also do better than the field-dependents on open-ended, long-answer test questions (Lu and Suen, 1995). Similarly, they score higher on music reading ability (King, 1983). Brown (1994) found them to be better problem solvers, because they could focus on the relevant details and not be distracted by irrelevant information.

Field-independents are also more likely to be men than women and may want to fix a problem more than understand it. They stress the importance of details, prefer to work alone, and are task oriented. Less concerned about making nice, they are quarrelsome and least apt to agree (Oltman et al, 1975). They stay on task and persevere. Goodfellow (1980) found that nursing students who passed were more often field-independent, whereas failing students, and those who quit, tended to be field-dependent.

The research generally reveals that field-independents function more autonomously and demonstrate greater detachment and a willingness to "go it alone". When the task is complicated or unstructured, independent types impose their own structure; they plow straight ahead rather than get hung up on the ambiguity or uncertainty of the situation.

Field-dependents are different. They are less detail oriented and are influenced more by what's going on around them. More likely to be female, they are holistic in their thinking and are less concerned about not understanding all the facts, as long as they "get the gist" of the big picture. They are relationship people and are better at resolving differences than their field-independent cousins.

Field-dependent people are more socially involved and attentive. According to Terry Musser's review article, they prefer to be physically closer to those with whom they are interacting. In the same vein, they show better recall for the faces of others and tend to remember social aspects of situations more than the non-social aspects. Field-dependents are also more likely to be self-disclosing; to know and be known by more people. Similarly, Witkin and Goodenough, in their 1981 book, *Cognitive Styles*, reported that they are frequently described as being very interpersonal; they have a well-developed ability to read social cues and to openly communicate their feelings. Others describe them as being warm, friendly, and personable.

It is clear that being field-dependent or field-independent influences how we perceive the world, and therefore, how we lead our lives. While field-independents are more inclined to say the ends justify the means, field-dependents are more concerned with how a goal is achieved than they are with the goal itself. Personal success and accomplishment of the task is a greater priority for the independents while, for the others, a philosophy of "do no harm" may guide their thinking to a greater extent.

Each has its pluses and minuses. For the pursuit of personal excellence it seems the independents may have an edge whereas the orientation displayed by the field-dependents favours interpersonal harmony. There is little doubt that in today's world we need the characteristics of both to maximize our ability to live well between our ears.

NO SUBSTITUTE FOR PRACTICE

"Practice does not make perfect.
Only perfect practice makes perfect."

– Vince Lombardi

I RECENTLY WATCHED AN INTERVIEW WITH THREE COMPETITORS bound for the Olympics in London. According to them, performance is never good enough if it doesn't win gold. They train 7-8 hours every day, 6 or 7 days per week. That's some serious practice time. Do you practice your skills that much? How much better could you be if you were even close?

The athletes talked about their greatest achievements. Their personal best times or scores were almost always achieved at competitive events. They don't run the world's fastest 100 meters or dive the cleanest dives during practice. World records are usually broken at well attended, big events like the Olympics. Why is that?

In addition to talent and practice, it is because they are more energized when people are present. The athletes are energized by their fellow competitors and by the crowd when adulation from the fans is at its highest. This energizing effect, caused by the presence of other people, was discovered by psychologist Robert Zajonc in 1965. He called it "social facilitation" and it affects all of us.

It means we get extra energy just from being in a social environment; a type of power from the people. And it doesn't have to be a competition. A solo violinist, with no competitor in sight, has her finest performance in front of an audience. Her skills are enhanced by the heightened sense of arousal, driven simply by the people listening and watching. It pushes performance to another level.

The bad news is that the energizing force of social facilitation drives both the good and the not-so-good skills. For example, if a swimmer's technique is a tiny bit out of whack and adds a hundredth of a second to his time during practice, it might cost him two hundredths of a second at the Olympics. The social facilitation effect isn't choosy. It will energize the good behaviour as well as the bad; both our strengths and weaknesses are amplified.

What does this mean for us non-Olympians? It means that Dad wasn't kidding when he said that practice makes perfect. Some of our Dad's said that perfect practice makes perfect, and they were right. If we've had enough practice it means the correct techniques have become our dominant response. Too little practice makes it more likely that our mistakes are the dominant response.

Suppose you are a golfer in a big tournament. Of course you have more good habits, but there are still those niggling bad ones. Because of the added energizing effect of the gallery, you should expect your slices to be some of your worst, and your good drives and putts to be some of your best. If you are a duffer, with more bad habits than good, your scores will hit an all-time low. But, if you are a scratch golfer or better, you will probably shoot your best game.

Practice is important because it assures that the correct response becomes the most dominant, and it is our dominant responses that are influenced most by social facilitation. A soldier on patrol in Afghanistan, facing an unruly mob, is definitely in an aroused state. He is energized by the crowd and his dominant response better be the right one. Now is not the time to have the wrong response spring forth and precipitate a catastrophe.

Although she did not discuss it using the language of social facilitation, Bonnie Docherty was clearly talking about the same phenomenon in a 2007 report on military training. She, and the soldiers she interviewed, recommended much more practice for the troops heading off to urban warfare. She quoted an experienced major who said, "800 people scare the bejeezus out of soldiers." They recommended over-training (more practice) for urban, counter-insurgency-type situations. The report is a strong endorsement for the importance of practice to insure that the desired response is always dominant, especially when facing a high energy crowd.

These examples all point in the same direction; there is no substitute for practice. When you perform in public—and when do we not—recognize the power of social facilitation. It is an energizing force that makes the skilled better and the unskilled worse. Practice all your skills to make them dominant, and live well between your ears.

THANK A VOLUNTEER

"Volunteers don't just do the work ~ they make it work."

– Carol Pettit

IN A FAR-REACHING STUDY OF 2,444 VOLUNTEERS IN AUSTRALIA IN 2004, Judy Esmond and Patrick Dunlop found the number one reason people quit volunteering was lack of recognition. They were taken for granted and given few thanks. Of course, volunteers aren't paid, so the only recognition they get is when they are thanked. A few, such as mayors, councillors, and volunteer firemen, are paid in some communities but should still be considered volunteers because the economic benefit, if any, is not enough to attract and keep them.

Do you volunteer without being asked? Small communities in particular are heavily dependent on the time and energy of volunteers who help with all kinds of events. But not everyone volunteers, whether they are asked or not. According to Esmond and Dunlop, people decline to volunteer because they don't have the time or don't believe their help makes a difference.

The ones who volunteer without being asked are the organizers—the really special ones. These organizers spend hours per day and half their night's meeting and planning to make sure they overlook nothing. They volunteer because of their strong giving spirit, or they spring forth from a committee that is part of a town council, church, or service organization. They accept responsibility to make events come off without a hitch, and I'm sure you've noticed, they're always the same people.

As plans progress and the event draws near it comes time for the organizers to recruit more volunteers—the helpers. They are the people who are stopped in the street or called on the phone and asked to help man a booth, tend bar, sell tickets, help in the kitchen, or a hundred different tasks depending on the event.

But, without the organizers, the helpers would never get the call, the event would not take place, and the village, town, or community would suffer a diminished cultural experience. Any sense of community dies without volunteers. The volunteer helpers are critical to an event's success and deserve our thanks, but they're not in the same league as the volunteer organizers.

What drives people to volunteer? The Australian study says the top five reasons motivating them are: values, reciprocity, recognition, understanding, and self-esteem. Values stood out from the other four. People who volunteer because of their values do so because of strongly held beliefs that it is important for the good of the community and the people in it. It is the most altruistic of the reasons.

Esmond and Dunlop did not differentiate between organizers and helpers, but rather focused on volunteers in general. However, as described above, there is a qualitative difference. The organizers have broader over-sight, more responsibility, and a greater commitment of time and effort. Driven by fundamental beliefs about the importance of the community and helping others, a large part of their motivation comes from within.

The other four motivators indicate people volunteer to satisfy a need. Reciprocity means people volunteer because they believe what goes around comes around and the day may come when they need volunteers. Recognition implies we volunteer so our efforts are noticed. Understanding means the person has the chance of learning something from volunteering, and finally, people volunteer to maintain a feeling of usefulness—it boosts their self-esteem. No doubt combinations of all these motivators are operative for both organizer and helper volunteers.

However, a strong sense of giving, embodied by the values motive, is a major part of what drives the organizers.

It's not important why volunteers do it, we're just thankful that you do. Our communities would be much less enjoyable without you. So, when you see the volunteers in your community, recognize and thank them for all they do, and live well between your ears.

II
Keep yourself psychologically healthy

Addiction, depression, low self-esteem, stress, anxiety, anger—none of these are big problems unless they belong to you or someone you love. This section is about minimizing mental angst, regardless of its source. Some of these psychological issues lie just under the surface. They nag at us and it's hard to put a finger on them. But, it doesn't mean that we can't do something about them; that we have to suffer our lot in silence.

We don't have to accept that, "it's just the way we are." Diet makes a difference, lifestyle makes a difference, social surroundings make a difference, relationships make a difference, our personality-type makes a difference. All these are addressed in this section.

ADDICTED AND DON'T KNOW IT.

"Addiction: When you can give up something any time,
as long as it's next Tuesday."

– Lemmy

A FRIEND OF MINE LAMENTED, "I CAN'T MAKE MYSELF DO THE THINGS I know I should. I want to lose weight, spend less, eat healthy, exercise more, watch less TV, and read more. What the hell is the matter with me? I seem to be incapable of doing what I should." Does it sound familiar?

Having an addictive personality is one possible cause of such problems. Compared to the average person, people with addictive personalities are more impulsive, tolerate more deviance, have lower self-esteem, have a higher incidence of depression and anxiety, and most importantly, are less able to delay gratification.

Phillip Zimbardo (2008), a Psychologist doing quality research for decades, says that people who live for today have a weak future perspective and are not good self-controllers. They are more susceptible to addiction. They are like toddlers—self-centred and hedonistic—wanting everything right now.

Your weakness might be for sweets, cookies, alcohol, nicotine, salt, fries, sex, money, or the chance to gamble? Those are some of many. We can also become dependent on anything that provides relief from pain, depression, or anxiety. Despite their best intention to lose weight, feel good, quit bad habits, or begin good ones, the addict's focus is on immediate gratification: satisfaction as soon as possible.

The thought of cancer, high blood pressure, diabetes, obesity, or even premature death does not dissuade the addict. For example, instead of less meat, fewer trans-fats, and more vegetables, the food addict says, "I want it all," and adds Lipitor to his diet to fix his high cholesterol and unclog his arteries.

We can be so blinded by the power of a drug we'll risk its God-awful side effects rather than muster the will power to change diet or life-style. For example, the clinical trials for Lipitor reveal the most common side effects are: "diarrhea, upset stomach, muscle and joint pain, tiredness, and tendon problems."

Other side effects include "serious muscle problems" as well as "kidney disease that may lead to kidney failure." If that's not enough, add nausea and vomiting, brown or dark-colored urine, tiredness, and yellowing of your skin and eyes. You'd think veggies and exercise would be a small price to pay to avoid such calamities.

There are more warnings, but you get the idea. How stupid are we? We can't blame the food and drug companies. If they didn't warn us that their food has no nutrition and that their drugs could kill us, we'd sue them. The problem is, the person with addictive tendencies is overwhelmed by desire and can't will himself to leave the lethal donut at the bakery. Instead, he turns to a pill that might kill him, just so he can have it all.

We know better. We know trans-fats clog our arteries, but gobble them down anyway. We know we're 70 pounds over-weight, but buy the chips for the kids. Why—so they can be 70 pounds over-weight? We know we should save more, read more, or be more constructive, but the little voice inside does not shut up. You've heard it. It says, "Go to the cupboard, eat it now, buy it now, do it now, just once more, and I'll get on track tomorrow."

Many of us have these addictive tendencies. If it's not one thing it's another that tempts us to abandon our best intentions. Don't despair. It isn't uncontrollable, it's just difficult. Acknowledge the problem, enlist the support of friends, take control of yourself, empty your house of the things that tempt or distract you, replace thoughts of immediate gratification with thoughts of future goals, and if none of that works, visit a good therapist, and live well between your ears.

GOT THE POST-HOLIDAY BLUES?

"No one needs a vacation so much as the
person who has just had one."

– Elbert Hubbard

ONCE AGAIN CHRISTMAS CAME AND WENT. THE MONEY IS SPENT, turkey is eaten, it's still below zero, and the forecast includes more long nights and short days. Just in case you have a mild dose of the post-holiday blues, don't despair. Blame them on Mother Nature and the gap. There's nothing wrong with you. It's wise to step back. See if your crappy feelings stem from something outside you, rather than thinking you have something wrong on the inside that's driving you crazy. So, why mother nature? And, what's the gap?

Mother-nature is giving us more hours of darkness than light and that means our bodies produce a bit more of the hormone melatonin which tells us we are sleepy. Feeling sleepy feels like being tired, and that can feel like mild depression. For two to six percent of the population who live in northern hemispheres, the extra darkness can result in a type of depression called Seasonal Affective Disorder or S.A.D.

In our part of the northern hemisphere, darkness is right on cue—it arrives early and leaves late—so it is possible the other ninety-four to ninety-eight percent of us might feel a bit depressed. So, the absence of good old mister sun shining down on our stuffed little bodies may cause some of our winter blahs. If you think that's the problem, go online and buy yourself a sun lamp for SAD, follow the directions and see if that helps. But first, read on.

Probably the biggest culprit causing our post-holiday blues is the gap. Any time there is a big gap or discrepancy between what we think is going to be a wonderful fun-filled time and what we actually experience, we will feel let down. We often have great expectations for the holiday season. From the time we were little kids, Christmas was a happy time associated with family, friends, food, days off, no school, gift giving, and tons of other good stuff, too plentiful to describe.

But that's when we were kids. With each passing year, more stuff interferes with our happy holidays. Money is tight, not everyone is able to get home, the baby is sick, uncle Bob drinks too much, and who knows what else. The truth is, what really takes place during the holiday season is often a far cry from what we expected or planned. And no matter how we might gloss over it, the discrepancy between what we expected and what took place can lead to disappointment that lingers and causes the blahs. The greater the discrepancy, the greater the disappointment, and the more potential there is to feel depressed.

What's the solution? Just move on. The days will get longer. You're a good person. You did what you could. You can only control yourself, and not Uncle Bob. Let it come and go and move on to the next day, week, month, and year. Life is good—it's just not easy. Get back to a routine, eat your veggies, get more sleep, and exercise. Learn to manage your expectations so they are in line with a realistic and positive future, and live well between your ears.

HAS ANYONE SEEN WILL?

"Nothing is easy to the unwilling."

– Thomas Fuller

DO YOU KNOW PEOPLE WHO COMPLAIN ABOUT BEING SICK OR NOT feeling well? Are you one of them? Do you feel worn out, tired, heavy, sore, depressed, or just plain crappy? There are many opinions about why, but let's look at two relevant factors: (1) the causes of poor health and (2) whether we can control the causes.

There are four lists of things that make us sick. A few may be missing, but you'll get the drift. The 'A' list is about diet and life-style: sugar, saturated fat, food in a box, too few colourful fruits and vegetables, lack of sleep, lack of exercise, smoking, drugs, alcohol, and other harmful toxins all cause sickness. The 'B' list is germs: bacteria, fungi, viruses, and other intruders. The 'C' list is internal medical problems: chemical imbalances, high cholesterol, high cortisol, a weakened immune system, worn out or abused organs, and myriad medical mysteries. The 'D' list is psychological factors such as anger, impatience, low self-esteem, depression, and anxiety.

When these enemies of health are under control we feel better. But which ones can we control? It may not be easy, but we can take charge of the culprits on the 'A' list. It means saying no to yourself; swapping your bag of chips for a head of broccoli; taking walks further than from the couch to the fridge; cutting or reducing consumption of liquor, tobacco, and other toxins. If you need help with this list, look for Will. He'll lock the fridge and restrain you until you restrain yourself, or until the need for real food replaces your addiction to fake food.

The 'B' list guys are harder to manage. You might try wearing a surgical mask, filtering your air and water, or just dig a hole, jump in, and cover it up. But wait—not so fast— we know germs take over when our immune system is weak. We also know we can strengthen our immune system by taking charge of the 'A' list. Ah-ha, we can slow down those pesky germs after all.

The 'C' list usually requires a medical doctor or nurse practitioner depending upon severity. They can diagnose the medical condition, check out all the organs, identify the type of germ overwhelming your immune system, and prescribe something to cure or relieve the problem. But many of these 'C' list things are caused by our continued neglect of the things on the 'A' and 'D' lists. When we don't take charge of the things we can control, our doctor grows tired of our repeat visits and refers us back to Will. Hopefully you can find him before it is too late.

Controlling the items on the 'D' list is more difficult. We cannot see the psychological factors sneaking up on us so we don't make the connection between them and our health. For example, the connection between drinking too much and tomorrow's hangover is easy to understand because it happens right away. But the health-damaging effect of low self-esteem takes longer to recognize. In the fifties, two cardiologists, Friedman and Rosenbaum, were the first to notice that "Type A" personalities have a higher incidence of coronary heart disease. Since that time, many studies have shed light on the risk posed to our health by some psychological factors.

For example, in 1995, Kirschbaum and colleagues found that people with low self-esteem produce more prolonged and higher levels of cortisol in response to stress. This is not good for low self-esteem, stressed-out people in a stressful world. It is a problem because sustained, high levels of cortisol are one cause of impaired cognitive performance, blood sugar imbalance, high blood pressure, lowered immunity, increased abdominal fat, unhealthy cholesterol counts, and more.

That's a nasty list, but do we care? Yes we do, but only when we hurt. The point is that simply knowing the cause of sickness doesn't help if you can't find Will Power. So keep looking for him, and in the meantime, live well between your ears.

FARMERS AND RISK:
TOGETHER FOREVER

"The farmer has to be an optimist or he wouldn't still be a farmer."

– Will Rogers

IF YOU'RE A FARMER, YOU'D LIKE SOME ANSWERS. WILL THERE BE RAIN, drought, hail, bugs, disease, late frost, early frost, early snow, a bad market, or major equipment problems this year? No one knows. Other than farming, is there any business where a person assumes so much liability in the face of so much uncertainty? I don't think so. It made me think about the psychological profile farmers must possess to enjoy their life to the max.

But before getting to that, the latest update from Agriculture and Agri-Food Canada forecasts a 2 percent decline in farm income. They say it's because higher expenses and decreased program payments will exceed projections for increased crop and livestock sales. At the same time, the consumer price index is forecasting a 2.2 percent increase in the cost of food at the supermarket. It's a familiar refrain: food costs up, farm income down.

To all this you may say, "Bull, farmers always have money." Perhaps, but they accept a boat load of risk for the money they do or don't have.

By any risk-reward analysis, food producers the world over are in the poor house compared to the processors, brokers, and retail food outlets. The small producer has no leverage, and in this global economy, won't have until there is agreement by the world's major food exporters on a fair and equitable price per tonne. OPEC gets away with it.

But there's much about Ag economics I don't know. What I do know is farming is a life you have to love because the financial reward is too small, relative to the risk, to be in it for the money. The other thing I know is that not everyone is cut out to be a farmer. So, what does the psychological profile for the happiest farmers look like?

In addition to the obvious things like being a good business person able to make decisions, the happiest farmers have a high tolerance for ambiguity, a valued characteristic according to psychologists. This means the farmer can function and remain level headed without too much distress in the face of uncertainty. We're not talking about your average uncertainty, but the tough kind: the kind that stems from lack of control when the financial stakes are high. Two uncontrollable biggies are the weather and the price received for their product.

It's these two factors that make it necessary to have a high tolerance for ambiguity. What independent business owner do you know, besides a farmer, who can't set their own competitive price for something they produce themselves, and whose financial security is dependent on something as unpredictable as the weather?

This doesn't mean farmers are not in control of their destiny. On the contrary, they exercise their control by making major decisions with little input from others. Unlike decisions most people have to make at work, decisions on the farm usually have big financial implications. Such things as when and where to purchase equipment (none of it cheap), how to set up seeding and harvesting equipment, till or no till, fertilizer and chemical decisions, and choices about timing and profitable strategies . At the same time, it is hard to imagine any other business upon which Mother Nature can wreak such financial havoc, and undo all the careful decision making with just one evening of hail or a night of frost.

When stuff breaks or goes wrong, almost daily, they're there by themselves to fix it. Each repair, sometimes make-shift, offers a unique opportunity for a sense of accomplishment and builds a level of confidence and independence not generated by most other careers. Their confidence helps sustain their optimism, without which, farming would be difficult.

Despite decades of declining numbers, many farmers still dot the landscape. They continue to manage their business and their lives in a low margin, high dollar, and high risk environment. Here's to greater marketing leverage and cooperative weather to help you live well between your ears.

STRESS: HOW TO COPE

"Problems are not the problem; coping is the problem."

– Virginia Satir

ARE YOU WORRIED ABOUT YOUR HEALTH? MAYBE AN ACHE THAT WON'T quit, a lump you just noticed, or a scary diagnosis. Coping is all about how we deal with threat and worry. How we cope can make us feel better or worse. Some people worry more than others; it depends on the coping strategy they use. How do you cope?

Do you pace the floor, withdraw to a quiet place, develop a plan, find someone to talk with, analyze the situation, fret and stew, or ignore it?

We each cope with worry differently; how we cope affects our happiness. According to a 2009 study by Hasida Ben-Zur, reported in the International Journal of Stress Management, effective coping can promote positive feelings, mental and physical health, and a day-to-day sense of well-being.

We each have a predominant coping strategy, but we may employ some combination of three: problem focused, emotional focused, and avoidance focused. Focus on the problem leads to greater peace of mind and a return to happiness. Avoidance is the least effective, and emotional responses leave us somewhere in the middle.

Direct attention on the problem is best and means we gather information, develop a plan, look for the silver lining, and approach it head on. Second best are the emotional strategies that lead you to seek support from others, join a support group, see the humour in the situation, confess your worries to a friend or spouse, or allow yourself to feel sad. The avoidance strategies are when you do nothing constructive; you decide to hide your head in the sand and hope it goes away. A common avoidance strategy is rumination: when you have the same worrisome and non-productive thoughts over and over again. Rumination is the least effective coping mechanism and leads to inactivity, depression, and helplessness.

Based on her research, Ben-Zur recommends starting with the coping methods at the top of the list and not even considering those at the bottom. When we gather information, make a plan, and approach problems directly, we take control of the only thing we can—ourselves. In fact, a repeated theme in psychological research is that things always improve when we learn to control our own behaviour and feelings, instead of trying to control those of others.

So, what makes some people more problem-focused than others? In general, they have a stronger sense of self-efficacy; they believe in their ability to be successful—to make a difference—and to take charge of their life. Self-efficacy is a concept first introduced by Albert Bandura in 1977. It stems from a history of success, from watching others cope successfully, and from people who believe in you. It's when you master your emotional responses and replace fear, stress, and sadness with positive outlooks.

What steps can you take to deal with problems that affect you? If it is a health concern, for example, you may compare symptoms with others, research it online, and keep records of the severity and incidence of the symptoms to provide relevant information to your Doctor. Do your symptoms subside with rest? Are they correlated with certain foods, times of day, or any other event in your life? Learn as much as you can; you may discover ways to help yourself. Are you doing the things your health care provider recommended? Should you be more active, drink less, change your diet, or reduce exposure to toxins such as pest and weed spray.

The emotional strategies are less direct. Nonetheless, they get you actively involved in recognizing and dealing with the issue. Getting things off your chest and discussing them with friends, family, or supportive others is a common remedy for things that worry us. And, keeping some humour in the mix keeps things in perspective. The best example of that comes from Riolli and Savicki (2010) who found that soldiers stationed in Iraq who maintained a sense of humour about traumatic situations were able to cope with them more effectively.

So, cope for contentment. Keep your head out of the sand, replace destructive rumination with problem-focused action, throw in some humour to lighten your mood, and live well between your ears.

BEHAVIOUR MODIFICATION
AT HOME

"The consequences of an act affect the probability
of its occurring again."

– B.F. Skinner

IF YOU WANT TO UNDERSTAND WHY THREE-YEAR OLD MARY IS A
screamer, Joe cheats, Alex sulks, and Jane never leaves the house, start by
understanding the consequences of their behaviour.

Decades of research in behavioural psychology confirm that we continue to do things when they produce positive outcomes, and we quit
doing them when they produce aversive consequences. This is a for-sure-
thing, not a maybe-thing. Behaviour and its consequences form contingency relationships, and there is always more than one at work. Discover
what they are, and life is less mysterious and more predictable.

Some people don't believe in behaviour modification. That's like not
believing in gravity; it is lawful and occurs whether you believe or not.
We use it all the time—usually in the form of negative reinforcement
and punishment. The nonbelievers often equate positive reinforcement
with bribery. It is no more bribery than getting paid to work, getting an
ovation for a good speech, or getting a ticket for speeding. It's what we

do if we want to encourage good behaviour, and teach people the rules of the game. For example, driving the speed limit is *negatively reinforced* because it results in *avoiding* a fine by driving the speed limit, whereas *receiving* a $500 reward for driving the proper speed would be *positive reinforcement*. I think the latter might make me drive the speed limit more often, although it's not likely to happen any time soon.

Suppose three year-old Johnnie has a melt-down at the dinner table. He yells for juice instead of milk, he doesn't want peas on his plate, and he throws a fit when his older sister tries to help. First—and this is important—you have to define the behaviours you want to increase and those you want to decrease. Effective behaviour modification requires that we know exactly what behaviours we want to increase and those we want to decrease. If we don't, we'll almost certainly end up strengthening the wrong behaviour. In this case, we want him to be quiet, eat his peas, and accept the milk. We've all seen it, so you know what I'm talking about. Of course, it's mostly a problem for other people's kids.

As long as he's fussing and screaming at his sister, it's a non-starter. The first thing you could do to quiet him down is to implement a 'time-out' procedure. For example, if he continues to yell at his sister—despite your requests for silence—take him and leave him in a quiet place where he cannot attract anyone's attention, watch TV, or do anything else he likes. In time-out he should be ignored until he is well behaved for some period of time—usually around 15 or 20 seconds. Most people use time out periods that are much too long. If you're going to use time-out effectively, you need to pay close attention. The moment he's quiet, he gets to re-join the people or the activity from which he was withdrawn. If he starts to howl as soon as he sees you, immediately put him in time-out again until he understands that only when he quits misbehaving will you end the time-out period.

If the truth be known, you might not even care if he eats his peas. You just want him to quietly accept the damn peas, accept his milk, quit yelling at his sister, use his spoon to eat his food, and interact in a civil way with those at the dinner table. Offer praise, recognition, and thanks when he initiates any sign of quiet conversation, pea acceptance, proper use of his spoon, or any other semblance of appropriate activity for the dinner table. If he screws up, it's back to time-out.

Positive reinforcement is more difficult for the parent because it means paying attention to the kid when he is being good. The problem is that when they're good, we normally leave them alone. It's only when they're misbehaving that they get our attention, and in that case, we inadvertently reinforce, and therefore increase, the bad behaviour because we interacted with them.

The more common, but less desirable, method to increase Johnny's table manners is to use negative reinforcement. It is when you make avoidance of an aversive outcome contingent upon being well behaved—like the speeding ticket. For example, by behaving well he can avoid things he doesn't like such as being scolded, lectured, chastised or ignored. This is what normally passes for parental discipline, and in the long run, it is less effective than positive reinforcement. It's less effective because the parents aren't forced to attend to the good behaviour—it is ignored—which is a sure-fire way to decrease the likelihood of its occurrence. The problem is that kids want your attention, and the only way they can get it, if you use negative reinforcement, is to misbehave because misbehaving causes you to interact with them.

What do we do to decrease the misbehaviour? We usually punish it in one of two ways. We either follow his bad act with scolding—a spanking in the old days—or we follow it with the removal of a positive event. You may take away his favourite toy, his food, his cookie, and remove him from any social contact. The first method, following bad actions with an aversive consequence, is the worst. It creates fear and emotional disturbances that usually aren't hallmarks of a good childhood. Withdrawing a positive consequence—taking away privileges or using time-out—is more effective.

Because we are people and not lab rats, make sure you explain these contingency relationships to the kid, no matter how young they are. Explain that the reason he's getting praise is because he is well behaved, and that the toy was removed and he was placed in time-out because he misbehaved. The better the child understands the relationship between what he does and its consequences, the quicker he learns.

There are times to use punishment; it's just not the preferred method. For example, running into the street without looking for cars, warrants punishment. It is better that Dad scare the crap out of him by yelling than have him run over by a car.

So, if you're a parent, teacher, or coach, try to catch your kids being good. In the long run, it is much more effective to notice and reward the good behaviour than it is to catch and punish bad behaviour. Learn to manage the contingency relationships, stick to your guns, and help the child and you live well between your ears.

WE ARE WHAT WE DO NOW

"Action speaks louder than words but not nearly as often."

– Mark Twain

BEHAVIOURAL PSYCHOLOGISTS SAY WE ARE WHAT WE DO. WHAT DOES it mean? It means our sense of identity—our sense of who we are—is based on what we do, not on what we did before or what we might do in the future. You're not a carpenter if you don't build. You're not a farmer if you don't farm. You're not a teacher if you don't teach. You can think you are all kinds of wonderful things, but if you don't do them it means nothing—just dreams, thoughts, and talk. There is nothing wrong with dreams and thoughts. Just don't count on them to provide a solid identity until you start living them. And, the only time you can live them, is in the present.

Countless talk show hosts, authors, and other new-age prognosticators have jumped on the live-in-the-moment movement as if it was a new idea. Really! There's nothing new about 'now', and there has never been another time to do anything. If you don't do it now, you aren't doing it at all. You can't do it in the past; the future isn't here yet; you're either doing it now, or not at all. It's an idea with a long history.

Someone once said, if you have one eye on yesterday and one eye on tomorrow, you're going to be cockeyed today. The poet Emily Dickinson (1830-1886) wrote, "Forever is composed of nows." Another poet, Ralph Waldo Emerson (1803-1882), said, "We are always getting ready to live but never living." Einstein, who died at 76 in 1955, weighed in with, "I never think about the future, it comes soon enough." William James (1842-1910), the father of modern psychology, offered this advice, "To change one's life: Start immediately. Do it flamboyantly. No exceptions." Charles Caleb Colton, the British writer who died in 1832 at the age of 52, wrote, "Time is the most un-definable yet paradoxical of things; the past is gone, the future is not come, and the present becomes the past even while we attempt to define it, and like the flash of lightning, at once exists and expires." And, in the mid-fifties, renowned psychologist Abraham Maslow (1908-1970) said, "The ability to be in the present moment is a major component of mental wellness." As you can see, there's nothing new about the live-in-the-now craze.

We all know we have to focus on making the most of today—tomorrow is not here, and yesterday is gone—but it is difficult. When not preoccupied with yesterday, we are often worried about tomorrow. The moments slip by. Soon, today winds up as yesterday, and we've done four and four-fifths of sweet tweet, except weaken our identity.

All this leads to the frightening conclusion that in those moments or, heaven forbid, days when we are doing nothing, we become nothing, going nowhere. Each tick-tock is gone forever. We can plan to do it later, but that means that right now we are planners or procrastinators doing nothing. Of course, having a plan is critical, but nothing happens until you execute the plan.

Our past is a fading memory of what was. Science can't even determine where memories reside, let alone know what they are. Besides, shaky memories only give rise to weak and inaccurate identities which cause other problems. Our future, until it happens, is a plan at best and a wish or dream (maybe even a nightmare) at worst.

Of course, there must be more to us than just doing or not doing in the present. There is. Our past experience does shape our lives: how we think, and why we do what we do. But the effect our past has on our identity pales in comparison to the effect of action taken in the present.

For many moments in the day we are TV watchers, snoozers, day-dreamers, and eaters. You see where this goes. Whatever we do—we are. If we do nothing much, then we are nothing much. When we spend weeks doing nothing worthwhile in the present, life feels empty or worse; we end up dwelling on the past which leads to depression, or dwelling on the future which creates anxiety. Doing! It's what fills us up, strengthens our identity, and is most rewarding.

So, here's to the people doing something right now. Without them, nothing gets done. Do what you've been putting off, and be the person you intend to be. Do it now, and live well between your ears.

PATIENCE: A VANISHING VIRTUE

"Patience is bitter, but its fruit is sweet."

– Aristotle

PATIENCE IS DEFINED AS HAVING THE CAPACITY FOR CALM ENDURance under difficult circumstances. It's when we don't act with annoyance or anger in the face of frustration or delay. For example, in busy traffic, patience is preferred to road rage. We are patient when we curb the impulsive desires that get us into trouble, or cause us to buy things we don't need, or do things we regret. If patience is nothing else, it's rare.

Last week I heard a man complain to a couple of friends about the big red pill he got from the Doctor. Apparently it didn't work, but it reminded me, as did the frustration in his voice, that we've come to expect everything immediately. In this case, the guy wanted a health issue cured by the big red pill. If he weighed an ounce, he weighed four hundred pounds. Not to be critical, but really—a pill? Diet and exercise might have helped, but the pill is quicker and that's the point. We're impatient and want it fixed now.

Historically, impatience is sinful. All the major religions extol the virtue of patience. For example, Judaism proclaims the patient man shows good sense. Christianity lists patience as one of seven virtues, along with chastity, temperance, charity, diligence, kindness and humility. Islam maintains patience is one of the valuable virtues which move one closer to God to attain pure peace. Buddhists say patience is one of the perfections to practice to realize enlightenment.

Psychologists view patience as the ability to exercise self-control; to regulate what we do and how we feel, in order to reduce our impulsive desires. For example, we control our impulse to buy a car or a box of chocolates if we leave the showroom floor or walk past the aisle of chocolates. Alternatively, we can do something as simple as count to ten, which distracts us from the immediate, I-have-to-have-it feeling. We can also control the urge by reminding ourselves that the benefits of previous impulsive acts were short lived or less satisfying than we imagined.

The people able to regulate behaviour and feelings most effectively are those who have an internal, as opposed to external, locus of control. First studied in 1966 by psychologist Julian Rotter, it's a concept that is still in vogue today. If you are an 'internal' you believe that positive and negative outcomes in your life are controlled by you. 'Externals' believe their life outcomes are controlled by others or by fate. Those people who have an internal locus of control are able to exercise greater patience.

What might cause our impulsiveness? Sigmund Freud proposed that an unconscious factor, the Id, energized by our sexual energy and the fear of death, controls our basic and relentless drive for immediate gratification. According to Freud, our Ego, that part of our personality which keeps us organized and grounded in reality, together with the Superego, best thought of as our conscience, are charged with the task of keeping our Id—the greedy, hedonistic, I-want-it-now mechanism—under control. Good luck! The Id appears to be winning the battle.

Perhaps we are weak willed because the advertising industry has crippled our patience and exploited our impulsiveness? We are inundated with reminders on TV, radio, bill boards, and the internet, to get it, have it, eat it, do it, feel it, or fix it right now. We have come to expect everything quickly. Stuff we didn't know about a few years ago, we now can't do without.

If it wasn't so annoying it would be comical. In less than ten minutes, my television reminded me that I should pick my McFlurry at McDonalds, get Spicy Mama at A&W, eliminate my deep wrinkles with Nutrogena, and get an educational foundation good for the rest of my life at ITT tech. I was reassured I could get all the right ingredients eating Tostitos, and even get cash at Toyota's nationwide tent sale. Famous footwear will sell me one pair of shoes and give me half off the second pair. And get this: Mazda only builds cars worth driving. That's good to know! Wouldn't you hate it if they made one that wasn't worth driving?

"But wait," as the guy on TV screams, "if you call right now, we'll send you a second one free—blah, blah, blah." There is no end to the commercials or the stupidity of the messages. If you feed Pedia-Sure (it doesn't even sound like food) to your soccer-playing-goalie-daughter it prevents her from looking like a fat donut through which the Pedia-Sure-fed-kids kick the ball. Yup, better feed your kid Pedia-Sure or she'll be fat, no good at sports, and who knows what else.

KFC has "cheap" chicken. Foster Farms' chicken is fresh within 48 hours, a nice way of saying the cute little cluckers were killed less than two days ago. But, the most exciting news came from Nexus Hair Salon. Nexus puts 92 percent of your split ends back together, and in two weeks your hair is together, and—get this—so are you! I couldn't believe it. You, not just your hair, are together in two weeks. No more need for self-help books or therapists.

Every one of these commercials carried the subtle message that the smart, attractive, and happiest people do these things without waiting another day. We're encouraged to be impatient, but don't let them get to you. Become more internal. Exercise self-control. Count to 10. Hell, count to 1000 if necessary. Let the desire for immediate gratification subside, and live well between your ears.

DOES YOUR NEED FOR A BLACK
AND WHITE WORLD HOLD YOU BACK?

"To be uncertain is to be uncomfortable,
but to be certain is to be ridiculous."

– Chinese Proverb

A FEW MONTHS AGO, A PERSON I'VE KNOWN FOR YEARS TOLD ME, "I have more debt than assets, I worry about everything, and I can't afford to change. I wake up panicky, sweating like a pig because money is tight. Things I used to do don't seem to work anymore. No matter how hard I rack my brain, I can't make it better. My life is going to hell, and I don't know what to do."

Money worries magnify our other problems so, if this sounds like you, seek out a certified financial planner (CFP) with the best financial planning software, and at least get help with the financial part of the puzzle.

But this is not about the obvious remedies: save more, spend less, and stay within budget. You already know that. Rather, there might be something about you—about your personality—that creates sleepless nights and too much worry.

Do you agree with these three statements: (1) The sooner we all acquire similar values and ideals the better. (2) An expert, who doesn't come up with a definite answer, probably doesn't know too much. (3) What we are used to is always preferable to what is unfamiliar.

If you agree more than disagree with them, you may be your own worst enemy. It means you can't tolerate ambiguity, and since today's financial and political climate is more ambiguous than ever, your intolerance is a problem. The world is more complex, business is more complicated, and the rate of change has quickened. These conditions lead to values that are different, not similar; questions that are tougher not easier; a need for creative solutions, rather than reverting back to your old ways.

Tolerance of ambiguity is defined by the American Psychological Association as: "the degree to which one is able to accept, and to function without distress or disorientation in situations having conflicting or multiple interpretations or outcomes." Agreement with the three sample statements above means you would likely score high on the complete Intolerance of Ambiguity Scale developed by Budner in 1962. Agreement means it is likely that your intolerance of ambiguity causes you to make a few bad decisions.

Our businesses, personal lives, and the world in general are more ambiguous than ever. They are rife with conflicting interpretations and outcomes. If we don't learn to tolerate them—indeed, to thrive in their midst—we are doomed to deal less effectively with the complex issues we face and everything, including our financial situation, will worsen.

Research shows that people who cannot tolerate ambiguity well see issues as black and white; they feel nervous or threatened by uncertainty. They react prematurely, discount information that is inconsistent with what they believe, give up sooner on tough problems, exhibit prejudicial tendencies toward unfamiliar situations and people, and retreat to polarized, simplistic opinions that are difficult to dislodge.

Preference for black and white over shades of grey makes you stubborn. You may overlook important alternatives in order to keep things simple, or react prematurely because you're anxious to get the conflicting stuff behind you. For example, you may say no to improved technology because you've just started to understand the old one.

And, don't forget, our demographics are changing. It is no longer white, Anglo Saxon, run-of-the-mill, white folks who move to town. South American, Sikhs, Arabs, Filipinos, First Nations, and others comprise a growing and economically powerful population base. Statistics Canada reported minorities accounted for 16 percent of the population in 2006, and by 2031, that number will double. The prejudicial tendencies found among the intolerant make it more difficult for them to prosper and enjoy peace of mind in an ethnically diverse population.

The ability to be more tolerant of uncertainty, to relish the cultural differences, to welcome what's new, and to roll with the punches, are all game changers. They make a difference in how we behave and how we are perceived by others. An increasingly diversified population will tend to push those who are intolerant to the sidelines where they'll find less opportunity and a weakened sense of belonging.

Adapting to a changing world is easier for those with a high tolerance of ambiguity because they are less threatened by difficult situations or a shortage of information. The tolerant are also more patient. It means they are better able to connect the dots when the information is plentiful and complex. They remain open to multiple solutions in the face of apparent contradictions.

Is it possible to become more tolerant of ambiguity? Yes, but it isn't easy. The research says tolerance increases when we become more familiar with new things, get more education, take the time and make the effort to experience things beyond our comfort zone, and begin to empathize with others. It also helps to be open to suggestion, exhaust all sources of relevant data, accept input from others, brainstorm solutions, and acknowledge that multiculturalism and complexity are here to stay. The world is less black and white, so find comfort in the shades of gray, and live well between your ears.

NEGATIVITY

"Anger is an acid that can do more harm to the vessel in which it is stored than to anything on which it is poured."

– Mark Twain

ARE THERE NEGATIVE PEOPLE IN YOUR LIFE; THOSE WHO COMPLAIN frequently about something or someone? I found surprisingly little research on what causes some folks to always see the glass half empty. Reading between the lines, it seems that negative people often see things as threats to themselves. But what is the connection between being negative and feeling threatened?

Being negative provides a means of deflecting attention away from one's self, thus avoiding evaluation, judgement, or criticism. The negative person is a type of bully and we try to steer clear of them. We are less likely to interact with them because we tire of their negativity and aggressive nature. So their purpose is served—they avoid evaluation, judgement, or criticism because the rest of us want nothing to do with them.

Being a bully may mean asserting a problem and magnifying it. For example, a person may say to their spouse, "you don't respect my need for some alone time, in fact, the minute I sit down to read or watch TV, you want me to do something else." If they argue, the bully sticks to his statement, while the other person maintains a defensive position, saying or doing things in an effort to diffuse the situation, or as a last resort, they may go silent and walk away. In any case, the person being criticized is put off guard; the bully gains control, reinforcing his position as the one who has been harmed.

Bullying stems from insecurity. They make a mountain out of a mole hill with their rants, and they become the authority figure appearing to be right. The recipient avoids all this by allowing the bully to prevail rather than making the situation worse.

So, are you a negative person? Do you notice yourself saying: I hate such and such, I can't stand it when ..., that is stupid, this coffee is too strong, the government sucks, don't eat there, I can't stand their food, or how dumb can they get. Perhaps you give orders in harsh terms as if you have the right to exercise control over the other. The negative person may be critical of successful people or complain that people whom he dislikes have life too good, and they don't deserve it. Negative people find fault; they view those who are different as inferior. They also blame others rather than accept responsibility for their own misfortunes.

No one sets out to be negative. It's a response to a threatening situation that exists more in the mind than in reality, and it becomes a bad habit. But if you're spring-loaded to negativity, how do you overcome it? Psychologist, Stephen Hayes (2005) of the University of Nevada, suggests a few techniques to avoid negativity.

For example, pay attention to your negative thoughts and the urge to speak or act negatively. Become conscious of what you were going to say, acknowledge that the negativity is non-productive, and figure out what triggered the urge. He also suggests that you think of your mind as another bodily organ. When you find yourself becoming negative in response to a stressful or threatening situation, remind yourself that it's the same as a hungry stomach rumbling. Instead of being negative, think, "There goes my mind again, worrying about something trivial."

We can also reduce our negativity by realizing we are safe. Analysis of our past tells us that the things we worried about usually never happened; we weren't evaluated, judged, or criticized unfairly, and our safety wasn't at risk. The same is true of the present, we usually are not threatened.

There is no need to deflect an attack by bullying or being negative if the threat will never materialize.

As with most psychological help, recognizing and understanding the problem is critical. Pay attention to how your words and actions affect others. Listen to yourself and recognize your negativity; replace it with either no comment or something positive. Control your thoughts and acts—they do become your reality—and live well between your ears.

The Big Five and You

"Personality is immediately apparent, from birth,
and I don't think it really changes."

– Meryl Streep

HAVE YOU NOTICED THAT PEOPLE DON'T CHANGE? IF THEY WERE energetic, selfish, and talkative as kids, they are that way most of their life. We change careers, hobbies, friends, food preferences, and other characteristics, but personality traits are more permanent. It's more noticeable among family members because we know them best. A traumatic event or exposure to new ideas or different cultures may cause someone to do an about face on one or more of these dimensions, but that is more the exception than the rule.

I'm not a big believer in the use of labels; we are never all one or the other. We're always combinations. The problem is, once attached, the labels tend to stick, usually more to the detriment than to the credit of the recipient. So tuck today's topic in your "information-only" category rather than in your "ways-to-describe-my-spouse" category.

Psychological research, from the 1930's to the present, perhaps best exemplified by Paul Costa Jr. and Robert McCrae's work in the 1990's, support a five factor model of personality. Different research teams approach the issue from different perspectives, but the consensus is that we humans are, at least partly, described by five broad dimensions: extraversion, neuroticism, agreeableness, conscientiousness, and openness. They are referred to as the Big Five. Yes, there are hundreds of other ways to describe people, but when submitted to statistical analysis, the many adjectives and adverbs we use to describe each other tend to fall under one or the other of these five.

Highly extraverted people are affectionate, joiners, fun-loving, talkative, active, and passionate. If you are low on the extraverted dimension, you are more introverted and described as reserved, a loner, sober, quiet, passive, and unfeeling. Of course, you may be somewhere in the middle, in which case you possess some low and some high characteristics of extraversion. But, typically, we are more one way than the other on each of the Big Five.

Highly neurotic people are anxious, temperamental, self-pitying, self-conscious, emotional, and vulnerable. A person low in neuroticism is calm, even-tempered, comfortable, unemotional, and hardy. Yup, being less neurotic is a good thing.

People who are high on the agreeableness dimension are soft-hearted, trusting, generous, acquiescent, lenient, and good natured. Those who are not agreeable are more ruthless, suspicious, stingy, antagonistic, critical, and irritable.

Highly conscientious people are hardworking, well organized, punctual, ambitious, and persevering. The non-conscientious folks are more likely lazy, disorganized, late, aimless, and quitters.

Finally, people high on openness are imaginative, creative, original, curious, and liberal. Their opposites, those who are not open to new experience, are down-to-earth, uncreative, conventional, prefer routine, not curious, and conservative.

What is the point? Why does it matter? Maybe it doesn't matter; we are who we are. The point is, for better or worse, we use our knowledge of these dimensions to understand people and to predict how they might behave.

For example, if your friend is self-conscious, emotional, and temperamental, you don't say things she may interpret as critical for fear of hurting her feelings—unless, of course, you are very low on agreeableness.

Similarly, we ask for trouble when we recruit a non-conscientious person to organize Joe's retirement party. It could be cake-less, gift-less, and totally disorganized, much to the disappointment of Joe. But again, if you are low on the agreeableness dimension, you may not care. In fact, you may think Joe deserves it.

People are complex. Different characteristics are more dominant depending on the situations; so one label is never going to be accurate. It's one thing to use labels to understand people, it's quite another to label someone with an inaccurate (and perhaps hurtful) name-tag. Remember what your mother told you: "If you can't say something nice, don't say anything at all." Be careful with your use of labels, and live well between your ears.

DO WE REALLY NEED REGULAR EXERCISE?

"Our growing softness, our increasing lack of physical fitness,
is a menace to our security."

– John F. Kennedy

APART FROM MAINTAINING A NUTRITIONAL DIET, IF WE COULD DO just one thing to live a healthy and vibrant life, it would be to get enough exercise. There is no shortage of scientific evidence supporting the many benefits of regular exercise. The obvious are that it strengthens and maintains muscles and bones. Without activity our bodies decline in every way. If you have aches, pains, digestive problems, unwanted fat, or any number of similar problems, regular exercise will help.

There are many reasons we don't exercise, none of them as compelling as the reasons we should. In 2001, P. Salmon confirmed that aerobic exercise—walking, running, cycling, or anything to increase your heart rate—produces anti-depressant and anti-anxiety effects, as well as providing enduring resistance to the negative effects of stress.

Hansen, Stevens & Coast (2001) found that riding a stationary bike, to achieve a sixty percent increase in oxygen volume for ten, twenty or thirty minutes per day, resulted in improved vigor and less fatigue, confusion, and negativity. The positive results increased when the exercise duration went from ten to twenty minutes, but beyond that there was no appreciable difference.

In 2000, Hassmen, Koivula, and Utela studied 3004 Finnish men and women ranging in age from twenty-five to sixty-four. Individuals who exercised two to three times per week experienced significantly less depression, anger, cynical distrust, and stress, than those exercising less or not at all. Those who exercised also reported higher levels of alertness and a greater sense of social integration.

Similarly, Lee and colleagues, studying 102 ethnic minority women, found that a seven-week walking routine produced a significant decrease in depressed mood even two to five months later. Working in India, Ray and colleagues found that five to ten months of Yoga produced greater shoulder, hip, and neck flexibility, as well as reduced anxiety and depression.

Results like these are common. There is no denying the positive effects of exercise. The problem is we do not get enough. Sometimes knowing why something works provides a more compelling reason to do it. Exercise works because it stimulates bodily systems; they function more efficiently.

The most immediate benefit is that exercise produces an overall sense of well-being. It stimulates our elimination systems. Our lung, liver, and kidney functions are improved; blood and lymph circulation—we have at least two times more lymphatic fluid than blood in our bodies—is enhanced, and the alimentary canal is made more efficient. All this reduces the toxins in our body and puts less strain on our immune system. It stimulates our nervous system causing muscles to relax and blood vessels to dilate which helps control high blood pressure.

Exercise also stimulates production of white blood cells which strengthen the immune system. It reduces the incidence of LDL, the bad cholesterol, and increases HDL, the good. It increases oxygen to the brain, thus improving mental function.

Finally, there is a critical relationship between activity, aging, and self-esteem that is worth mentioning, especially since most of us are not immune to aging. There are three types of self-esteem: verbal, interpersonal, and physical, which combine to shape our overall sense of self-worth and confidence. The decline in activity that occurs with age lowers physical self-esteem. What makes it worse is that low self-esteem is also associated with greater stress, anxiety, depression, and cynicism. High self-esteem, on the other hand, is associated with faster recovery from injury, confidence, optimism, internal locus of control, better job performance, humour, and the ability to care for self and others.

Research indicates that physical self-esteem stems directly from dissatisfaction with our: health, agility, athletic ability, neatness and cleanliness, body shape, build, and proportion, weight, coordination, and our clothes. All of these characteristics decline naturally with age, so if we don't become more active, we greatly increase the probability of suffering from the psychological maladies that accompany low self-esteem, to say nothing of the reduced bodily functions which come with inactivity.

The truth is: regardless of age, regular exercise is necessary to live well between your ears.

For a test to measure self-esteem go to www.livewellbetweenyourears.com

Depression, Food, and
Psychological Assets

"I am not what happened to me. I am what I chose to become."

– Carl Jung

DO YOU FEEL SAD, HOPELESS, WEAK, TIRED, AND LESS INTERESTED IN getting out and about to do things you once found pleasurable? If the answer is yes, you might be depressed. It is an insidious problem. It can make you weak, sad, despondent, and disinterested, causing you to lose all motivation to do anything, which compounds the problem.

Three hundred and forty million people—five percent of the world's population—suffer from clinical depression. It's closer to ten percent in developed countries. One in four women suffer from situational depression which, if it lasts longer than four months and grows disproportionate to the precipitating event, becomes clinical depression, complete with its own diagnosis and probably a prescription for Zoloft or some other SSRI (selective serotonin re-uptake inhibitor). One in ten men and one in twenty teenagers suffer from depression.

The American Psychological Association defines depression as: "A mood or mental state that can vary in severity from a fluctuation in normal mood to an extreme feeling of sadness, pessimism, and despondency." It is a continuum; some days you feel very depressed, and other days it is mild.

Sad events, such as loss of a loved one, loss of a job, loss of status, or lost mobility due to sickness, age, or disability, are some of the seeds of depression. The seed bed for such depression-triggering events is made more fertile when we do two things: ingest the wrong stuff, and reduce meaningful activity. These two choices are more critical than the triggering events themselves. Let's look first at ingesting the wrong stuff.

The neurotransmitter, serotonin, is the chemical linked most often to depression. Sugar, alcohol, caffeine, nicotine, diet pills, and antihistamines deplete the availability of serotonin. Low levels of serotonin results in inefficient transmission of messages throughout our nervous system, which causes depression.

The problem is our body either produces too little serotonin, or what it does produce is re-absorbed too quickly. Either way, it is unable to fulfill its role as an efficient transmitter of messages from one nerve cell to the next. The re-absorption problem can sometimes be successfully treated with a prescription for an SSRI. If the problem is a shortage of serotonin, taking the supplement 5HTP, its natural precursor, may help (Schimelpfening, 2011).

The link between a healthy diet and freedom from depression is well established. Plenty of fresh fruit and vegetables, along with essential vitamins (B3, B6, D), minerals (zinc and magnesium), and fatty acid (omega 3) will help send depression packing. As far back as Hippocrates in the 5th century we've known that, until we develop nutrient-rich eating habits, we will continue to experience mental and physical problems.

The key is to eat for fuel and not for taste. Maintaining a life style free of sugar and refined and processed food greatly reduces the risk factors for poor mental and physical health. It is hard to go wrong if you get your groceries from the produce section and stay away from all food that comes in a box.

The second factor causing a fertile seed bed for depression is the reduction of meaningful activity. It leads to psychological bankruptcy. Think of all the skills, activities, creative abilities, hobbies, sports, social interactions, special talents, special relationships, and group memberships you have ever had. Each of those is a psychological asset. They shape who you are—your sense of identity or self-concept. We can lose them due to inactivity, age, disability, accidents, or simple neglect. As these assets are allowed to decline we become a smaller, weaker, less robust version of ourselves. As we lose these psychological assets, just like depleting assets in the bank, we become psychologically bankrupt. We notice the decline, notice the difference, and experience it as depression.

To fight depression, don't worry about the events that trigger it. They are part of normal life. Instead, resolve to ingest only healthy stuff and to rebuild your psychological assets. Set goals, visit more, develop skills, get active, be creative, get involved, and live well between your ears.

WHERE DOES THE MONEY GO?

"A fool spends money he doesn't have on things
he doesn't need to provide pleasure that won't last."

– Unknown.

THE US DEPARTMENT OF LABOR STATISTICS REPORTS THAT AMERICANS
spend an average of one hundred and forty six hours per year searching
for things to buy. A survey of seven hundred readers of *Money* magazine
found that more than half had, in the previous six months, made a major
purchase they regretted. Market research indicates two thirds of all buys
are unplanned; kids as young as eighteen months recognize product
logos; we watch an average of forty thousand TV commercials per year.
A 2002 Stanford University study estimated that sixty million Americans
are addicted to shopping. They have one of the lowest savings rates
among industrialized countries, and rack up over two trillion dollars in
credit card debt each year. And Canadians are right there with them.

According to the Organization for Economic Co-operation and
Development (OECD), which has tracked these and other statistics for
years, the Canadian savings rate dropped from 13 percent of our household income in 1990 to 1.1 percent in 2009. Comparable figures in the

USA show a drop in savings from 7 to 1.2 percent. Why do we continue to buy?

We buy because we want it, we need it, we like it, our neighbour has it, it's different, it replaces our old one, it looks good, it looks interesting, it relieves boredom, it makes us happy, and because the advertisement on TV convinced us. You get the idea—there are many reasons—some more complicated than others.

But look around you. Your prize possessions have gone from treasure—to stuff —to junk—to crap, in no time flat. Sometimes the glow wore off your prize purchase before you got it home! Most things you did not need, nor have they made you happier. In fact, a 2005 British study found that, since 1957, we've seen a three-fold increase in wealth and gadgets, but a sixteen percent decline in happiness.

Advertisers make us believe we need something, and they promise we'll feel better if we buy it. They present the problem, tell us how to eliminate it, and then glamorize the payoff. If we're not careful, we talk ourselves into it in much the same way. How does this happen?

Consider a TV Ad for a new bed. The opening shot is a worn out looking couple on the edge of their bed. The announcer says, "Are you tired of not sleeping well? Do you wake up feeling drained, sore and grumpy?" The scene shifts to a big new bed, with the same people waking from the best sleep ever. They look happy and ten years younger, and the announcer asks, "Don't you deserve a good sleep?" And, consciously or subconsciously, you answer "yes" to all three questions.

What is the psychology behind this? First, they point out the problem—waking up tired with an aching back. Then they lead you to make mini-agreements throughout their ad, and finally, they tell you the bed will solve the problem. They paint a glowing picture of relief and satisfaction. Their plan is to get you to relate to the problem, connect the dots, and head for the store.

There is plenty of psychology at work, but the mini-agreements—getting you to say yes as often as possible— are the most powerful. Psychologists have known for years that the need for consistency between our thoughts and actions is a strong motivational force. The advertiser leads you to agree, and you think, yes, I do wake up tired, sore, and grumpy, and yes, I do want to feel and look as good as those people, and yes, I do deserve restful sleep. Having made these yes-yes-yes agreements, it is more psychologically consistent to take the plunge and buy the damn bed than it is to continue to sleep on your sagging bag of springs.

Of course, it's not always that simple. Maybe you actually need a new bed. But, beware of the mini-agreements; they lead you to spend money you don't have, for stuff you don't need, to give pleasure that won't last. Don't buy it unless you need it, and live well between your ears.

BAD EARS

"I wasn't sure if she said she was bad, glad or sad. My reaction had
a 66% chance of being wrong. Poor hearing sucks."

– Me

YEARS AS A DRUMMER, PLUS AGE-RELATED DECLINE, HAVE LEFT ME A
tad deaf. But my inability to hear like a kid provides some laughable
moments. One happened today.

As I entered the house and kicked off my boots, after sweeping snow
from my deck, I heard the TV Ad say, "To order your rat bastard, call the
number on your screen."

What? I know one or two, but never thought they had the nerve to
clone and market their unsavory selves. But there it was—an ad for rat
bastards—right out of my television.

I had to hear it again. So I did what I always do when I can't understand
my TV. I used a great invention for us moderately deaf guys—the PVR. I
backed it up and listened again. It wasn't a rat bastard I could order. It was
a new gadget to keep your food fresh, called wrap plastic.

The day the audiologist checked my hearing, she explained that I
heard vowels, but had trouble hearing consonants. I sat in her little sound
booth and repeated the words I heard through the headphones: mouse,

thin, Anne, and many others. They came through loud and clear, and I wondered when she'd test me on the difficult stuff. But there was no more testing; we were done, and she asked what I thought. "I think I did pretty well" I said, proudly relieved that I wasn't deaf after all. She smiled and said, "Not quite."

I'd gotten most of the words wrong. It wasn't mouse, thin, and Anne; it was house, win and can. I can't differentiate—hell, most often I can't even hear—the consonants. They are higher pitched and more difficult to hear. And consonants provide most of the meaning. You can understand almost any sentence if you leave out the vowels. But, if you leave out the consonants, it's a different story. Mostly, I just guess or nod my head as if I understand.

I wouldn't know if someone said they needed to take a nap or a crap. In either case I won't ask for clarification; I'll just watch to see if they head for the couch or the toilet. To say there's room for error is an understatement. Our 26 letter alphabet has 21 that we hearing-challenged folks don't hear too well. And when spoken by a woman or a child they are harder to hear since their voices are higher pitched and softer in the first place.

It happens most when I watch television. Did the bad guy tell the cop that he shot him or fought him? Hearing is more difficult if the speaker has his back turned, or sports a bushy mustache. Jeez, movie director, we can't see his freakin' lips! And understanding is impossible when they throw in shrieking violins to set the mood. The consonants are spoken more softly, so they are the first to be drowned out by the music.

The remedy isn't more volume. The audiologist said more volume helps only partially because consonant sound waves fade quickly once they are 3 or 4 feet from the speaker. If I sat that close to my TV, I'd go blind too! Again, my PVR comes to the rescue. It also provides exercise.

Imagine it: The wounded guy with the mustache mumbles a consonant-rich secret to the cop, just as the string quartet cuts in. I don't know what he said; I click on pause; relocate my popcorn; lower my recliner; spring out of my chair; scramble to my TV; crouch down with my ear to the speaker; crane my neck up to see the guy's lips—the screen is three feet higher than the speaker to which my ear is pressed—screw with my rewind button till I locate the scene; hit play; and then strain to hear, and squint to see what the victim said.

So what's the good and bad news about partial deafness? The good: It provides the odd laugh and improves fitness and flexibility. The bad: You miss a lot of meaning, and it takes longer to watch TV. The moral: Expect to need hearing aids, or look after your ears to live well between them.

ANGER

"What is begun in anger ends in shame"

– Benjamin Franklin.

HOW MAD DO YOU HAVE TO GET AT YOUR CHILD, SPOUSE, OR ELDERLY father, before it does some damage? Anger always ends badly. Accompanied by faster breathing, poor digestion, increased heart rate, and the pumping of adrenalin into the system, anger prepares us for fight more than flight. When out of control, it is destructive—it makes life uncomfortable or dangerous for family, co-workers, or friends— and it burdens the perpetrator with guilt, remorse, and dissatisfaction. According to an American Psychological Association (APA) brochure on anger management, anger makes you feel, "at the mercy of an unpredictable and powerful emotion."

Frequent or prolonged anger leads to ill health. In 2012, Smith, Uchino, Berg and Florsheim found that continual marital discord is associated with a higher risk of Coronary Artery Disease. Similarly, Ewart, Elder, Smyth, Sliwinski and Jorgensen (2011), studied adolescents and found that regardless of ethnic origin, gender, or body size, people with combative anger who try to control others experience greater frustration and elevated blood pressure. If you're unlucky enough to be on the receiving end of anger, you live with one of the greatest health hazards of our time—stress. According to a 2000 report by the U.S. Department of Health and Human Services, stress-induced illnesses account for fifty percent of all illness in the country.

Causes of anger can be understood if we look at the frustration-aggression model. It was first proposed by psychologist John Dollard and his colleagues in 1939 and it remains current to this day. It simply states that goal blockage creates frustration, which leads to aggression and anger.

Examples of goal blockage are plentiful: A daughter denied the opportunity to date, insufficient money to raise a family, a promotion that doesn't come, and retirement that is out of reach. For some, more than others, when such blockages persist, the frustration mounts disproportionately and produces anger that becomes unbearable or worse—destructive.

We've all heard stories about extreme action taken by people who weren't promoted, or by those who lived with rejection or social isolation. They can't handle it, it bubbles up inside, and boom—they lash out with an aggressive response. They may argue, yell, throw stuff, or go on a violent rampage.

Recent research indicates that genetics can spring-load some people to greater anger. In 2009, Reuter, Weber, Fiebach, Elger, and Montag, at the University of Bonn in Germany, reported that a gene, called DARPP-32, helps explain why some people fly into a rage at the slightest provocation, while others remain calm. The gene affects levels of dopamine, a brain chemical linked to control of emotions. The German researchers administered a DNA test to determine which of three versions of the DARPP-32 gene people were carrying. Those who had the "TT" or "TC" version portrayed significantly more anger than those with the "CC" version.

You can't change your genes, so what can you do about anger? The APA brochure has many research-based pointers. Acknowledge that anger is normal and that your ability to manage it requires improvement. Increase your tolerance for frustration, often as easy as counting to 10 before you react. Breathe deeply from your gut, not your chest. Communicate your expectations calmly and avoid using the terms "never" and "always." Angry statements such as, "You never freakin' listen." are not only inaccurate they imply that your anger is justified. Uncontrolled anger is an insidious problem that only creates misery. If it is a problem for you or a family member, seek professional help.

Albert Einstein, like Benjamin Franklin, had some words of wisdom: "Anger dwells only in the bosom of fools." For the good of everyone, listen to them both, and live well between your ears.

ARE YOU A WORRYWART?
MAKE A PLAN

"Don't worry, it may never happen."

– Written on a small box of matches I gave
to my Dad when I was fifteen.

DO YOU SOMETIMES LAY AWAKE TORMENTED BY A FLOOD OF WORRIES? Excessive concern about the past is referred to as rumination—a topic for another time. Today's topic deals with worries about bad events in the future which prevent us from being carefree and happy today. They start with a "what if". What if this lump is cancerous, it doesn't rain, I get sick, I lose my job, I have a heart attack, I don't have enough money, or my daughter gets pregnant?

It is helpful to be a bit of a worrywart. We experience it as anxiety, a precursor to fear, which is a healthy response to a future threat. For example, it makes sense to think about your health if it causes you to take better care of yourself, to eat properly, and get enough rest and exercise. However, if you fret and stew obsessively, it becomes a major stressor and takes a heavy toll on your health. According to a 2000 report by the U.S. Department of Health and Human Services, stress is implicated in 50 percent of all illness.

Too much worry and stress cripples our ability to live well. When it graduates from mild concern about something that might happen, to fear that the outcome is a certainty, it becomes irrational and more destructive. It wears on you until sleep and other bodily functions are disrupted. Your adrenal glands pump stress-producing cortisol into your system which contributes to confusion, fatigue, and anxiety.

Our ability to manage stress depends, in part, on whether we believe we are in control of life's outcomes. People who believe that their life outcomes are dependent upon powerful others and events beyond their control are said to have an external locus of control (Rotter, 1966), and they worry more. Research by Samantha Scott and her colleagues in 2010, provides more recent confirmation that externals worry more than those with an internal locus of control.

Those who are more internal believe they control their life's outcomes, and they are able to cope more effectively (Benight and Bandura, 2004). When you believe that you—and not outside forces—are responsible for your future, you are better able to evaluate your possible choices and the consequences of each. At that point, you can commit to the choice you made, and live with it without second-guessing yourself. As long as the facts don't change, you can put the concern in the "I've-got-it-handled" category and move forward.

For example, if you have money worries, your choices are: spend less, earn more, borrow, or do nothing—each with its own consequences. Of course, the externally controlled person may head for the casino or buy a lottery ticket, since solutions are out of his control and he bets on luck, producing more worry.

The difficult part comes after you decide whether to borrow or not. That's when you have to actually commit to earn more, spend less, or both. Should you look for part time work, seek a better job, or sell off assets to live a less shiny version of your life? The choices may not thrill you, but they are a constructive start.

Commitment to a solid plan of action reduces worry. It enables you to reassure yourself that you considered your choices carefully, and that you are doing the best you can. If the worry pops back into your mind you can neutralize it by recalling your plan—the details, facts, choices, and consequences you accept—to help live well between your ears.

RUMINATION

"What's done is done. Get past it."

LAST WEEK, THIS COLUMN WAS ABOUT WORRY. THIS WEEK, IT'S ABOUT worry's cousin: rumination. When we worry, we do so about real or imagined problems in the future. But, when we ruminate, it's about things in the past. Ruminators over-think life events related to work or relationships. For example, you might obsess about why your friend or relative quit talking to you. She doesn't respond to your messages, and it has been months since you enjoyed a good conversation. You try to remember all the talks you had and go over them repeatedly to understand what upset her or what you could have done differently.

It is impossible to change the past. No amount of re-hashing the problem will change the outcome and bring relief. Mental re-runs will not change anything, but focus on the past does contribute to depression. The American Psychological Association defines rumination as: "Obsessional thinking involving excessive, repetitive thoughts or themes that interfere with other forms of mental activity." It is a common feature of Obsessive Compulsive Disorder.

Women are almost twice as likely to suffer mood disorders and depression as men, according to a 2002 Public Health Agency of Canada report. Similarly, in the US, Blazer and his colleagues (1994) found that 21 percent of women, compared with 13 percent of men, suffer major depression at some point in their lives. The difference starts in adolescence.

Susan Nolen-Hoeksema et al (2008), arguably the leading researcher on rumination, suggests that women react to sadness and depression differently than men. When women experience negative moods they focus on possible causes and "what if" scenarios in an effort to understand their feelings about the event. In contrast, men try to distract themselves and direct their attention to something else, or engage in physical activity. The result is that women are more likely to ruminate than men. They go over the past events repeatedly, wondering what went wrong, and they start to obsess about the matter.

Women are more concerned about relationships, and as Nolen-Hoeksema said, "relationships are great fuel for rumination." In an article on stress management, Elizabeth Scott (2013) said that, rumination can be oddly irresistible, and can steal an hour of your attention before you even realize that you're obsessing again. Left unchecked, it contributes to stress and hypertension, a more negative state of mind, and less positive behaviour. Scott's review of the research also linked rumination with negative coping and self-sabotage behaviours, such as binge-eating and binge-drinking.

By all accounts, the obsessive nature of rumination, once started, is difficult to shut off. It can be reduced, according to Nolen-Hoeksema, when you engage in activities such as hobbies, meditation, or prayer to fill your mind with positive thoughts. "The main thing is to get your mind off ruminations for a time so they die out and don't have a grip on your mind," she says. It also helps if rumination is replaced with problem solving. For example, take concrete action to phone or visit your friend or relative instead of obsessing over why you haven't heard from her. Nolen-Hoeksema also says it helps to practice the opposite of rumination—adaptive self-reflection. It is when you proactively focus on concrete aspects of the event, not to dwell on them, but to examine your role to make sure that, going forward, you do everything possible to avoid negative outcomes that lead to obsessive concern over events in the past.

But, whether it is worry about a threat in the future or rumination about a problem from the past, how can we do everything possible when we haven't been able to so far? Both worry and rumination have one thing in common: they are more likely to occur among people who believe the outcomes in their life are due to chance, fate, or powerful others, rather than things within their control. If you want to reduce either one or both, take positive action to prove to yourself that you control you—and live well between your ears.

HERE'S TO THE PRODUCE
AISLE AND THE GYM

"If I'd known I was gonna live this long.
I'd have taken better care of myself."

– Eubie Blake at age 100

"A healthy body is a guest-chamber for the soul;
a sick body is a prison."

– Sir Francis Bacon (1561 – 1626) – an English philosopher, statesman, scientist, lawyer, and author

MY BRAIN IS ON STRIKE THIS WEEK, SO THIS COLUMN IS ABOUT ME. IT
is too preachy and I apologize, but it might inspire someone, so here goes.

A year ago I decided to return to the gym. I work out for 1.5 hours
per day, three days per week. I now run 35 minutes (2.5 miles) without
stopping, but it's taken me a while to get there. I work my upper body
with sit-ups, push-ups and weights for the next 60 minutes; not really
killing myself.

Don't let anyone tell you that you can form a habit in 30 days. I've crawled out of bed and made it to the gym for months and I wouldn't call it a habit yet. What is habitual is my desire to stay up late, get up late, watch TV, plop in my chair to write, and pig-out on monster cookies, filled with chocolate chips and M and M's, on those rare occasions when I let them in the house.

I returned to the gym for one primary reason: I felt old age sneaking up. Through my fifties, my ex-wife and I went to the gym three days per week and cycled and ran many miles on the weekends, so I knew, without doubt, that exercise would help. In addition, because she is a holistic nutritionist, we ate a super-healthy diet.

We ate only raw food for two years, and were vegan in the years that followed. We ate or juiced all kinds and colours of fruit and vegetables and bought wheat grass by the pallet. What went in our mouths came from plants—it was organic, non-GMO, and non-processed. Junk food was as welcome as a turd in a punch bowl.

I've clung to most of these habits because I believe they promote health and well-being. Now days, my main meal is a salad: a large bowl of spinach with a tomato, an avocado, half an apple, slices of bell pepper and cucumber, and pecans, topped off with honey mustard dressing. Breakfast is a rice protein smoothie made with almond milk and frozen fruit. Nothing changes from day to day unless I eat out.

I snack on steel cut oats and raisins. I cook a week's supply in the crock pot. Another snack is a veggie wrap—a spinach tortilla filled with mushed black beans (another source of protein), onion, tomato, avocado, and salsa. When I crave warm food, I steam a few heads of broccoli, make a veggie stir fry, or boil corn on the cob. I also bake a piece of wild salmon quite often.

I avoid food that comes in a box, bag, or wrapper, and buy most of my groceries from the produce aisle. Unless I have company, I don't have red meat, dairy, or bread in the house. But when I eat out or have visitors, anything goes, and I usually love it. I also have some very bad habits.

Until very recently, I smoked a half pack a day, and I could be the poster-boy for diet coke (about six cans per day). So what's the point?

The point is I feel good, and when it comes to diet and exercise, there is a chance you can learn from my experience. I've spent many years on either one side or the other of the diet and exercise issues. I'm convinced that if you spend two-thirds of your food budget in the produce aisle, and get your heart rate up so you sweat 3 or 4 times per week, you'll feel better (physically and mentally) in less than a week, and you'll rarely be sick.

It seems to work for me. I'm 5'9" and 168 pounds; my average blood pressure (I'm in the habit of checking it regularly) is 107 over 76. I don't take medicine. I've never had a flu shot. I don't get colds, and the last time I was sick was in 1967, when I had the Hong Kong flu. Since then, I can count on one hand the times I've seen an MD—nothing to be proud of considering the importance of regular checkups.

With the exception of the cigs and diet coke, why not try it? Get some exercise, eat like a rabbit, and live well between your ears.

WHY CAN'T YOU WAIT?

"Patience is bitter, but its fruit is sweet."

– Jean-Jacques Rousseau, French philosopher

IF YOU COULD HAVE $50,000 TODAY, OR $250,000 IN TEN YEARS, WHICH would you take? What about $100,000 today versus $1,000,000 in fifteen years?

These are the type of questions psychologists ask when they seek to understand our preference for immediate rewards, rather than larger rewards in the future. It is called delay discounting because we discount the value of the larger reward—we think it's too far off or too uncertain. Instead, many of us opt for the smaller, immediate reward because we can't wait, and our apparent need for immediate gratification takes over. It's a trend consistent with our 'instant everything' mentality, but it comes at a price.

The inability to delay gratification blocks some of our important needs, such as those to save money and maintain health. We just can't seem to help ourselves. A $40,000 car is an easy choice compared to a better retirement years from now, if ever. Similarly, thoughts of a healthier you sometime in the future, pale in comparison to the thought of the ice cream in the freezer.

The research indicates that the folks who want it all right now have many unflattering characteristics: They are more likely to be impulsive and non-compliant (Rosenbaum, 1986); they often experience mood swings (Ahn et al, 2011); they are more likely to have grown up poor (Block, 1983); they come from an unstable background (Griskevicius et al, 2011); they like to gamble (Callen, 2011); they are more likely to be obese, practice risky sexual behaviour, and have more problems with substance abuse; they are often younger (Lockenhoff, 2011); they are likely to be more extraverted (Hirsch et al, 2010).

Many of us have more of these characteristics than we care to admit. The research offers two broad suggestions to increase our ability to delay gratification.

First, visualize the delayed outcome as gloriously, and in as much detail, as possible. Sport psychologists tell us that athletes who win visualize each movement necessary to accomplish a difficult task. Success stories frequently reference the importance of a visualized desired outcome. A clear mental picture of a life filled with abundance and good health will help. Psychologists have known for years that we are motivated to behave consistent with our thoughts and attitudes. But, when our minds are filled with defeatist thoughts, our behaviour is counterproductive also. If we can visualize the positive outcomes of delaying, it helps curb our impulsivity.

Second, stop and think through all the ramifications before you act. For example, if impulse buying is a problem, talk to yourself about the amount of money you burn up. Get a financial calculator, learn to use it, and ask yourself tough questions before you spend. For example, the $40,000 you spend on the new car would be worth $135,454 if it grew at five percent in your investment account for the next 25 years; it would be $217,097 if it averaged seven percent. Do you really want to spend that much for a car?

Ask and answer the questions out loud—it has a stronger impact. Consider these questions: Did you suffer because you were without a new car or gadget yesterday? Does what you have work for now? Is it important to have no money worries at retirement? If you answer no, yes, yes, drive your old car home, do without the gadget, and be happy.

What about the ice cream? Ask yourself if you'll die without it? Are you happy about the bowl you ate yesterday—and the day before that? Do you really want to lose 20 pounds of paunch in a few months? If the answers are no, no, yes, then throw it out, or give it to the cat.

No one says that doing without is easy. Get the financial calculator, learn to use it, think out loud before you act, and visualize you in the future. With a little luck, we'll be better waiters, and we'll live well between our ears.

DOES STRESS MAKE YOU SICK?

"The greatest weapon against stress is our ability to
choose one thought over another."

– William James- father of psychology in North America

LOOK AROUND YOU. THERE ARE TOO MANY PEOPLE SPENDING TOO
much time at the Doctor. Research tells us that stress causes more than
its fair share of physical and emotional problems—from cancer to the
flu to anxiety and depression. A survey by the American Psychological
Association found that one-third of the population live with extreme
stress, and 48 percent say it has increased over the past five years.

What causes stress? It's caused by environmental, internal, or social
events that signal danger and sets off a chain reaction—your fight or
flight response—at the centre of which is your hypothalamus. About the
size of an almond, this stress trigger is located just above your brain stem.
Within seconds, many organs and regions of the brain spring into action
and produce major chemical changes in the body which, in the face of
real danger, serve us well. All this hormonal and electrochemical activity
prepares us to deal with the stressful event; we attack it head on or escape
from it. But most of today's stressors are different. They are subtle, more
complicated, last longer, and are not easy to attack or avoid.

A thorough review of the literature by Hawkley and her colleagues (2007), put financial strain and social isolation near the top of the stressor list. Many people live pay cheque to pay cheque, and for those trying to support a family, the stress is endless. Obviously, living alone can produce social isolation, but so can living with someone if the warm and supportive bond is gone. In that case, you might be less stressed and healthier if you live alone. There are many other stressors. A few of them are unrelenting pain, disability, sickness, and dysfunctional relationships, all of which can lead to prolonged stress.

The problem is that our bodily and chemical reactions haven't evolved much since we swung from trees. Today's stressors aren't lions springing out of the bush; they are long term money shortages, unpredictable jobs, shaky markets, unfamiliar technology, sour relationships, or any of hundreds of changes that are in our face and uncontrollable. Unlike an encounter with a lion, which is over in a few minutes, our present-day stressors impact us for months. One common feature is that most of the stressors are things we can't control, and when we lack control, stress compounds until it exhausts us and makes us sick.

Dr. Hans Selye (1956), a famous Canadian endocrinologist, discovered decades ago that we can adapt to short term stress, but when it continues for long periods our ability to adapt breaks down and we suffer. When the chemicals our body produces to handle short term stress are pumped into our system for weeks and months on end, the result is not good.

When we are stressed, sugar gets dumped from our liver into our blood, our heart works harder, blood pressure increases, vessels constrict to reduce the flow of oxygen and nutrients to non-essential areas of the body, and our digestive process slows down. Perhaps most importantly, when this chain reaction is prolonged due to continuous stress, our immune system is weakened; our ability to fight disease is compromised, and we're at greater risk for diabetes, heart disease, intestinal problems, and who knows what else.

So, how can we manage stress? We have to deal directly and constructively with the stressors we can control. Allwood and Salo (2012) and Ben-Zur and Zeidner (2012) say we can lessen the effects of stress when we meet it head-on, using a rational method of coping, instead of an avoidant, hide-your-head-in-the-sand strategy. Hiding from stress, rather than dealing with it, causes greater threat which produces more stress.

The most common suggestion for dealing with the uncontrollable stressful events is to be mindful. Acknowledge stressors, realize they're out of your control, let them pass through your mind, and then boot them to hell out of there. I know, it's much easier said than done. But think about it—when you truly have no control over the stressful event, fretting and stewing does no good. Rumination makes it worse. Once you've taken every rational step to counter-act the stressor, try to practice mindful meditation twenty minutes a day. Let all thoughts and memories flow freely through your mind—without reacting to them—and live well between your ears.

THE SMARTER WE GET THE SLOWER WE GO (TSWG)2

"In the midst of movement and chaos,
keep stillness inside of you."

– Deepak Chopra

WOULD YOU LIKE TO CHANGE YOUR LIFE, START A BUSINESS, INCREASE income, travel the world, learn to play music, or any of a hundred things your little heart desires? Not enough time, money, or talent you say? Nonsense! You've already accomplished the impossible. You need only decide what you want and commit to it. Don't worry about the details. When not resolved on the conscious level, details get worked out in your unconscious. Besides, the caterpillar doesn't worry about how to be a butterfly.

At conception your little cells had a plan—a blueprint—but they didn't think. A good thing too, or they would have given up. The grand plan of the universe nudged you forward, and not knowing any better, you let it; you went with the flow. In those first few months, every aspect of your being was quiet, and you progressed faster than at any time since.

Not plagued by a need to control, you were totally receptive to your world in the womb, and a few cells became more cells—trillions of them—performing complicated maneuvers still not understood by science. Some joined to form soft stuff, hard stuff, outside stuff, and inside stuff. In nine months, they formed enough stuff and moved out.

Now this is life; it can't get any better. To be out of that dark place, into the light—wow. But disappointment loomed large. You sensed life was better for the real people, the ones who could walk and talk. Had you been older, sadness and depression would have been unbearable. How in the world do people get to be so big and move so fast?

You spent months strapped in a seat, a plastic chair with wheels, a pen, or attached to a spring-loaded bouncy thing. Giants came and made faces and noises you didn't understand. You seemed doomed to accomplish nothing, despite being on the steepest learning curve of your life.

Had clear thinking and analysis been possible, you would have given up all hope and never tried. But, fortunately for you, questioning and thinking did not happen, and you simply let your potential unfold. You watched, listened, smelled, felt, and tasted everything that came close enough. You progressed most quickly when you did not resist or question anything; simply paid attention. But, as you got older, you began to get "smarter" and development slowed.

For example, when you were almost two, you were so smart it took months to learn how to use your spoon to get food in your mouth without it scattering in a three foot radius. The reason: You were getting smarter and began to think that eating, playing, waving, and talking, were all part of the same process. You thought your new found skills and abilities were all there was; that there was nothing else to learn. Just get the stuff on the spoon, more or less close to your mouth, and some of it would go in. Your ill-informed smartness got in the way of progress.

Again, between two and three, it took forever to learn how to not be negative. You noticed it again at age six; in fact, the whole negativity thing has been a life-long struggle. With each passing year you "knew" more things were impossible, more people were wrong, and your way of doing things was correct.

With age came more talking than listening, more analyzing than observing, and more judging than accepting, all of which slowed your development. In fact, as an adult, analyzing, resisting, judging, and figuring, pretty much stopped your development altogether and it convinced you of your limitations. You became too smart for your own good. You knew too much. You sometimes even mistook what you believed for the truth.

Looking back, development that seemed totally impossible progressed quickest when you were quiet. When listening, watching, feeling, smelling, tasting and soaking things up took priority, everything else fell into place. You've already accomplished the most difficult. Pursue your goals, like you did before too much "smartness" sapped your potential, and live well between your ears.

TEND TO YOUR BELLY

"The only way to keep your health is to eat what you don't want,
drink what you don't like, and do what you'd rather not."

– Mark Twain

"Those who do not find time for exercise will
have to find time for illness."

– Edward Smith-Stanley (1752-1834) – English statesman,
three times Prime Minister of the United Kingdom

FALL IS A TIME OF RESOLUTIONS, ALMOST MORE THAN NEW YEAR'S.
When we were most impressionable, a new year began when we went
back to school. For many of us it still feels that way. Starting a new grade,
beginning a new year at college, or watching the kids do the same, signals
a new beginning. Those were exciting times, filled with potential. But for
many of us, that over-the-top feeling is gone. We're not bursting at the
seams; the joy of life is elusive—and we miss it.

What's the fix? Retailers say buy stuff; pharmaceutical companies push
pills; air and cruise lines offer exotic vacations; you get the idea—endless

lies promise youth, wealth, health, good looks, and happiness. But today, let's look to our belly for the solution.

This summer I made a few new friends and visited people I hadn't seen for years. I noticed a common complaint: people are tired of being out of shape. The truth is many of us are beginning to look a few months pregnant. If we believe the research on the topic, early belly fat is the thin edge of the wedge. If we don't nip it in the bud, more fat collects in our gut. Soon we accept it as normal, and before long we look ready to give birth—men and women.

The cause is visceral or abdominal fat, a by-product of high trans-fat diets. It migrates to our middle and grows to surround the organs and fill the space in our belly. Allowed to flourish, it eventually looks like we swallowed a little beach ball, and it's inflating. According to Dr. David Haslam (2010), of the National Obesity Forum in England, "Visceral fat is dangerously toxic and pumps poisons into the bloodstream. It causes inflammation in the colon and the artery walls, and is a major cause of heart disease, diabetes and some types of cancer." The culprit foods are commercially baked products such as donuts and cookies, processed foods, chips, crackers, breakfast food in boxes, frozen desserts, fast food, frozen dinners, candy, and the list goes on.

Reviewing some of the British research in 2010, Jane Feinmann reported that, "Visceral fat affects mood by increasing production of the stress hormone, cortisol, and reducing levels of feel-good endorphins. So, along with killing you, visceral fat, it seems, can make you feel low." Ah-ha! Belly fat can explain our reduced vitality.

Nutritional research is unequivocal. If we continue to eat wrong and sit on our collective asses, we will get lazier, weaker, dumber, and sicker, regardless of our denial. Some of us have spent so many years eating poorly and getting little exercise, we've forgotten what feeling good feels like. We wouldn't know a vibrant healthy feeling if it jumped up and bit us on the ass, and for some of us, it would take many bites before we'd notice a difference.

How do we regain our healthy sparkle? We already know; we've heard it for years. Eat right and exercise. Eat non-processed food, plenty of plants—colourful ones—and don't eat as much meat.

How much exercise? Most research says 30-60 minutes per day. Get your heart rate up enough so the need to breathe makes it difficult to carry on a conversation. For some of us, that will mean a brisk walk. If it feels good in a month, start walking a little faster or—heaven forbid—jog or run. Maybe ride your bike several miles each day. Do something besides sit at home or drive your car, and get those legs moving to bump up your heart rate!

The kids are back to school, and it's time to re-kindle the joyful optimism we once felt. Tend to your belly. Resolve to avoid trans-fats, eat lots of veggies, and develop the habit of 30-60 minutes per day walking, jogging, or riding a bike. Let some air out of the beach ball; become less pregnant. Try it a month at a time. Prove that it works, and live well between your ears.

IS NERVOUSNESS A PROBLEM?

"Anxiety is a thin stream of fear trickling through the mind.
If encouraged, it cuts a channel into which all other
thoughts are drained."

– Arthur Somers Roche

DOES NERVOUSNESS OR ANXIETY INTERFERE WITH YOUR ABILITY TO perform? It's when you are mildly to extremely fearful and you have no control over it. Your palms sweat, your mouth dries up, your hands tremble, your voice cracks—or worse—your brain decides not to work. It can get to the point where clear thinking escapes you, and the simplest tasks require all your concentration. It is often accompanied by tense muscles, shortness of breath, stomach cramps, and a rapid heartbeat. We've all felt it when we've had to give a speech, sit for an interview, or perform in front of others. As Roche's quote suggests, left unchallenged it can become debilitating.

It's a terrible feeling of incapability. It happens when you are not confident in the situation and you're expected to be. It's when one or more people are in a position to evaluate you and you fear looking incompetent or out of control. It gets worse when you have time to think about it. The reaction can be as mild as butterflies in your stomach, severe enough to keep you house-bound to avoid social contact, or some place in between.

Nervousness is defined as a state of restless tension and emotionality in which people tend to tremble, feel apprehensive, or show other signs of anxiety or fear. Anxiety is a bit more severe. The American Psychological Association defines anxiety as, "a mood state characterized by apprehension and bodily symptoms of tension in which an individual anticipates impending danger which may be real or imagined, internal or external." The nervousness or anxiety may correspond to an identifiable situation such as an upcoming test or unfamiliar social situation. It may also be a more generalised fear of the unknown or, most disconcerting, just plain fear that is so out of control you don't know what caused it.

According to the Anxiety Disorders Association of America (ADAA), "Anxiety disorders all involve irrational, seemingly uncontrollable and frightening thoughts, which often result in avoidance behavior. And in all cases, the person with the disorder is fully aware that their behavior is irrational."

A recent study, conducted by the World Health Organization, says the odds of developing an anxiety disorder have doubled in the last 40 years. The Public Health Agency of Canada reported that 12.6 percent of Canadians suffer some form of anxiety in any given year. There are five types of anxiety disorder: general anxiety disorder, panic attacks, phobias, obsessive compulsive disorder, and post-traumatic stress disorder. They can occur singly or in combination. Each of the categories is comprised of more specific sub-types. For instance, three common phobias are: agoraphobia (fear of going outside), claustrophobia (fear of confined spaces), and arachnophobia (fear of spiders).

You do not have to be a part of the 12.6 percent to feel nervous. Simply being uncertain and in a position to make mistakes in front of people can create the feeling. Some remedies for nervousness are: focus on the present moment: take 10 or 20 deep breaths and remind yourself that your world is not coming to an end, visualize something positive, quit focusing on how inept you appear, and re-focus on the task. It helps to direct your attention to one single thing outside your body. If you can't get your mind off your nervous cramps, sweaty palms, trembling hands, or scared look on your face, you're headed for a personal meltdown which forces you to escape from the situation.

These suggestions help mask the symptoms of nervousness, but the best solution is prevention. That means practice until the task becomes second nature. For example, if you have to speak in public, prepare a report for your boss, or undergo an interview, the more practiced you are, the less nervous you'll be. Rehearse your speech many times, know the report like the back of your hand, and anticipate the interviewer's questions.

The door to nervousness opens any time you have to do something for which you are not well prepared and you are in a position to be evaluated. So, before the thin stream of fear becomes a raging torrent, practice what you are unsure of until you are 100 percent prepared, and live well between your ears.

WHY LISTEN TO YOUR GUT?

"Common sense is instinct. Enough of it is genius."

– George Bernard Shaw

DO YOU DISREGARD YOUR GUT FEELINGS AND YOUR DREAMS? IT MIGHT be a mistake. The more we learn from recent research on consciousness and unconsciousness, the more it makes sense to pay attention to our intuition, gut-feel, dreams, and solutions that come out of nowhere.

J. Bargh and E. Morsella, in their 2010 review article, make the case that our unconscious mind is a huge data processor that influences our perception, evaluation, and motivation more than previously believed. Furthermore, it happens without prior conscious awareness. It's a radical idea, since we typically think of these things coming to mind because of conscious thought. They conclude their article by saying, "Unconscious processes are smart and adaptive throughout the living world."

Plants, fish, birds, and animals accomplish miracles—reproduction, swarming, migration— without conscious awareness. The implication is that we humans can benefit if we figure out how to harness the power of the unconscious. What's exciting is that technology may help us do it.

Functional magnetic resonance imaging (fMRI) has shown that sounds, images, and other signals first register in our mid brain stem. At that location, we have no conscious awareness of them, even though our brain is sensing them. However, with enough intensity, the signal radiates from the brain stem to our prefrontal cortex, where they enter conscious awareness. It's somewhat analogous to a dog whistle; the sound is there (the dog can hear it), but we can't hear it, even though the MRI says the sound is registering in our brain.

Our unconscious mind appears to store an enormous amount of information from both the environment and our past history. It operates non-stop (24/7) to organize and seek meaning from all we are exposed to, even though we are not conscious of it at the time. As mentioned above, we remain unaware of it because it lacks sufficient intensity. The information may lack intensity because it is about a painfully traumatic event and we repressed it. Or, it may simply be that we have no need for the information at the moment. Research tells us that some information from our unconscious mind manages to migrate into consciousness.

In a recent TV series, hosted by Charlie Rose, a panel of scientists, who study the brain, claimed that the unconscious mind has the capacity to push information into consciousness—especially when the information is helpful or needed to solve a problem. For example, we've all failed to come to a difficult decision only to discover that if we slept on it, or took a long walk, the solution presented itself. The scientists' explanation is that during that mental down-time your unconscious mind goes to work on the problem, without your awareness, and comes up with a solution.

Bargh and Morsella, together with the panel of scientists, agree that the unconscious mind is more capable than our conscious mind of making sense out of complicated and conflicting information. Based on the study of children's cognitive development, they offered additional evidence that unconscious processes play a larger role.

They cited research showing that unconscious or non-conscious processes are heavily involved with language acquisition from birth to the age of 2-3 years. At that age, children have no conscious awareness of learning a language, they just learn it. They don't have fully developed neurological pathways, yet they can master the rules of any language to which they are exposed. They grasp all the appropriate intonation and local nuance, a feat that would be extremely difficult as an adult.

Similarly, research has shown that 2-3 year olds can learn separate identities for 100-200 monkeys based on facial appearance alone. Try doing that as an adult with a fully developed cortex. It won't happen.

These findings confirm that the unconscious mind plays a larger role in complicated learning and decision making than previously thought. Psychologist, Timothy Wilson (2002), from the University of Virginia, says, "there appear to be two kinds of thinking: the slow deliberate conscious kind and the adaptive unconscious kind." It is the latter that the little kids used to learn language and recognize 200 different monkeys.

The evidence from the kids suggests we should not disregard our gut-feelings, dreams, or thoughts that seem to come from nowhere. Allow for the possibility that it's your unconscious trying to tell you something, and live well between your ears.

III
IN SUPPORT OF SCIENCE AND EDUCATION

SCIENCE ISN'T PERFECT, BUT IT'S THE BEST YARDSTICK WE HAVE FOR separating fact from fiction. Despite increased access to information, the proliferation of conspiracies and the belief in the preposterous, in the absence of data, is at an all-time high.

Public policies have to reflect science rather than myth, religious preference, and political partisanship. The stakes are too high for anything else. The absence of policy is just as dangerous as stupid policy. Both have to be corrected (and it can only come from science) or we'll have trouble ahead.

For the past several decades our kids have been short changed by the education system. We lower standards when we should raise them. We lower self-esteem when we're trying to raise it. Popular opinion rather than science shapes policy decisions, and we routinely confuse what we believe for the truth.

Education:
Are we doing all we can?

"Live as if you were to die tomorrow.
Learn as if you were to live forever."

– Mahatma Ghandi

ANOTHER CROP OF HIGH SCHOOL GRADUATES ARE MOVING ON. BUT TO what, and are they as good as they can be? Many parents and teachers feel the education our kids get isn't what it used to be—that the quality is, somehow, less.

What do you think? If you believe there is a problem, do you blame the government, department of education, the local system, the teachers, parents, students, or what? It may be more productive to blame no one, and instead, make an individual commitment to, (1) convince our government to set a goal to be number one in education in the world, (2) hold students and teachers accountable for higher standards of achievement, with tougher curricula in all subjects, and (3) decide to value education in thought and deed, at least as much as we do our sports teams. But wait. There is impressive data that say we don't have a problem.

This data no doubt influences policy makers and curriculum designers, and it says our kids are doing well compared to many places in the world. The Organization for Economic and Co-operative Development (OECD) initiated a survey to assess high-school students as they approached the end of compulsory education. It's called the Program for International Student Assessment (PISA), and students from 65 countries were surveyed in 2000, and every third year since. And guess what? The survey says, on measures of reading, math, and science, Canadian students are well prepared, "with enough knowledge and essential skills to enjoy full participation in society."

In 2009, Canadian students ranked 5, 10, and 8 on reading, math, and science, down from 2, 6, and 5 in 2000. Even with this slight decline, congratulations are due our teachers, administrators, and students for ranking in the top 10 to 15 percent. On top of that, we like to point out that our students scored better than USA kids; they ranked 16, 30, and 17 on reading, math, and science.

But—and it's a big but—the survey also indicates the proficiency level at which the students function. The levels range from one to five. At level one you're barely bright enough to wipe your nose. The bad news is that even though the Canadian kids achieved a high ranking, their actual skill and knowledge level, as measured by these proficiency scores, is slightly below the midway mark of level three.

Therein lies the problem: we look at our rank, we rejoice at beating the USA, and come away believing all is right in the world. But the truth is, based on the proficiency scores, we are only among the best of the not-so-good. Because rankings are emphasized more than the proficiency levels, we are lulled into thinking we're great. Unfortunately, we accept the status quo and do not expect more. Some analysts of the PISA report even used words such as "excellent" to describe Canadian students' ranking and our education system. Are you kidding? We can't be excellent if we're below the middle of proficiency-level three.

Some clarification of our students' scores comes from an additional survey. Canada added a Youth in Transition Survey (YITS), taken every two years. This survey is an attempt to learn more about paths to higher education, progress of immigrants, the role of parents, and rural/urban differences. To date, these results indicate that immigrants score 4 percent below average on reading, but after five years in Canada, their scores improved to 4 percent above average. I wonder why? Do immigrant parents hold higher expectations for their kids which accounts for the upward shift?

Rural students scored 3 percent lower on reading than city kids. But it's not a rural or urban environment that makes the difference. It is the expectations parents hold for their child's academic achievement that is most influential. When parents place a high value on education and expect their kids to do well academically, we see a 6 percent increase in reading scores, regardless of whether they are urban, rural, or foreign born.

And what about Saskatchewan, how did our kids fare? On reading, we ranked sixth out of ten. We were 4 percent below Alberta, which led all ten provinces, followed closely by BC, Quebec, and Ontario. It's not a big difference, but why can't we be number one? In fact, why can't we be number one by a long shot? Becoming number one is one governmental decision away if they truly made it a priority. Saskatchewan has the resources. We are a rich province, our parents are capable of holding high expectations, and our children are not inherently dumber. If the government and the department of education simply decided to be the best in the world, we could be. Not tomorrow or next year, but with focused attention it would happen.

Do you want long term industrial and social benefits for everyone in the province? Then create the smartest work force on the face of the earth. At the very least our kids would compete more successfully for jobs, access to higher education, and scholarships, both here and around the world. And if we maintained that focus, we would reap the benefits for decades.

Let's be known for something besides Roughriders and Potash. "I'm from Saskatchewan, we have the highest education scores in the world" carries more weight in the world than, "I'm from Saskatchewan, the home of the Roughriders." As a culture we are dangerously close to paying more out of pocket for stadiums than for education.

Think about it. Are we doing all we can? Getting our students to number one in the world is achievable. We're not that far away, and the benefits of gearing up to get there would be incalculable. Commit to urge government, boards, teachers, and students to make it a goal. Approach it with the same zeal as we show for our sports teams. Hold high expectations for academic achievement of students, and allow teachers to hold them accountable.

With sustained focus, Saskatchewan kids and our education system can be number one in the world on PISA's reading, math, and science scores. The spin-off benefits would be immense, and we would live well between our ears for generations to come.

GRADUATION TO WHAT?

"Education is the key to unlocking the world,
a passport to freedom."

– Oprah Winfrey

GRADUATION IS ARGUABLY THE ONLY TIME IN YOUR LIFE WHEN ONE decision—to stop now or continue your education—will impact so much. Do you want to expand your horizons, make tons more money, multiply career options, increase job security, make some of your best friends ever, and reward yourself mentally, materially, and quite possibly spiritually, with many of life's riches not otherwise attainable—or not? If the answer is yes, then continue your education.

Of course there are exceptions. But, if exceptions happened for everybody, they wouldn't be called exceptions. No other period in your life allows you to accomplish so much and have so much fun doing it. Economists estimate that over your total earning years the wrong decision costs you $800,000—and that's the average! Some professions requiring a University degree allow you to earn that and millions more. And, you're living in one of the best countries in the world to do it.

Of course, what most grads want to do straight out of high-school is make some money. What can they earn? In their lifetime they can earn plenty. Check out these income numbers from Statistics Canada. Averaged across all age groups, the average annual income for those with less than a high school education is $20,100; with a high school education it's $28,000; with a trade school certificate it's $34,600; College graduates earn $36,700; University graduates earn $57,500. Over a 40 year working career the University graduate will earn an average of $2,300,000. If they have less than high-school, they'll earn $804,000—a difference of $1,496,000. The news looks good for University grads; not so hot for the high school grad.

But statistics can be misleading. Suppose our grads are short-sighted, and all they look at are the income numbers of those who are 20 to 24—going no further. In that case, the numbers tell a far different and misleading story. Averaged over only 4 years, the annual incomes for less than high-school, high-school, Trade school, College, and University are: $14,800; $14,200; $20,300; $16,500; and $15,000 respectively. The ones going to college and university during those years probably only have part-time jobs, so it's no wonder they earn so little.

If the short-term numbers can be believed, who in their right mind would elect to go to University to earn $15,000, when they can go to trade school and earn $20,300, or not continue their education at all and earn almost as much? The difference is even greater if the grad gets a job mining or working in the oil patch. If those were the only numbers they looked at, I'm not sure anyone would fork over the tuition to continue their education and delay their entry into the work force. But, over the long haul, there's a big difference. Out beyond age 24 is when they start to make some serious money. Given a normal life span, the average student who does not pursue higher education will earn much less.

But, it's not only about income. Without advanced education, your job is less secure, and your standard of living will be much lower. A February, 2012 MSNBC report says, "today's knowledge-based global economy is highly competitive and will only become more so in the foreseeable future. The nations, states, and communities that are the most successful in developing human talent, particularly college-level knowledge and skills, will enjoy significant advantages. Conversely, those nations, states, and communities [and little old you if you make the wrong decision] that fall behind educationally are likely also to fall behind in competing for good jobs and in achieving or maintaining high standards of living."

You need to continue your education. In China alone there are enough kids scoring at the highest level to whip our fat behinds and send all of our fifth- and lower-ranked kids scrambling and looking for work in Zimbabwe by age thirty.

Imagine the message home if you make the wrong decision: *"Dear Mom and Dad. Hope you are fine. Last night our moon-shine still caught fire and scared off our goat and chickens. Wish we could afford to come home. I should have gone to University."*

And the reply comes back, *"Dear Chris, we are both fine. Sorry to hear about the fire. No booze, no milk, no eggs, no meat; what in the world are you going to eat. Sorry we can't help. We've downsized too and rented the house to Wei Li. She's a real nice girl from China; a consultant for Chi-Can Digital who speaks English, Mandarin, Arabic, and Hindi. Good luck. Love, Mom and Dad."*

Make the right decision. You're in the first period and there's time on the clock. Get excited and think big. The statistics are not lying. Continue your education—in this country it's there for the taking—and live well between your ears.

Beer cans, good times,
AND GADGETS

"People who develop the habit of thinking of themselves as world
citizens are fulfilling the first requirement of sanity in our time."

– Norman Cousins

Peter Mansbridge, Charlie Rose, Fareed Zakaria, and George
Stroumboulopoulos are impressive guys. While they may not be happy
(who really knows?) it isn't due to lack of money, influence, or opportunity. They've created plenty of each.

Peter is chief correspondent for CBC news and anchor of CBC's
National News. Charlie hosts his own show on public television in the
USA. Fareed, a prolific journalist and very bright guy, hosts Global Public
Square on CNN Sunday mornings, and George, hosts a regular talk show
on CBC.

They are thoughtful, well-educated, complex people who, one day at a
time, shape beliefs. Two were born in North America and two were not,
but unlike many North American men in particular, if you peeled back
their skull and looked inside, you'd find much more than beer cans, good
times, and gadgets.

Not to be critical, there's nothing wrong with beer cans, good times, and gadgets. You'd find a few under my skull too. But these days there needs to be much more. If we don't pay attention to world affairs and start valuing education and the interconnected nature of the world, our culture will lose its place near the front of the line. We cannot remain at the forefront of technology, development, and most things good if we don't crawl out of our cocoon and pursue knowledge, excellence, and understanding more successfully.

It's not just these four. Many talented men and women make their mark in many fields every day. Do they have anything in common? Google them, or others you have in mind, and find out. Whoever they are, I'll bet their road to success is long, and they've shown great tenacity. They are competitors. Yes, they have talent, but they weren't necessarily born with more than you. Do they work harder at their craft? Probably. Do they pay closer attention? Probably. Are they better educated? Probably. Are they smarter? Maybe, but it's not likely the difference maker.

What accounts for their success? Don't say it's who they know. Yes, at some point it may have helped, but more importantly, it's their work ethic and what they know. As you watch these four, it is easy to believe that what got them to the top, and keeps them there, is perseverance, curiosity, and global interest, more than blind luck or happenstance.

For the benefit of future generations, and to assure the good life as we know it, we need to create family, educational, and cultural environments where talent like theirs can take root and flourish. Pay attention to the news anchors, producers, editors, talk show hosts, politicians, documentary guests, sports casters, weather women, and leaders of any sort who create, broadcast, govern, manage, or one way or another, shape our culture.

Who are they? Where are they from? Are they first or second generation immigrants? Somewhere along the line they were encouraged to be creative, open to ideas, tolerant, and to hold high standards for their work. They value education, do not settle for the status quo, and are citizens of the world as much as they are citizens of their local community and country. No doubt, there are young people in your community who fit the description, but there could be many more.

With awareness, we can move our children in that direction. Are your kids on pace now to compete with the Peters, Charlies, Fareeds, and Georges of the world? If not, why not? Don't say it's not important. In your heart you know it is. Do we help our children think big enough and make them aware of their many options?

Regardless of race, religion, or background, if the majority of North Americans don't trade in our okay-is-good-enough attitude for one which stresses challenge and excellence, the up-coming generation of kids and grandkids will experience less fulfilling lives, a lower standard of living, and resentment for feeling left out. We see it now, and it's accelerating. The world is more competitive than it was a few years ago. The spoils will go to the tolerant, complex, well educated, and worldly children. Home court advantage is disappearing. Make sure their world is more than beer cans, good times, and gadgets, and live well between your ears.

ARE WE GETTING ENOUGH
TELEVISION?

"Television isolates people from the environment, from each
other, and from their own senses."

– J. Mander, Four Arguments for the Elimination of Television.

NIELSEN, THE TV RATING COMPANY, REPORTED IN 2009 THAT THE
average viewer spends four hours per day watching television. Other estimates put the number closer to five. Time on the internet is not included.

TV-Free America, a non-profit organization in the USA founded
in 1994 to raise awareness of excessive television watching, provides
some interesting statistics. Forty-nine percent of people say they watch
too much TV. There have been 4,000 studies examining TV's effects on
children. The average child watches 1,500 hours per year, and over that
period, sees 20,000 thirty-second commercials. By the time a kid finishes
elementary school, he's seen 8,000 murders on the tube, and by age 18,
he's seen 200,000 violent acts.

By way of contrast, the average child spends only 900 hours per year in
school, and 3.5 minutes per week in meaningful conversation with their
parents. This dismal statistic probably means that, "Please clean up your
room", "Stop teasing your brother", or "Have you done your homework?"

do not constitute a meaningful conversation. A lengthy discussion about the importance of taking responsibility for their choices would be more to the point.

There are other facts that the TV-free America folks want us to know. The number of TV commercials seen by the average person by age 65 is 2 million. The percentage of broadcast time devoted to advertising by local stations is 30 percent. The percentage of time devoted to broadcasts about crime, disaster, and war is 53.8 percent, while the percentage of time devoted to public service announcements is 0.7. As influential as television is, numbers of this magnitude and the differences between them demand our attention.

Parentstv.org, a sister to TV-free America, considers the biggest problems to be the promotion of sex, profanity, and poor role models. That may be true, but many argue that what is more damaging is the promotion of intolerance and violence. For instance, Psychologists have known for decades that, when exposed to enough violence, children and adults are desensitized to it, less shocked by it, and are more likely to go along with, or even commit, violent acts. Violent crimes are reported every day, and TV and movies offer it steadily.

As far back as the seventies, psychologist Phillip Zimbardo (1975, 2007) and Stanley Milgram (1965, 1974) demonstrated that people could be easily led to do the unimaginable if they were in positions of authority or they thought others were doing the same thing. For example, they would administer what they believed were near lethal electric shocks when they thought others were doing the same thing, or when authority figures showed no disapproval. The volume of research leaves no doubt that exposure to violence on television leads to violent acts.

Unfortunately, heavy TV viewing also means we have plenty of opportunity to compare ourselves with the near-perfect television stars. Studied by psychologists for half a century, social comparison is something we do whenever we're given the chance, even though we're not always aware we're doing it. It is impossible to watch TV as much as we do and not compare ourselves with the people we see. The actors, anchors, models, talk show hosts, and guests appear smart, well spoken, good looking, well built, well dressed, rich, and usually famous. When we compare ourselves with these people, we come up short.

Social comparison is one of three major contributors to self-esteem. When we watch these celebrities our self-esteem comes under attack because we can't help but compare, and we usually don't look or sound as good. We forget that these stars are at the top of their game. Besides, we never see what they look like before their two hours of hair and makeup, and we forget that the Teleprompter guarantees they never flub their lines.

We don't see the blemishes and cellulite. We don't know about their failures and worries. Their nervousness and mistakes are hidden from view, and yet we compare ourselves with them and come out on the short end of the stick. A steady diet of this type of comparison, and self-esteem will drop. And, if you follow this column, you know that low self-esteem contributes to physical and mental problems we are much better off without.

It seems safe to conclude that too much TV hurts us, and we should watch it less. At least remind yourself that most of what's on there is make believe, and that violence makes the news because it's sensational. Make no mistake, if you got nipped, tucked, groomed, clothed, and coached for several hours before you stepped out your front door, you would look and act like a celebrity too. Don't allow the people who are crammed into your flat screen to serve as your standard for anything, and live well between your ears.

What's Wrong With Our Boys?

"If you don't design your own life plan, chances are you'll fall into someone else's plan. And guess what they have planned for you? Not much."

– Jim Rohn, American entrepreneur and motivational speaker.

IN THEIR SCIENCE-SUPPORTED 2012 BOOK, *THE DEMISE OF GUYS: WHY boys are struggling and what we can do about it*, Phillip Zimbardo and Nikita Duncan present alarming facts. If you are a boy, parent of a boy, teacher, or on the school board, please read it.

Their book states, "Girls outperform boys now at every level, from elementary school through graduate school. By eighth grade, only 20 percent of boys are proficient in writing and 24 percent proficient in reading. Young men's SAT scores in 2011 were the worst they've been in 40 years. Boys are 30 percent more likely than girls to drop out of both high school and college. In Canada, five boys drop out of school for every three girls who do. Nationally, boys account for 70 percent of all the D's and F's given out at school." And the bad numbers don't end there.

Why do so many boys struggle and fall behind? The authors emphasize too many hours of video games and pornography, but there are at least two other big reasons: (1) We push them to read before their brain is ready, and (2) most of the guy-stuff he was good at, policy makers have made illegal.

Boys spend 13 hours per week playing video games, compared to 5 hours for girls, and the time boys spend watching porn is over the moon. According to Sonya Thompson at the University of Alberta, one of every three boys is considered a heavy porn user; the average boy watches nearly two hours of pornography every week. One of the consequences is that boys are beginning to treat their girlfriends like sex objects. Heavy porn watchers, as young as 14, don't spend as much time with girls. They develop dysfunctional relationships; sexual interests are satisfied more easily, and with less rejection, watching porn than they are with actual girls.

Boys' brains are wired differently than girls; the neural connections required to read develop less quickly. Trying to teach a boy to read in pre-school, kindergarten, and perhaps grade one—if his brain isn't ready—does more harm than good. As Zimbardo says, "If a boy is forced to learn before his brain is ready, he is unintentionally conditioned to dislike the task, and early negative experiences create resistance and resentment for learning in particular, and school in general. Since 1980, there has been a 71 percent increase in the number of boys who say they don't like school, according to a University of Michigan study." Could this be why kids in Finland, ranked first in the world on academic tests by the OECD (Organization for Economic and Cooperative Development), don't start formal schooling until they are 7 years old?

Many of our children do not have the technical and verbal skills to compete in today's society, and boys are hard-wired to miss the boat. Their genetic and socially based skills and abilities—the masculine ones—are not needed as much as in past years, and when they are not needed they begin to feel useless. The 'git-er-done' mentality, that used to be critical for a young man's success, is no longer as critical. In rural areas most of their role models are 'git-er-done' guys, so the boys are spring loaded to develop high masculine skills. But, in today's technical environment, high masculine skills are not in as much demand in the work place. There are a few career fields left where high masculine skills are important and in demand, the most obvious is in the oil-patch. But the oil field can't accommodate all the boys, and when you look around the work sites, many of the good jobs are now filled by young women.

From conception, boys are bathed in testosterone. It guarantees their masculinity,but what have we done? We took away, or made illegal, most of the things that little masculine creatures need to build their can-do attitude. No more monkey bars where daring feats impressed the girls. No more sling shots, BB guns, or 22's, the condoned use of which, taught them that they were trusted. Fewer co-ed gym classes where boys proved they could jump higher and run faster than girls. Fewer opportunities to sit on Dad's knee and drive the car, or help with household repairs, or drive the grain truck at incredibly early ages. Is there a boy-relevant task left for him to master? Yes there is. He can kill monsters, acquire nations, and win the Daytona 500 on his video game. And how much good do you think that does?

It's bad enough that we try to get him to read, almost before he can poop on his own. It gets worse when he figures out the world needs fewer guys who can drive 18 wheelers, and more guys with engineering degrees who can design fuel-efficient vehicles. And, let's not forget, gender equality helped to assure that the girl next door got the job he wanted—not to mention the fact that she had a higher GPA, better references, and was more articulate.

I'm not suggesting that we cut the boys any slack or revert to the old days. On the contrary, world competition means he should forgive his elders for their screw-ups and get busy building his skills. The rest of us can urge policy makers to enact laws based on science. We need to replace monkey bars and co-ed gym classes with a curriculum to build something useful in kindergarten and first grade: maybe a kids' art park, a hydroponic vegetable garden, or anything requiring skill sets that come with masculinity. But, for now, if you have preschool boys, you have a decision to make. Will you send them to preschool, kindergarten, or where? It's up to you. At the very least, don't worry about teaching your boy to read till he's ready. Make sure your decision helps both you and your boy to live well between your ears.

PREJUDICE AND SCIENCE:
SWORN ENEMIES

"Science replaces private prejudice with public,
verifiable evidence."

– Richard Dawkins.

THE AMERICAN PSYCHOLOGICAL ASSOCIATION DEFINES PREJUDICE AS, "a negative attitude toward another person or group formed in advance of any experience with that person or group. Prejudices include an emotional component (ranging from mild nervousness to hatred), a cognitive component (assumptions and beliefs about groups, including stereotypes), and a behavioural component (negative behaviours, including discrimination and violence)."

A key feature of prejudiced beliefs is they are held in spite of facts which contradict them. You may prejudge someone when you don't have the facts and simply be wrong, as when you make an error in judgement. But, maintaining a prejudice when the known facts contradict it is more than just wrong, it's an attack on peaceful harmony between people.

Do you know anyone who is prejudiced against Quebecois, Mormons, First Nations people, Torontonians, Albertans, Americans, Asians, or folks who speak with an accent, to name a few? I bet you do.

Canadians aren't prejudiced. Well—you might be. Sometimes people admit their prejudice but turn around and tell you they believe it is the truth. They know the facts don't bear it out, but they continue to hold the prejudiced belief regardless of the facts. It's as if you know your brakes don't work, but you convince yourself they are normal and continue to drive.

Believing that members of a certain race or nationality are lazy, stupid, dirty, or immoral qualifies as prejudice. Prejudice is hateful, even in the abstract, so imagine the hurt if it is directed at you. For example, some Christians believe anyone who doesn't celebrate Christmas won't go to heaven and should be feared. That's a large number of people, including, but not limited to, Jehovah's Witnesses, Buddhists, Hindus, Muslims, Sikhs, and many others for a total of four billion, seven hundred and eighty one million, one hundred and eleven thousand. That's one hundred and twenty six times the population of Canada! If you plan on going to heaven, at least it won't be crowded.

"Is it true that they won't go to heaven, and should I be afraid of them?" the child asks. You can't blame the kid for asking. It's how we answer him that is important. The parent, attempting to do the right thing, might say, "Well son, many people have different beliefs. We believe God's word and it's important that you do too." If his questions about the nature of God continue, the parent's interpretation of the "facts" may leave him more confused than he was when he started. That's the nature of prejudice. It's a touchy subject—this business of truth, facts, and interpretation. Prejudices, and the fear, dislike, and assumptions about other people they arouse, are difficult to combat. They are strongly held, resistant to change, and passed from one generation to the next.

We often confuse what we believe for the truth. Besides, our version of the truth may not be a fact? There has never been so much information available to so many, but is it accurate? We know some is and some is not. Social media, blogs, advertisements, and most of what is on television can be factually incorrect, but much of what we find at Wikipedia or Google is reliable information. Educational TV such as the History Channel, TLC, and National Geographic appear to offer factual information most of the time.

The simple truth may not be so simple; the simple facts not so factual. Keep questioning, keep seeking facts, recognize that what you believe may not be the truth, and live well between your ears.

Is that the truth or just what you believe?

"Scientific criticism has no nobler task than t
o shatter false beliefs."

– Ludwig von Mises

I spoke to a guy the other day who told me climate change was a hoax. I asked him, "Is that the truth or just what you believe?" He looked at me with a vacant look as if to say, "Is there a difference?" I also spoke to a church-going lady who maintained that Buddhists won't go to heaven. I asked her the same question and got the same reaction. Sometimes our beliefs are a long way from the truth.

Does it matter whether personal beliefs are the same as the truth? We know that beliefs influence behaviour, so as the gap between belief and truth gets wider, it can make a difference or even be dangerous. For example, if someone believes alcohol does not impair their motor skills, we hope he doesn't confuse that with the truth—and we certainly don't want him driving the school bus.

What's the difference between the truth and what we believe? We only have one yardstick to measure the truth, and that is science. As beliefs receive more scientific support they move closer to the truth. Science crosses all boundaries and doesn't care if the evidence comes from a Buddhist, a Christian, a Jew, a liberal, or a conservative. Science is based on controlled experiments, isolation of the operative variables to study the effects, and replication—the ability of other researchers to find the same results when investigating the same thing. If those conditions are not met, the idea loses traction within the scientific community, and we don't hear much about it.

Why do we cling to worn out beliefs when they are contradicted by science? In psychology, denying new information is referred to as confirmation bias, which is most powerful when the beliefs are tied to our identity, as with religion and politics. It means we are more willing to accept new information when it confirms what we already think.

But, when new information threatens our core values, it is harder to accept. Centuries ago, a core belief of major religions was that the earth, not the sun, was the center of our galaxy. Beliefs to the contrary, while they turned out to be true, were not just denied, they could get you killed. Even today, strongly held beliefs cause wars. Maybe the warriors should be governed more by science.

Unfortunately, belief about global warming is one of those hardest hit by confirmation bias, and one where it's important to distinguish between belief and truth. Some believe it exists and others don't. Since climate change is an issue with such major consequences, it is important to distinguish between the truth and what we believe—not unlike the bus driving story where confusing the two could cost lives.

If 255 independent scientists analyzed your water, and all agreed it had become dangerous to drink, would you let your kid drink it? Even if you knew none of the scientists, what is the safest choice?

Something similar happened recently when 255 scientists, from the prestigious National Academy of Sciences, signed an open letter in the May 7, 2010 edition of *Science* magazine. It essentially said: We acknowledge there are a few conflicting reports, but we all agree that the vast majority of scientific data calls for long term action to deal with the reality of global warming before it irreparably changes many of the life supporting eco-systems of the planet.

Even if these scientists are of different nationalities or political stripe, surely you wouldn't bet against them? So, is all this the truth or just what

I believe? At least for the big issues take the time to find the science—ask your politicians to do the same—and live well between your ears.

No more dumbing down

"Education is the most powerful weapon which you can use to change the world."

– Nelson Mandela

THE US ELECTION HAS BEEN OVER FOR TWO MONTHS. I DON'T MISS THE campaign lies but I miss their TV appearances, the pundits' views, and trying to ferret out fact from fiction. I am a US political junkie: more so than most Canadians since I lived and worked there for 27 years, and eventually became a citizen, giving me dual citizenship status. I returned to Saskatchewan, but I still follow their news because our nations' futures are tightly interwoven.

I'm writing this in mid-November, 2012, (two months before you are reading it) and it looks as though the Democrats and Republicans are going to quit bickering and agree (or at least set the stage to agree) on spending cuts and tax reforms that reduce costs and increase revenue, enough to address their huge deficit over the long run, and move them toward a balanced budget in the medium run. If they do both, it will put them on firm economic footing so they can follow through on the other things they have to address, the most important of which is education. The US is seriously dumbing down.

It will dumb down even further if they cannot successfully accomplish two things: (1) rein in the anti-science mantra that's become the rallying cry for the religious right to whip up support for the idea of Creationism as opposed to Evolution, and (2) speak out and vote against extremists who downplay the importance of education. The US election highlighted several paths to jobs and prosperity. Certainly they have to focus on energy and infrastructure in the immediate future, but they also have to re-energize and re-vitalize their education system at the same time.

On the education front the Yanks are in a bit of a pickle. The OECD (Organization for Economic Co-operation and Development) ranks their kids 17, 31, and 23 on reading, mathematics, and science respectively, out of a total of 65 countries. Canada fared better (5, 10, and 8 on reading, math and science), but as closely linked to them as we are, we can't afford their dismal scores. If they don't fix their education system, the resultant decline in the standard of living in the US, our largest trading partner, will affect us adversely. What remedies can be taken to re-build leadership roles in education, science, and technology in both countries?

You will find one example of an attractive solution if you go KhanAcademy.org. Created in 2006 by Bangladeshi-American Salman Khan, a graduate of the Massachusetts Institute of Technology and Harvard Business School, it grew out of his effort to teach math to his young cousin via YouTube. It now has more than 3,500 illustrated online lectures on almost every level of every subject imaginable and shows no sign of slowing. It has been heaped with praise and garnered support from the Bill and Melinda Gates Foundation and elsewhere. The Khan Academy is impressive; it holds tremendous potential for fixing much of what's wrong with education across North America.

The need to read and do math and science at advanced levels is more important than ever before. Through the centuries, those societies that favoured education and worked to incorporate the best available technology always fared better than their more ignorant neighbours. With their test scores and education declining, the US is at risk of becoming an ignorant neighbour. To maintain the standard of living in both countries there has to be significant improvement in education so our kids can compete with immigrants from the highest scoring regions: Shanghai, South Korea, Finland, Hong Kong, Singapore, and Urban India. Only if we do that successfully, will our kids have a fighting chance to prosper and live well between their ears.

BE SLOW TO JUDGE WITHOUT
THE FACTS

"Science is facts; just as houses are made of stones, so is science made of facts; but a pile of stones is not a house and a collection of facts is not necessarily science."

– Jules Henri Poincare

ALL OF US HAVE A BIT OF PSYCHOLOGIST IN US; ALWAYS TRYING TO figure out the "whys". Why do people lie, cheat, blame, or argue? On an international level, why is there mutual distrust between Iran and the West, or between China and the USA. The situations are complex, but none-the-less, the powers that be (and us sitting in our living rooms) search for causes and explanations so we can better understand our world.

But, when we lack sufficient information, we make mistakes. It leads us to blame the victim or say that, "all things happen for a reason", or "it is God's will", or "the universe is unfolding as it should." These are all ways of saying, "I don't fully understand the facts."

Attribution Theory originated with Fritz Heider in 1958, was refined in 1967 by Harold Kelley, and continues to this day. It is the study of how people explain the behaviour of themselves and others. Psychologists who study attribution theory have discovered three common errors we make when we don't have enough facts.

The first, referred to as the fundamental attribution error, is our tendency to overestimate personal characteristics and underestimate situational or environmental factors as causes of behaviour. For example, without knowing the facts, we are more likely to falsely blame a school yard fight on the aggressive nature of the attacker, rather than on what might have been said or done to provoke the attack. Similarly, some countries' desire for non-weaponized nuclear capability gets blamed on the leaders' war-mongering nature, without much consideration given to situations that arise due to neighbouring countries having nuclear capability, or the need for alternate sources of energy.

The second error we make is referred to as the actor-observer bias. It is when we say our own behavior is due to the situation, but we believe the identical behaviour of someone else stems from their personal characteristics. For example, if you fly off the handle at your kid, you say it's due to the persistent disobedience of your child. However, if another parent does the same thing, you are inclined to think he or she is abusive. Similarly, nations chalk up their own aggressive behaviour to the fact that the situation warranted it, while foreign countries see aggressive behaviour in another as a character flaw.

The third error we make is referred to as self-serving bias. This leads us to take credit for our success, while blaming our failures on the situation. For example, you believe you won the trivial pursuit game because of your superior intellect, but if you lose, you blame it on the fact that your opponent has more experience with the game, or that you received the hardest questions. Likewise, the government takes credit for a strong economy, but when it weakens, they are quick to put the blame on falling energy prices or a poor commodities market.

The problem is that these errors are real; they occur in the absence of enough accurate information. They result in false blame or false credit which can be devastating to relationships and even to the well-being of societies. To avoid making these errors, we have to make sure we have all the facts. The judicial system does this by spending millions of dollars on lawyers, judges, forensic science and courts. Among countries, billions are spent on espionage, surveillance, and other data gathering techniques in order to have all the facts. These three simple attribution errors are only neutralized when we have enough information. Until you have that information, be slow to judge, and live well between your ears.

QUIT PUTTING IT OFF

"Procrastination is one of the most common and deadliest of
diseases and its toll on success and happiness is heavy"

– Wayne Gretzky

YOU SHOULD SEE YOUR DOCTOR FOR YOUR OVERDUE CHECK-UP, BUT
you can't. You should phone your sister, but you can't. You should clean
the garage, but can't. You should lose some weight, but can't. You should
get some exercise, but can't.

If it was true that you really couldn't do all these things—that something or someone was stopping you—you would be furious. However, it's
probably not a "can't" thing; it's more likely a "don't" thing. You should
lose weight, but don't. Should clean the garage, but don't. Should prepare
for next week, but don't. Should see the doctor, but don't.

It's not that you can't take action, it's that you don't. Your fury should
be directed at you, and nothing or no one else. It's an insidious problem
because you have the ability to take control, but you don't. It's called procrastination, and it's a bigger problem for some than for others.

In a 2007 issue of the Psychological Bulletin, Piers Steel, from the
University of Calgary, wrote a lengthy and thorough review on the
subject. He says, "to procrastinate is to voluntarily delay an intended

course of action despite expecting to be worse off for the delay." It plagues all of us at some time and is a chronic and debilitating problem for one in five people. We are all familiar with the consequences of procrastination: failure to achieve, jobs done poorly or not at all, frustration and anger with ourselves, and missed commitments, to name a few. What is not clear is the cause.

According to Steel's review article, if you do not procrastinate you probably are conscientious, self-controlled, steadfast, well organized, motivated to achieve, and less concerned about negative evaluation. Conversely, if you and procrastination are best buddies, you are likely less conscientious, less self-controlled, easily distracted, impulsive, less well organized, low in need for achievement, and have low self-esteem. It is not accurate to say these things cause procrastination. They co-exist with it, and therefore, provide a clue about where to start looking for help.

In addition to the personality characteristics, two features of the avoided tasks themselves produce procrastination. When the task is (1) negative or difficult, or (2) has a more distant payoff, you are more likely to put it off. For example, starting a new diet is not much fun, and a skinnier you is months away. Or, you'll clean the garage later, but right now there's something on TV. It's not that you even like the program, but the TV's turned on, you're in your chair—and oops—there goes another hour. Once again, impulsiveness trumps planning. The things we should do, but don't, pile up to make a bad situation worse.

It is difficult to stop procrastinating, especially if you are easily distracted. The internet, ipad, iphone, and no end of electronic games and gadgets derail your best intentions. With hundreds of channels, you can find something to watch rather than contact your lonely aunt. You can farm on Facebook, text your friend, and forward dubious jokes about big boobs, dumb men, and foreigners to everyone you know, rather than wash the car or do your taxes. Yup, if you are spring-loaded to impulsiveness or easily amused, procrastination probably visits you often.

To make matters worse, it is persistent. Steel's review indicates it is much like a personality trait, which is more difficult to change than a bad habit. Traits are more ingrained; they become part of who we are. But there is hope. If you are serious about procrastinating less, here are some things to try: Set goals which specify what you plan to do, establish a complete-by date, create a daily schedule, and stick to it.

A family I know in Sacramento did something different to alter their schedule. They decided that every other day would be a non-media day in their home: no texts, email, computer, TV, electronic games—nothing. They are happy with the change. Their non-media days have fewer distractions and they get things done. So, if you want to quit putting it off, try to structure your time and reduce your hours of electronic engagement, and live well between your ears.

KEEP TO THE SANE SIDE

"The object of life is not to be on the side of the majority, but to escape finding oneself in the ranks of the insane."

– Marcus Aurelius – A Roman Emperor
for 19 years in the 2nd Century AD

ARE YOU ON THE SANE SIDE? IF YOU READ THIS COLUMN, YOU KNOW I extol the virtue of science over myth, peace over war, and similar dichotomies. I like to think I'm being objective, and that the truth mirrors what I believe about these issues. But, maybe I'm all wet, and don't know my butt from second base. You decide.

Consider where you stand on this list of issues: climate change, conservation, fair taxation for rich and poor, giving to the needy, democracy vs. dictatorship, love over hate, like over dislike, natural vs. fake, eat for health vs. eat for taste? These are more than just political or free choice issues. They have major consequences! There is an obvious, inherent goodness here that is recognizable—isn't there? I'm sure you sense it.

There are more bi-polar sentiments: equality vs. a widening gap between rich and poor, fact vs. fiction, astrology vs. astronomy (the world didn't end), respect for wealth vs. greed, acceptance vs. rejection, tolerance vs. intolerance, kind vs. mean.

Good God, to be on the sane side of these choices cannot be that difficult. For example, National policies about international conflict are not executed by the Department of Attack: it's the Department of Defence. And where are you on the need for folks to have 30-round assault rifles? Yes, we need more of those. Jeez-Louise, in what hole have these assault rifle proponents stuck their head?

I have been a psychologist for 43 years, and I assure you, the reputable research says that exposure to violence begets violence.

Owning a gun, a fly rod, or any tool leads to mentally rehearsing how to use it. If you're a bow hunter, you envision using it; you handle it, you practice with it, and someday you may stalk the thanksgiving turkey with it. Good for you. The same is true for your hammer, fly rod, and whatever else—including your assault rifle. When we own something, we think about how we are going to use it, and that paves the path to action.

We model behaviour we see. Parents are role models for kids. Kids learn from them. They don't "sort of" learn from them, they actually learn from them, so be careful what you do or say in their presence. We don't "sort of" think of how we are going to use our guns, we actually think about how we will use them—and thoughts lead to actions. If you own an assault rifle it's going to be natural for you to think about how you'll use it. The guy who retrieves his 30 round assault rifle from its storage spot is not thinking deer or turkey, he's thinking people. Hello!

Lunacy has become the norm and common sense is not so common.

I'm not a big fan of organized religion. I find it hypocritical. But at least they have a code by which to measure right and wrong. They're often among the first to ignore the code, but they have one. Christians, and followers of practically every other religion, grew up understanding the 10 commandments, or something that closely resembles them. Even most atheists and agnostics have a moral code that roughly corresponds, so it shouldn't be that difficult to identify the sane side.

So what's the point? The point is it must be hard as hell for some people to live a contented life when the first thought in their head, or first words out of their mouths, supports myth over science, war over peace, attack over defend, waste over conservation, intolerance over tolerance, cruel over kind, harsh over gentle, and all the other preferences that should not be prevalent in a sane world. Examine your belief systems, get closer to the sane side of these issues and live well between our ears.

Resolve to favour Science
and reject myth

"The saddest aspect of life right now is that science gathers knowledge faster than society gathers wisdom."

– Isaac Asimov

OKAY, LET'S GET SOMETHING STRAIGHT. ASTRONOMERS ARE SCIEN-tists and astrologers might as well read tea cups. If you're wondering why the world didn't end on December 21, 2012 it is because the theories of our demise were concocted by an assortment of New Age prognostica-tors caught up in their own web of astrological pseudo-science.

With 2013 upon us, it made me think about all that happened in 2012. That led me to the many predictions made for the end of the Mayan Calendar, a few days ago, on December 21. Those who have been follow-ing the prophecies made in anticipation of this winter solstice know what I'm talking about. I admit that the confluence of wars, extreme weather, and other catastrophic events could lead the gullible to the conclusion that an evil force was afoot. The predictions were all over the map—end of world, reversed magnetic poles destroy satellite communication and internet functions, more extreme weather, collapse of the electric grids— you name it.

The Mayan civilization ended their calendar on 12/21/2012 because the planetary and galactic alignment on that day signaled the end of one cycle of 25,800 years and the beginning of another. It is understandable that they didn't bother to create a new calendar since the need for a new one was hundreds of years in the future.

In a November, 2012 report from Missouri Southern State University, Mark Claussen, an astronomer with the National Radio Astronomy Observatory in New Mexico, said the Mayans did an outstanding job of accurately forecasting cosmological movement. He also said that, from an astronomer's perspective, nothing about their discoveries supports the occurrence of wide spread catastrophes.

Conspiracy theorists, and others who view the world through a doomsday-tinted lens, are inclined to succumb to extreme explanations for things. Why is that? One reason is that science may eventually determine they are true. But most are not. People gravitate to conspiracy theories because they do not tolerate ambiguity well. They like certainty and prefer to see things as black or white. Even complicated theories or myths are more satisfying to them than not knowing. It reassures them that the world is orderly and not random.

Conspiracy theorists also believe their life outcomes are influenced more by factors outside their control than within their control. The increasing rate of change, and uncertainty in the world, provides fertile ground for conspiracy theories. They do not trust authority, are more cynical and sinister, see patterns were none exist, overlook science, and have a bad case of what Psychologists call confirmation bias. It means they seek out and accept information that confirms their initial belief, and reject that which does not. Conspiracy theories are more prevalent than ever before, and are held by an alarmingly high percentage of the population.

Surveys by Robert Brotherton (2012) at the University of London in the UK, revealed that 40 percent of Americans and Brits believe the US Government was in some way complicit in the 9/11 terrorist attacks. Thirty-one percent of Brits believe Princess Di's death was no accident; fifty-nine percent believe their government is not telling the truth about the four bombings in central London in 2005; twenty-five percent believe climate change is a hoax; one third of the population believes governments are hiding evidence of alien visitations; ten percent believe that the US government created the AIDS virus to control certain populations; and, of course, by now, almost ninety percent of the population believe that a conspiracy lay behind the assignation of JFK in 1963.

Any theory, whether conspiracy or not, needs the support of replicated research from independent scientists in order to be believed. Consensus among a majority of scientists must be accepted as the best explanation for contentious issues, or society is doomed to wallow in ignorance. Before science set us straight, we believed many strange things: angry gods threw down lightning bolts, the earth was flat, the mentally challenged were possessed by demons, our planet was the centre of our universe, and blood-letting was a cure for disease.

We've learned to follow the money if we want to understand. It's time to also follow the science. To reject science is to institutionalize ignorance and gradually poison your mind. Resolve to favour scientific explanations instead of blindly boarding the myth and conspiracy bandwagon, and live well between your ears.

The big killer:
Short-term decisions

"Long term thinking improves short term decisions."

– Napoleon Hill

NOW THAT YOU ARE A FEW YEARS OLDER, TO RETURN TO YOUR WEIGHT at graduation comes with a problem. It would take too many months of green leafy veggies, nuts, and sweat-breaking exercise. The value you place on the fit-as-a-fiddle you is no match for the pleasure of your couch and the uproar of your taste buds, as they cheer for boxed food and sugar.

Psychologists say it's a problem of discounting; we discount the value of the future event. It means the further away the desired goal (a slim you), the less you value it, compared to the chocolate that you want right now. Decisions to favour long-term outcomes are difficult; the benefits are too far removed from day-to-day life.

Whether you make the long or short-term decision depends on the magnitude of the benefit (how much weight will you actually lose), and the length of the delay (how long will it take to lose the weight). The more pounds you can shed over the shortest period of time, the easier it will be to resist the chocolate and get on your bike.

The same is true for every long-term benefit. There is always the problem of delay. Our desire to buy new crap wins out over having sufficient money to live well in retirement. The new motor home fulfills an immediate desire for fun family camping but reduces future security. Politicians' short-term desire for re-election motivates them to cater to the loudest lobbyist with the most cash rather than address the more serious and unpopular long-term issues, such as an aging population, global warming, and cyber security, to name a few. The absence of long-term decision-making is killing us.

The further out in the future the long term benefits are, the more they are de-valued or discounted. It makes decisions in favour of immediate rewards preferable but wrong. But, eventually the future will be on our doorstep, and it will be too late.

Whether we want to restore our waist-line, our health, our financial security, or the world's precious resources, we cannot continue to shoot ourselves in the foot with dumb and selfish decisions to satisfy immediate wants rather than long-term needs. Why do we all fall prey to such short-sightedness?

Joshi and Fast (2013) discovered that a decreased sense of power weakens our connection with our future; it pushes us toward the short-term course of action. Is that why you make dumb short-term decisions; because you feel less powerful, less in control, and less able to shape your future? Today's rate of change, information overload, and the complexity of our world, have caused too many to throw up their hands and conclude, "I can't make a difference anyway so why even try." Once they cross that mental threshold, they forego the best decision in favour of short-term gratification.

More fact finding, education, and open-mindedness may help. Smith, Wigboldus and Dijksterhuis (2008) found that abstract thinking vs. concrete thinking increased individuals' sense of power. It also makes us smarter and tilts the needle in favour of long-term decision making. According to Mark Ylvisaker (2006) of the Brain Injury Association of New York State, abstract thinking is associated with better foresight, judgment, insight, reasoning, creativity, problem solving, and mental flexibility. It helps us to see the big picture and connect the dots, rather than throw up our hands and opt for the easier choices that have more immediate benefits.

The consequences of repeated short-term decisions are dire. The more we cater to the short-term, the more we neglect the long-term, and the sicker everything becomes: people, animals, air, water, top-soil, as well as personal and international relationships. It's time we educate ourselves, hone our abstract thinking skills, make the necessary long-term choices, and live well between our ears.

THE KHAN ACADEMY:
AN ANSWER TO SCHOOL WOES

"The school is the last expenditure upon which
America should be willing to economize."

– Franklin D. Roosevelt

AS I WRITE THIS, GRADUATION IS A MONTH AWAY. I AM REMINDED THAT graduates will miss their friends but not the mind-numbing boredom. According to a 2009 survey of its 34 member nations, the Organisation for Economic Co-operation and Development (OECD) found that 58 percent of Canadian school kids are bored. We rank sixth. It matters more than a little, because boredom seriously hampers learning.

Social media outlets such as You Tube and Vice have used interactive technology to make learning fun, but the classroom has not followed suit. Sadly, learning the important, academic stuff has taken a back seat. However, help has arrived!

The Khan Academy is an individualized, online, educational system that makes it easy and enjoyable to gain the knowledge you're supposed to get at school. Students, parents, teachers, and some of the most education-savvy folks in the world, have given it stellar reviews. It works, it's inexpensive, and it's more fun—a winning combination.

A brief description on their website (khanacademy.org) has this to say: "We offer a free, world-class education for anyone anywhere. Khan Academy is an organization on a mission. We're a not-for-profit with the goal of changing education for the better. All of the site's resources are available to anyone and are completely free of charge."

The academy grew out of a You Tube video that Salman Khan, a graduate of MIT and Harvard, first put together in 2004 to help his young cousin learn mathematics. Since being formally founded in 2006, it has spread around the world. It has garnered hundreds of testimonials, but none more powerful than the fact that 100 percent of its funding comes from a who's who list of benefactors, including the Bill and Melinda Gates Foundation, Google, The O'Sullivan Foundation, and many others.

Each student needs a computer or tablet with access to the internet. So far, over 4,100 videos cover a variety of topics for K-12, including math (the most common), biology, chemistry, and physics. More recently, others have been added to cover finance, history and more of the humanities. Each video is about 10 minutes long, excellent in its clarity, employs interactive features and lively graphics, and is designed to build full mastery of the content at each step before moving on to the next.

It is a system that provides huge economies of scale. There are about 3,200 high schools in Canada, with at least one calculus teacher for each of them. What if the 10 best calculus teachers put their best lessons and interactive graphics online? They could reach 500,000 students at a time and offer the best calculus instruction possible. Do the same for physics, chemistry, algebra, and the humanities, and imagine the potential for increased quality and decreased costs.

There are approximately 650,000 teachers in Canada. According to the OECD, the average base salary for secondary school teachers is $34,588, for a total payroll (including primary and secondary-school teachers) of approximately $22.5 billion each year. While the top 10 calculus teachers work their magic online, the others, freed from preparation time, would be available to facilitate all aspects of the process, and provide extra help and explanation for those who need it. Increased quality could lead to huge savings.

The Khan Academy now offers instruction in 24 languages; it serves 6 million students per month. It is destined to become an integral part of education systems around the world. If you are a teacher, administrator, or a parent wishing to enhance your kids' learning experience, spend some time on their website. Jump right in, share it with your kids, and live well between your ears.

IV
HAPPINESS

WE ALL WANT TO BE HAPPY. THERE IS MORE WEALTH IN THE WORLD than ever, but we're less happy. We have more knowledge, computing power, means of communication; more of almost everything, except contentment. The field of positive psychology has boomed in the past decade and we're seeing consensus regarding the factors (psychological and otherwise) that contribute to and detract from happiness. These topics, as well as topics related to having a meaningful life and not fearing life, are explored in this section.

WHAT'S HAPPENING TO HAPPY?

"Happiness is not something ready-made.
It comes from your own actions."

– Dalai Lama XIV

ISN'T IT GREAT WHEN YOU'RE HAPPY—SMILING, HUMMING, CONTENT, and brimming over with a life-is-good feeling? In an ideal world these are everyday feelings, or at least once in a while feelings, but not distant memories. Nearly everyone complains that happy is harder to find these days. A 2005 British survey found that only 36 percent of the people were "very happy" compared with 52 percent in 1957. This downward trend is similar in other developed countries. Why does the average person report being less happy? Does it have to do with money, stress, relationships, or what?

For the very poor, money does buy a bit of happiness; it assures food in their belly and a roof over head. But once those survival needs are met, money has little effect on happiness. In fact, polls tell us that since the fifties, we've seen a three-fold increase in wealth, but only static or even declining happiness.

Maybe stress caused by change and a hurried, complicated world contributes to unhappiness. It must be part of the answer since research indicates that many of the things that reduce stress also promote happiness, such as exercise, rewarding work, and creative activities. Another British study found that 48 percent of respondents said having good friends contributed most to happiness, followed by health at 24 percent.

Okay, assume the research is valid; that some of us are not as happy, and that happy is harder to find. How do we reverse the trend and increase happiness? We can make more friends, and get rid of all the stress in our lives. Both are easier said than done but, no doubt, they would help. However, there is current research putting the spot light somewhere else, saying that happiness is closely tied to personal virtues, character strengths, and how we live our daily lives.

This most recent, and comprehensive, research on happiness comes from Martin Seligman and his colleagues working in the field of Positive Psychology. With over twenty books and hundreds of research articles, he is highly regarded in his field. Not long ago, I heard him speak about happiness at a conference in San Francisco.

He defined three distinct routes to happiness. The first is what he calls the "pleasant life" in which we really only manage to "fidget 'til we die", searching for happiness in new toys, warm sandy beaches, and whatever else we believe provides some fleeting joy. Such happiness vanishes like smoke.

The second route is through the "engaged life". It produces the type of happiness you feel when you're in the zone with a sense of flow. Characterized as more intense, it's when time stands still, and you are totally absorbed.

Third, the "meaningful life", leads to more persistent happiness, achieved not with things, but by a life focused on service to others. These three paths to happiness redefine the meaning of happy. We are happiest when we direct our pursuits to all three, with the last two carrying the most weight. But how do we do that? What else is involved?

In 2005, Seligman, Steen, Park, and Peterson identified six important virtues and the character strengths found in each. These virtues and strengths move us toward the engaged and meaningful life, where happiness comes from how we live, and not from the latest gadget or vacation.

Wisdom, the first virtue they talk about, includes the character strengths of creativity, curiosity, open mindedness, love of learning, and a sense of perspective. Courage, the second virtue, has authenticity, zest, bravery, and persistence. A third virtue they called humanity is comprised of kindness, love, and social intelligence. Justice, the fourth virtue, includes fairness, teamwork, and leadership. Their fifth virtue, temperance, lists forgiveness, modesty, prudence, and self-regulation as the character strengths. Finally, the sixth virtue, transcendence, includes appreciation of beauty and excellence, gratitude, hope, humour, and religiousness.

An impressive list! To possess all of them in abundance seems a tall order. But, then again, who said being happy is easy? When all is said and done, deep down happiness is what our hearts desire most. So build those character strengths, hunt for the routes that work for you, and live well between your ears.

CREATIVITY:
A FOUNTAIN OF YOUTH

"An essential aspect of creativity is not being afraid to fail."

– Edwin Land

"The chief enemy of creativity is 'good' sense."

– Pablo Picasso

ARE YOU FEELING OLDER THAN YOU ARE? THE AVERAGE LIFE EXPEC-tancy of a Canadian child at birth is 80.7 years. If you have already made it to 65, your average life expectancy is over 85. Of course, illness may take its toll. Some will die sooner, others will live longer, but 85 is the average. That means most of us have time left on the clock and we don't want it spoiled by feeling old, tired, bored, or heaven forbid, all three. What can we do to feel young, passionate, and more energetic?

Eating healthy and getting exercise does wonders for our physical health, but our feeling of mental well-being doesn't always follow suit. Boredom, uselessness, and fatigue lead to the blahs and depression, and no one wants a steady diet of that. Instead, become a creative person.

Before you say, "I don't have one creative bone in my body", consider the following. Non-creative types say they never feel free to get out of their comfort zone and risk failure. Studying 111 Central Europeans in 2011, Keri reported a significant contributor to creativity was lowered inhibition; let go and run the risk of looking like a dummy. Keri also reported that greater creativity occurred among people of slightly higher intellect (that includes you for sure), and those with a strong primary social network of family and close friends, as opposed to everyone on your Facebook and Twitter account.

Other factors contribute to creativity. Basadur (2011) suggests that creativity comes when you pay attention to developing your "generation stage". It means you allow yourself to encourage a relentless discontent with the status quo which helps you generate new and different ideas or solutions to problems. We often support the status quo, and pooh-pooh any notion of creativity, because we associate it with lefties and weirdoes. Creative pursuits have often been associated with a Bohemian, "artsy" life style in contrast with the nose-to-the-grindstone protestant work ethic we grew up with. However, Richard Florida's 2002 book, *The Rise of the Creative Class*, provides repeated examples of creativity flowing from folks with both characteristics; they have a tremendous work ethic, and also subscribe to the laid back values associated with an easier life-style. In fact, he makes it clear that creativity flourishes most when strong work ethic meets non-traditional thinking. It means the more tolerant we are, and the more diverse our surroundings, the less inhibited we'll be, resulting in greater creative ability. And, since we have control over our tolerance, over the diversity we expose ourselves to, and over our ability to reduce our inhibitions, we must also have control over becoming more creative. So there! Maybe you do have a bone or two of creativity. You just have to allow it to show itself.

What else can we do to become more creative? In 2011, Dane, Baer, Pratt, and Oldham found students generated more creative responses to real world problems when they were instructed to rely on non-typical problem solving styles. For example, if they typically solved problems in a rational logical fashion, they were instructed instead to abandon their rationality and try to come up with solutions on a more intuitive basis. Similarly, those who were predominantly intuitive were asked to be rational in their approach to the problem. Creativity increased for both groups when they adopted a problem-solving approach opposite to what they normally used.

And why do we want to be more creative? It will help us feel young, rejuvenated, full of life, and less bored, tired, and empty. Abraham Maslow, the famous psychologist who spent a lifetime understanding what motivated people, lamented the absence of creativity in adulthood with this statement, "The key question isn't what fosters creativity? But it is why in God's name isn't everyone creative? Where was the human potential lost? How was it crippled? I think, therefore, a good question might be not why do people create? But why do people not create and innovate."

Even Sophia Loren, the iconic movie star, said after a lifetime of creative work, "There is a fountain of youth. It is your mind, your talents, the creativity you bring to your life and the lives of the people you love. When you learn to tap this source, you will truly have defeated age."

So go for it. Try painting, drawing, sculpting, music, pottery, ceramics, writing, poetry, model building, carving, photography, or whatever your mind can conceive. Be sure to drop your inhibitions and fear of failure, enlist your family and close friends' support, say to hell with the people who think you're not engaged in "real work", let your mind go to places it doesn't often go, develop a healthy disregard for what has become your status quo, make growing old more fun, and in the process, become more creative so you can live well between your ears.

THE GAP:
WHEN REALITY FALLS SHORT OF EXPECTATIONS

"Anger always comes from frustrated expectations."

– Elliott Larson

NOT LONG AGO I SPENT A FEW HOURS WITH A FRIEND I HADN'T SEEN for years. While I listened to him talk about his life, I felt badly. He said, "This is not what I ever wanted." He sounded desperate.

He felt extreme dissatisfaction with his spouse, his boss, his job, and where his life was headed. But, were these people and situations the real problems, or was there something else—something about how he viewed his world—that caused him such unhappiness? I suggested that the problem might be the gap between the reality of his life and what he had always expected life would be like—ideally.

He was quick to respond, "I don't know what you're talking about, but I know what's wrong. I'm broke flatter than piss on a plate, I don't get enough respect, and it's her and the direction I'm headed that's the problem; it's not some kind of gap. My life sucks."

My friend grew up in a stable, loving, middle class family, and for a variety of reasons, his life hadn't turned out the same way. When life doesn't match our expectations, we become upset, discontent, and often angry and aggressive. The greater the gap, the greater is our negative emotion. The longer we have to put up with the gap, and the less we see it ever being resolved, the more frustrating it becomes.

Since 1939, when Dollard and his colleagues put forward their frustration-aggression hypothesis, psychologists have repeatedly confirmed that frustration, caused by blocked goals, leads to anger and aggression. It gets worse when you feel you are running out of time.

You can fix it if you change your reality, change your expectations, or change them both. There are hundreds of things you can do to change your reality, but they are often disruptive and impractical. For example, my friend could divorce his wife, switch jobs, or move away, but if his expectations stayed the same, the gap between his new reality and his expectations could become greater, and so would his frustration. It might be more practical to change his expectations, albeit difficult since they'd been forming since childhood.

Our most important expectations correspond to Maslow's (1970) need hierarchy, identified as: our biological needs for food, shelter, sexual expression, rest, and release from tension; the need for safety, comfort and freedom from fear; the need to belong and feel loved; the need for self-esteem, a sense of worth, confidence and competence; and finally the need for self-actualization, whereby we can fulfill our potential.

We desire and expect these needs to be met in certain ways, but when they aren't, we become frustrated. My friend's income, sex life, job, and future outlook, did not meet his expectations. He was angry with those people and situations that he believed stood in his way. He grew up expecting the kind of life he'd had as a kid. But it was impossible for his current family situation to ever match the idealized version of the family he recalled.

We all experience gaps between reality and expectation. We can deal with the little gaps. It's the big ones that wear us down and make us want to run away. When the gaps in your life are large, and you feel stuck and dissatisfied with what you have, maybe you have to change what you expect. Change your expectations so they match a life with less—less stuff and less than perfect relationships. Instead of expecting your ideal, what if you shifted your thoughts to accept the imperfections and simply do your best to improve them. Expect improvement instead of perfection. Make life better by closing the gap rather than complaining about it. Before you give up, try to change what you expect, and live well between your ears.

THE BRIGHT SIDE OF DEATH

"As a well spent day brings happy sleep, so a life well spent brings happy death."

– Leonardo Da Vinci.

ARE YOU AFRAID TO DIE? ACCORDING TO THE NATIONAL INSTITUTE OF Mental Health, 68 percent of the population fear death. Why so many?

In her 1969 book, On Death and Dying, Elisabeth Kubler-Ross, after interviewing 200 terminally ill people, identified five stages we go through after diagnosis of a terminal illness. In the first stage, denial, we don't want to believe it is true. We ask for a second opinion, or believe a mistake has been made, or convince ourselves we can delay it by changing our life-style. As death becomes imminent, denial is replaced by anger, characterized by bitterness and resentment because of events we'll miss: birthdays, summer rains, social ties, plus endless pleasures we once took for granted. A common feeling is "why me—why now?"

The third stage, bargaining, is when we start making deals. We may want to live one more year to make amends. You make promises to God if He'll just give you a second chance. As the time draws near, we picture the end of life, and we ruminate about the past, both of which trigger depression—the fourth stage. Finally, the dying person learns to accept the inevitable, and experiences a certain sense of peace.

According to Kubler-Ross, not everyone experiences all five stages, and not always in the same order. But why is there such negativity—denial, anger, bargaining, and depression—when facing death? In addition to the volumes of faith-based religious claims for life after death, there is a growing body of research which says that our "mind", "soul" or "essence" lives on after death.

In 2011, an Ipsos/Reuters survey of 18,000 people in 23 countries, found that 51 percent of respondents believe there is an afterlife. Twenty-three percent believe they will just "cease to exist" and 26 percent simply aren't sure what happens when we die. According to a 2009 CBS survey of North Americans, as many as 78 percent think there is an afterlife.

But, why don't we look forward to an afterlife, or at least think of it as an adventure? After all, the Christians who have lived good lives—at least they'd probably all say they had—believe they are going to heaven. You'd think they might welcome death in order to get there. Hindus, Buddhists, Jains, Sikhs, and others believe in the reincarnation of souls in each life until eventually, due to accumulation of good karma, they become one with God. Jews believe in what they refer to as a "world to come", a spiritual realm.

Judging by the statistics, the religious doctrines, and the concern expressed by Kubler-Ross's interviewees, simply believing there is an afterlife is not sufficient to ease our qualms about dying. It would be helpful if we had proof of an afterlife. Maybe we do. Some research hints that we may have nothing to worry about; that life goes on.

The evidence for a positive outcome of death comes from children who claim to remember previous lives (the strongest evidence), followed by evidence stemming from near death experiences (NDE's), out of body experiences (OBE's), apparitions, and after death visions. All of these phenomena have competing explanations, but none-the-less, they suggest that there is a duality of body and mind; that our essence lives on and is carried forward in another body or realm. If true, death should be preceded by anticipation, and welcomed more than shunned.

The most compelling evidence for existence after death comes from Ian Stevenson and his colleagues. They investigated children who claim to remember previous lives. It happens mostly around the age of 2 or 3. Stevenson, a Canadian Psychiatrist who died in 2007, at the age of 89, was the Director of Personality Studies, Department of Psychiatric Medicine, University of Virginia. He spent years traveling the world, investigating and documenting reports from children that suggested the existence of reincarnation. It is an area of research fraught with methodological problems. His research was thorough and he sought to eliminate all competing explanations before concluding that reincarnation was the most likely explanation.

In 2001, Nancy Hurrelbrinck briefly described one of Stevenson's cases: "A Lebanese toddler picked up the phone repeatedly and said, 'Leila, Leila'—the name of someone she had never met or heard about. Later she began to describe Leila's family in rich detail. The toddler could remember lying in a hospital, longing to speak with Leila, the living daughter of a Lebanese woman who had died thousands of miles away in Virginia. The child could name all the woman's relatives, and recalled wanting to ask her brother to ensure that her daughters received her jewels." The most compelling explanation was that the toddler was reincarnated as Leila's deceased mother, and consequently, knew many details of her young daughter, her husband, and the whole family, all of whom were part of her previous family.

Near death and out of body experiences have been thoroughly documented by Bruce Greyson, M.D., Department of Psychiatric Medicine at the University of Virginia. In a 2010 issue of the Psychology of Religion and Spirituality journal, he reported that near death experiences occurred in 12-18 percent of over 100 cardiac arrest survivors. The incidents occurred in cases where the patient met all three clinical signs of death: the absence of cardiac output, absence of respiration, and the absence of brainstem reflexes. All the NDE survivors reported similar experiences: feelings of peace and joy, a sense of being out of their body (81%), a cessation of pain, an unusually bright light radiating love, sensing some other realm (often of great beauty), and encountering deceased people.

His article argues convincingly against the possibility that any physical, physiological, or medically known phenomenon could account for the complex mental activity experienced by these 100-plus survivors.

The evidence suggests that while the brain is clinically dead, the "mind", at least in these cases, is separate from the brain and is not dead.

Rather than "mind", some religions call it the soul; others refer to it as an essence. Whatever it is, we don't yet understand it, but such findings offer support—beyond mere faith alone—that death may offer some life-like experience involving souls, people-like entities, or some type of awareness after death.

Rather than fear it, let's look on the bright side of death; a side filled with adventure which helps us live well between our ears.

MEANINGFUL LIFE

"A life of short duration...could be so rich in joy and love that it could contain more meaning than a life lasting eighty years."

– Viktor E. Frankl

DOES YOUR LIFE LACK MEANING? EACH DAY MOST OF US ONLY MANAGE to get up, get ready, eat, go to work, fart around, eat twice more, nibble on junk, and go to bed. Such routine imparts little meaning, and we're left with the sense that life is empty.

Psychiatrist Victor Frankl, in his book *Man's Search for Meaning,* says the main motive that drives us humans is our search for meaning. He differed from two other influential thinkers of the day: Freud, who believed we were driven by our endless search for pleasure, and Adler, who said it was a search for power that drove us.

In a 2011 article in the Psychological Monitor, Neel Burton offered further insights into Frankl's conclusions about a meaningful life. As a prisoner in Nazi concentration camps, Frankl observed that those who survived longest in concentration camps were not those who were physically strong, but those who retained a sense of control over their environment.

Marveling at the men who walked through the huts to comfort others and share their last bread, he said, "they may have been few in number, but they offer sufficient proof that everything can be taken from a man except for one thing: the last of human freedoms—to choose one's own attitude in any given set of circumstances." Those men were internally not externally controlled. They believed that they, not their oppressors, were in control of their ability to lead a meaningful life and make a difference.

Further support for Frankl's view comes from renowned psychologist, Abraham Maslow, who said, "The ability to be in the present moment is a major component of mental wellness." For Maslow, the highest order of motivation is the need for self-actualization—to become all we are capable of becoming. When we do that, we live a meaningful life. More recently, Martin Seligman (2005) and his colleagues studying positive psychology, conducted many studies which show that life becomes meaningful when you find your true passion and follow it in service to others.

So how do we find this elusive, meaningful life? Frankl, Maslow, and Seligman offer clues. They tell us to seek out a like-minded person, place, or community where you can most fully engage in your passion. Beyond that, they would say you should strive to gain control over your outcomes; set your goals and relinquish your right to pursue them to no one.

If these three men are right, and if you can take control and execute, then a meaningful life should follow. It seems like a tall order, but don't despair. There are many examples of people facing massive odds and coming out on top. I recently read about Spencer West, a 31-year-old from Toronto, who was born with dysfunctional legs. At age 5 he had them surgically removed at his pelvis. In June, 2012, he climbed Mt. Kilimanjaro on his hands. It's a 19,340 foot peak! He took control, set a goal, and executed. He did it to inspire others, and he speaks about it to groups around the world.

His story, as well as those of others who have overcome great challenges, serve to remind us that if they can lead meaningful lives, we can too. Their achievement, in the face of tremendous odds, puts life in perspective. If we're honest, we have to conclude that we have no business whining. Rather, we should take control, pursue our passion, execute to the best of our ability, and make our life meaningful so we can live well between our ears.

LET'S KEEP IT THAT WAY

"...happiness does not consist in amusement. In fact, it would be strange if our end were amusement, and if we were to labor and suffer hardships all our life long merely to amuse ourselves.... The happy life is regarded as a life in conformity with virtue. It is a life which involves effort and is not spent in amusement...."

– Aristotle

IF YOU ARE A CANADIAN AND A NEWS JUNKIE, YOU ALREADY KNOW that you rank number five in the world. When you found out, the first question you probably asked—after patting yourself on the back—was, "why don't I feel like it?"

An April, 2012 report on world happiness, commissioned by the United Nations, says Canadians are the fifth happiest compared to citizens of 156 countries. Denmark, Norway, Finland, and the Netherlands are ahead of us; the USA ranks 11th.

The study was commissioned because of increased concern in many countries about the decline of happiness in the face of increased prosperity. The interest in Gross National Happiness (GNH) first came to light in 1972, when the King of Bhutan proclaimed that his country's goal would be happiness over wealth. At the time, the idea was totally foreign to developed nations, but since then, GNH has gained traction. A few countries, most notably France and England, have officially begun looking at it, and pollsters in many countries are coordinating efforts to obtain data on happiness.

The average score that put Canadians in fifth place is 7.6 on a 10 point scale. When you look deeper, the data isn't quite as cheery. While the average Canadian is three quarters of the way to "very happy", two-thirds of us scored somewhere between 5.8 and 9.3. Fifteen percent of us scored between 4.1 and 5.8. And, if you happen to be one of those who scored 4.1, you're a tad less happy than the average person living in Afghanistan.

The UN report identifies external and internal factors associated with happiness. The external ones are income, rewarding work, good community and governance, and values and religion.

People need enough money to look after their most basic needs of food and shelter, so until those needs are met, money makes them happy. Beyond that, money is not a major contributor to happiness. This was also found in a British survey. Thirty-six percent of the people reported being "very happy" in 2005, compared with 52 percent in 1957, and incomes tripled over the same period. Apparently, the money enabling you to take exotic vacations, buy more electronic gadgets, drive a new car, and live in a big house, improves your life style, but doesn't bring a greater sense of well-being; you can still feel unhappy or discontent.

People in rich countries are happier than those in poor countries, but it has more to do with better governance, greater trust, full employment, better quality jobs, and greater freedom and independence, than whether you have lots of money. According to a World Health Organization study, referenced in the UN report, job security, interesting work, and autonomy are up to three times more essential for happiness than the size of your pay-cheque.

Happiness is not tied to absolute dollars as much as it is tied to the discrepancy between the haves and the have-nots. The greater the gap between your financial status and that of the rich, the more it contributes to your unhappiness, even though your actual income may be relatively high. In many developed countries the gap is wider than it used to be. The same people who called themselves middle class in the sixties, if they were totally honest, might find lower-middle—or just plain lower class—a more accurate description today.

Good community and governance is largely about trust. People report greater well-being when they feel they can trust each other, their government, their banks, courts, and other institutions and businesses. The UN report also indicates that freedom to hold and express personal values and religious beliefs is associated with happiness and well-being. It goes on to say, "religious belief and practice is more common in countries where life is harder (less income, life expectancy, education and personal safety)." It concludes by saying, "After controlling for those factors, there is no difference in life satisfaction between more and less religious countries."

Most of the external factors, and their relationship to well-being, have been summarized here. The internal factors, and what two prominent psychologists say about becoming happier, are discussed in the next column. In the meantime, since a move to Denmark, Finland, Norway, or the Netherlands is probably out of the question, be thankful you live in Canada. Let's keep it that way; continue to demand that our government and institutions are transparent and trustworthy; value the freedoms you have; push for more, and live well between your ears.

Feeling as happy as we're ranked

"I am happy and content because I think I am."

– Alain-Rene Lesage

Last week, I summarized a 2012 report on happiness, commissioned by the United Nations. I promised to complete it this week, and introduce two psychologists whose ideas move us toward that elusive goal—happiness.

The UN report ranks Canadians the fifth happiest people in the world. Upon hearing this, a skeptical friend asked, "Hmm, shouldn't I feel happier?" Most of us want more happiness; more of that deep-down, life-is-good feeling, which researchers refer to as 'well-being'. It's the feeling they want to measure when they ask, "All things considered, how happy are you over-all?"

In developed countries there's been a three-fold increase in income over the past 40 years accompanied by stagnant or declining happiness. Our headlong rush to create wealth and increase goods and services has had an unintended side effect, and the UN wants to know why.

The report looked at the effects of external factors—income, work conditions, governance, and values. In a nut-shell, income has little effect on happiness after our needs for food and shelter are met, while transparent governance, quality jobs, and freedom of expression play a major role.

The personal (internal) factors associated with life satisfaction are: age, gender, relationships, physical health, and mental health. Well-being is greater to age 40, and from 40 to 50 it hits its lowest point. It increases again between 50 and 70, and beyond age 70, declines due to deteriorating health. Women have a slightly greater sense of well-being than men; the difference increases marginally with gender equality. Education impacts well-being indirectly since it improves job security, employability, and speed of promotion.

As expected, the report states that physical health has a large impact on individual life satisfaction. It also states that people in good relationships are happier than people without relationships, while people with few relationships are happier than people in poor relationships.

The data indicate that poor mental health contributes most to unhappiness. The report summarizes the statistics related to mental health and states, "among the working-age population in advanced countries, mental illness accounts for as much disability as all the other diseases put together." But those of us not mentally challenged or disabled (as far as we know), may still feel stuck with the short end of the well-being stick. Are there psychological factors we can work on to move us toward greater happiness? Yes there are.

In his 2005 book, *Flourish*, Martin Seligman, a renowned psychologist and father of positive psychology, says well-being is built on five components: positive emotion, engagement, relationships, meaning, and accomplishment. Positive emotion comes from the sensory pleasures that make us feel good such as vacations, shopping, and eating. Engagement is when we're in the zone, time stands still, and we're totally absorbed. Relationships have a powerful effect on well-being, much like moisture to a plant. Meaning is provided when you do things to benefit others, and accomplishment provides a sense of pride leading to well-being. The resulting acronym—PERMA—suggests a permanent foundation for fulfillment.

Zimbardo and Boyd offer advice to achieve greater well-being. In their 2008 book, *The Time Paradox*, they identify six major attitudes toward time and how they impact our lives, often without our awareness. They claim that moderate attitudes toward the past, present, and future contribute to well-being, while extreme attitudes lead to unhealthy patterns of living. We are less happy when we fail to maintain balance among our time perspectives.

It took 10 minutes online to complete the Zimbardo Time Perspective Inventory (ZTPI). I discovered my time perspectives are not in balance. On five of the six, I was close to the ideal. According to his test, I am a planner with a strong future orientation; not bothered by past events. But my pathetically weak orientation toward pleasure in the present is way out of balance. I place too little attention on achieving pleasure in the present, making it difficult (if not impossible) to feel happy. Upon reflection, I think he's right, and I intend to work on it.

If, like my friend, you want to feel as happy as you're ranked, I recommend you Google Seligman and Zimbardo. Take their tests, read their books, and live well between your ears.

HAPPINESS:
THE EFFECTS OF MONEY, FRIENDS, AND PERSONALITY

"There is no way to happiness. Happiness is the way."

– Buddha

FOR MOST OF US, THE HUNT FOR HAPPINESS IS AN ENDLESS SEARCH. You think you have it; then it's gone. Gleibs, Morton, Rabinovich, Haslam, and Helliwell (2013) investigated the effect of financial capital and social capital— money and friends—on happiness. They, like many others who ask the same question, conclude that money contributes to happiness to a point, but once your basic needs are met, money no longer helps.

Economists base their models on the assumption that we meet our needs by consumption of goods in a free market. They conclude that since consumption requires money, more money leads to more happiness. Wrong. A recent British survey found only 36 percent of the people were "very happy" in 2005, compared with 52 percent in 1957, despite there being a three-fold increase in wealth. Results are similar in other developed countries.

So what about friends, do they contribute to happiness? Another British study found that 48 percent said that having good friends contributed most to happiness, followed by good health at 24 percent. Psychologists believe that satisfaction of our higher level needs for love, belonging, intimacy, self-esteem, respect, and self-fulfillment contribute to happiness. Since relationships with other people are necessary for most of these needs to be met, it makes sense that social relationships, friends, and lovers might contribute more to happiness.

Some psychologists believe that happiness is also a product of personality traits (DeNeve & Cooper, 1998) or internal factors that predispose individuals towards optimism or pessimism. This suggests a genetic basis for happiness. However, the absence of positive social relationships is thought to negate any up-beat tendency due to genetic make-up or personality.

Gleibs and colleagues agree that social relations provide a more stable and enduring basis for happiness than does money. But what about personality types: do some personality-types enjoy more happiness than others?

Psychological research by Paul Costa Jr. and Robert McCrae in the 1990's supports a five factor model of personality. While psychologists differ on the details, they agree that we are at least partly described by five personality dimensions: neuroticism, extraversion, conscientiousness, agreeableness, and openness; referred to as the Big Five.

In 2008, Weiss, Bates, and Luciano studied 973 twin pairs (365 identical and 608 fraternal) to better understand the connection between genetics, personality-type, and happiness. They found that greater happiness was observed among those who scored low on neuroticism, high on extraversion, and to a lesser extent, high on conscientiousness. When you look at the characteristics of each type, their results make sense.

Highly neurotic people are anxious, temperamental, self-pitying, self-conscious, emotional, and vulnerable. A person low in neuroticism is calm, even-tempered, comfortable, unemotional, and hardy. So yes, people who score low on the neuroticism scale should feel happier.

Highly extraverted people are affectionate, joiners, fun-loving, talkative, active, and passionate. If you are low on the extraverted dimension you are more introverted and described as reserved, a loner, sober, quiet, passive, and unfeeling. Again, it makes sense that the highly extraverted would be happier.

The highly conscientious people are hardworking, well organized, punctual, ambitious, and persevering. The non-conscientious folks are more likely lazy, disorganized, late, aimless, and quitters. These are characteristics that may be associated with happiness, but probably not to the same extent as the other two, which is exactly what the twin study found.

The remaining two of the five personality types—agreeableness and openness—showed no significant relationship to happiness one way or the other.

To be clear, none of this research proves that our genes, our personality, our social relationships, or our wealth, is a reliable predictor of happiness. However, considered together, they do point to changes we can make to be happier. We can try to be less neurotic, more extraverted, and more conscientious to enable us to live well between our ears.

HOW TO JUST DO IT?

"You have power over your mind - not outside events.
Realize this, and you will find strength."

– Marcus Aurelius

JUST DO IT. IT'S EASIER SAID THAN DONE. THERE ARE MANY EXAMPLES: start your diet, stay on your diet, exercise, clean the spare room, organize your tools, quit smoking, quit drinking, or tear yourself from the TV. Are you one of the millions who don't just do it?

Piers Steel, in his 2011 book entitled *The Procrastination Equation,* noted that 90 percent of the population admit they procrastinate. Twenty-five percent see it as a major problem. According to Steel, procrastinators are less conscientious, less self-controlled, easily distracted, impulsive, less well organized, low in need for achievement, and less confident in their ability to be successful.

Negative tasks and those with a payoff in the distant future are the ones we neglect. For example, dieting is negative and the payoff—a fit, skinny you—is months away. Throwing the chips in the garbage and eating nuts and leaves is painful, and it takes so damn long to drop even five pounds. "What the hell," you say as you gobble your chips, "I'll start getting skinny tomorrow."

What do you do when "just do it" doesn't work? Most solutions employ some version of set goals and think good thoughts. Yeah, yeah, yeah, you know all that, but you're still fat, the spare room is still a mess, and you still watch too much TV.

Try this. It might get you motivated. It's a slightly different approach, doesn't require much energy, and when I was the Psychologist in charge of student practicums in a behaviour modification class, I saw it work.

It's a first step, and it's simple. It involves keeping records, one of several protocols in behaviour modification programs. For example, if you want to lose weight, buy a note book, get a pencil, keep the book close, and record what and when you eat and drink. Omit nothing. Record everything as you do it. Don't worry about the calories, just jot in your record book: "handful of chips" or "the whole damn bag." The main thing is to get up off your butt and record everything you eat. Every time your will power fails, and you indulge in another trans-fat boo-boo, record it.

If you want to watch less TV, do the same thing. Record when and what you watch. Keep track of when you start and stop watching, and for every thirty minutes that you're not watching television, make a stroke in your book. Five strokes mean 150 minutes—two and a half hours of TV abstinence. Don't cheat. Thorough record-keeping is an easy way to control bad habits.

Your notebook and pencil can clean that cluttered room too. Whenever you think of cleaning it, make a mark in your book and keep track of the marks. Soon, a sense of, "this is ridiculous" will overcome you, and rather than mark it down, you'll get started on it. Also, keep track of the time you actually spend cleaning the room. For every 10 minutes you're involved in cleaning, make a mark in your book. Keep doing it; keep accumulating marks and soon the room will be clean. Don't feel guilty if you aren't cleaning. Just remember to make a mark in your book for every 10 minutes you are cleaning.

Making yourself exercise is more difficult. Record when and how long you do it, and work up to your goal. In addition, reward yourself with a special treat for every hour, or mile, you spend walking, running, or whatever. For example, for every half hour of walking, allow yourself to watch one hour of TV. If you don't do it, you don't get to watch. Stick to it and don't cheat.

It's all about control. If you can't control yourself, you're screwed. Success is a decision away. Decide to record and reward the desired behaviour. Decide you've had enough—enough of whatever you do, or don't do, that makes you unhappy. Just do it, and live well between your ears.

COMMITMENT AND HAPPINESS

"The quality of a person's life is in direct proportion to their commitment to excellence, regardless of their chosen field of endeavor."

– Vince Lombardi

I HAD IT ALL WRONG. FOR THE PAST FOUR YEARS OF RETIREMENT I thought that as long as I avoided commitment—something I'd been bound to all my working life—happiness would follow. But commitment wasn't the problem. The problem was, the careers I was committed to in the past were not my passion. I had mistakenly concluded that if I rid myself of commitment, I would be happy. I should have rid myself of the jobs.

On the nine hour drive home from my cousin's place last week, I was pondering this stuff, as is my predilection. I reminded myself, with an undercurrent of pride, that I was fortunate to not have any life altering commitments whatsoever—not to a job, not to a person, not to anything. I somehow took pride in being a loose spirit; I walked around, sat on my ass, watched TV, played my drums, and wrote every now and again. I was responsible to no one and committed to nothing.

But, what about my writing? Maybe I need to be committed when it comes to my writing. After all, commitment is necessary to achieve goals isn't it? Yes, I answered, it is. So, I thought, maybe it's time to rethink the commitment thing. Since you love to write, perhaps you should be committed to it. It began to make sense. I'm sure it makes sense to you in seconds, but it had taken me four years to figure it out. Four years to figure out that commitment to something would be good for me.

Because I don't always manage myself well, I decided I needed an affirmation that I could repeat often, and plaster around the house to focus my attention. I need such reminders; without them I slip into old habits. I fussed over the words as I drove east on the Yellowhead Highway. The verbs had to be active not passive; I wanted them to jump out at the reader. Good affirmations are in the first person, present tense, and they should address all the key elements. For me, the key elements are: commitment, writing, benefits, and of course — jumping words.

The affirmations are now up; font-size 22, and boldface. They're on the fridge, over the sink, beside my computer, by the door, and where I keep my keys. They each say the same thing: "My commitment to write, so the words jump off the page, makes me happier, healthier, and wealthier every day." We'll see how it goes.

I occasionally use Maslow's hierarchy of seven needs to explain what makes us tick. If I apply it to my newly committed life, the first two — food and safety — I have met. My need for love is met since my kids love me and I dearly love them. My sense of self-worth is okay. My need for knowledge is helped along by reading. My need for orderliness is satisfied by a simple and routine life that allows for the unexpected. Lastly, my need for self-actualization — to be all that I can be — wasn't getting much attention, until I discovered my affirmation on the Yellowhead.

Martin Seligman, the father of positive psychology, said deep down happiness is found on two paths: the engaged life, when you're in the zone and totally absorbed, and more significantly, the meaningful life, when you act with passion in service to others. I know that when I write I'm in the zone and engaged. I don't know if I'm of service to others, but I am more committed, so happiness may be around the corner. I'll let you know. In the meantime, decide whether commitment will lead you to more happiness, and live well between your ears.

V
RELATIONSHIPS

ABOVE ALL WE ARE SOCIAL CREATURES. NOTHING IS MUCH MORE important in our lives than our ability to have and maintain good relationships with our spouse, children, friends, co-workers, and the people in our community.

People fall in and out of love and divorce rates hover around 50 percent. Much of the dysfunction and emotional hurt stems from disintegrating or troubled relationships. This section sheds some light on factors that build and ruin relationships.

Some of the issues this section addresses are: why does communication go bad, and why are some leaders effective and others not? Why do people feel the need to control others; what problems does that create, and how can we deal with it? This section also looks at what attracts us to each other in the first place and what continues to fuel attraction to make it last.

Relationships:
Questions to facilitate communication

"Effective communication is 20% what you know
and 80% how you feel about what you know."

– Jim Rohn

Valentine's day, the day set aside to boost romance in our lives, is at the gate. As it approaches, millions of people consider ways to renew their love and caring in a long-term relationship, or to stoke the flames of a new one. Nothing is much better when it's good, or much worse when it's bad, than a relationship with your husband, wife, girlfriend, or boyfriend.

When it is good the endorphins flow, you're in love, and you can't seem to get enough of each other. When it's bad, you wonder how the hell you got into this pickle. To fall in love is easy. You don't need a map; you just get there. To stay in love is work. You need a GPS just to stay on the path.

For now, let's assume you have your mate, for better or worse, richer or poorer, and you have no intention of abandoning ship. You've had him or her for years, or perhaps you're just getting started. In either case, you want to strengthen the relationship, and fan the flames of caring, laughing, and mutual respect. If it takes some kind of rating system to accomplish that—so be it—you want your journey to be pleasant, not endured.

The purpose of today's column is to share with you a rating system I came up with to facilitate a constructive talk with your partner about your relationship—one to help you do the work and fan the flame. It might help; it might not. It is very simple: four short questions about three things that matter in a relationship. The kicker is—you have to compare your answers. As with any system, there's no point in using it if you don't commit to it. So, if you fear that talking about your love-life will only prompt rancour, then best leave it for another day. But, if you think your mate will accept a little nudge to breathe life into a sagging relationship, give it a whirl.

There is no substitute for honest communication, and what better place to begin than with someone who was, and may still be, the love of your life. It is a touchy subject. For some couples, merely contemplating the idea might ratchet up your blood pressure. Just relax, prepare to learn something new, and resolve to listen at least as much as you talk.

Three factors play a major role in relationships. The first is comfort. It includes warm, abiding love and caring for the other. It places emphasis on being considerate, predictable, and family oriented. When you value comfort, you enjoy sitting close or holding hands in an emotionally safe environment. You understand the importance of stability in a relationship and are capable of meeting those needs.

The second factor is growth. Are you mutually supportive of personal growth? Are you like-minded when it comes to attitudes, beliefs and values about religion, politics, and life-style choices? Are you as intellectually curious as your mate, and finally, do you share similar dreams for the future. For example, vacations and retirement are desired by both, but if one of you imagines them on the farm, and the other has their heart set on palm trees and beaches, there could be a problem.

The third factor is intimacy. This is more difficult to talk about because it involves both emotional and sexual intimacy—things we often leave unsaid. It includes initiating intimate discussion and behaviour as well as sharing deep seated feelings and thoughts about your personal desires and fears.

The discussion of these topics is most productive when you provide honest feedback about your preferences, while being respectful of those of your partner. Don't assume your loved one knows everything about you—about what you want and don't want. Unless you have told them, or shown them, they probably don't know.

So how do you get this communication started? First, independently of each other, answer four questions about comfort, growth, and intimacy. The four questions are the same for each factor and they are: How important is this factor to me? How important is this factor to your mate—in your opinion? Does my spouse, or 'would-be' spouse, satisfy me on this factor? And finally, do you satisfy your partner on this factor?

Start out with the first factor, comfort, and on a scale of 1 to 7, indicate your feelings about each question, where 1 is "not at all" and 7 means "very much". Assuming you don't sense trouble brewing, continue with the task.

When you finish, you will have four answers about each of these three factors—comfort, growth, and intimacy—for a total of 12 ratings. Now, the comparing and talking begins. Remember to listen at least as much as you talk. Compare how you rated each question on each factor. How well do you know your spouse or significant other? The more similar your ratings are to each other, the better. For example, if you both like to snuggle up on the couch, share some popcorn with the kids, and relish the peacefulness of each other's company, you likely have similar ratings on your four questions dealing with comfort.

There may not be such similarity in all areas. You each rated how much your spouse satisfied you, and how much you believe you satisfy your spouse. How do those ratings compare? For example, do you satisfy your mate as well as you think? Is intimacy as big a deal for him or her as it is for you, and vice versa?

For couples contemplating a long term relationship this is a worthwhile comparison. It gets the differences out in the open. In the early stages of a relationship couples overlook differences, thinking they'll go away. But once love's initial lustre is lost, the differences start to matter. If not discussed, they can poison an otherwise great relationship.

So try answering the four questions about each of the three important factors and compare your answers. Hopefully, the discussion leads the two of you to greater similarity. If it does, declare some measure of victory and take a break, have a drink, go for a walk or, better yet, go to bed, and live well between your ears.

WHY WE JOIN

"If there isn't a them, there can't be an us."

– Jodi Picoult

I RECENTLY CAME BACK FROM A TRIP TO SEE MY TWO SONS AND THEIR families: one in Illinois and one in Colorado. The one in Colorado surprised me. When I arrived there on Thursday afternoon he told me I could go with him to a meeting of his Lodge. "Lodge", I blurted out, "when did this happen?" I was surprised. Like most fathers and sons, the two of us are similar, but I have never been a joiner and didn't think he was either. I was a Lion for five months a long time ago, but that's been it.

He filled me in on some details. For a year and a half he had attended every monthly meeting without knowing whether or not they would accept him as a member. Finally, the lodge took a secret vote and unanimously welcomed him to the fold.

As we arrived at the meeting, I was surprised again to see that the members were older than him. Many were older than me! We milled around, the mood was informal and friendly, he introduced me to a few people, and shortly thereafter, the meeting began. Early in the business portion of the meeting they introduced the guests in attendance. There were two: me and another guy. I was shocked at the loud applause when they introduced my son's guest. The clapping wasn't for me—I'd only been there ten minutes. It signaled to us both that he was a highly regarded member. I was proud of him. Here was a roomful of men, none of whom I knew, who respected my son.

The whole experience made me wonder what I had been missing. Why do people join clubs? I asked my son. He thought about it and said, "Maybe for the camaraderie." I would argue that in his case, one of several reasons is that it makes him feel special.

The most prominent psychological explanation for why people join is Tajfel and Turner's (1979) Social Identity theory. It states that people join groups because it strengthens their identity and increases self-esteem. My son is proud of his membership, proud of the people, and proud of its exclusivity. At this meeting they passed a motion to reduce membership from 33 to 30. I know of no other organization that wants to shrink instead of grow.

I suspect most clubs and organizations will say their members join to lend support to a charitable cause. Elks support and promote community needs, Shriner's support Children's Hospitals, and Lions support humanitarian goals. In fact, all similar organizations, Optimists, Kiwanis, Rotary, and others pledge support for an array of good causes.

Not to minimize the desire to do good deeds in the world, a more personal reason may be that group membership meets some important human needs. Looked at from the perspective of Maslow's need hierarchy, membership helps meet three of five broad needs: the need for safety and security (there's no doubt all these guys would have my son's back), the need for belonging and attachment, and the need for self-esteem.

Interestingly, there are more men's clubs, lodges, and service organizations than there are women's. In 1964 there were 26 major men's clubs in North America and 8 for women. Many of the men's organizations began allowing women members in the 1980's, but membership is still largely male. Are women's needs for safety, belonging, and self-esteem met some other way?

It seems obvious that male dominated service groups do not provide an attractive forum for women, since they are composed of more men. History tells the women they are less likely to experience a sense of belonging or have their esteem needs met in a group of men. And, there is no reason to suspect that women will find greater safety hanging out with a bunch of what Kylie O'Brien—commenting on the first ever exclusively female club formed in London, England—called a bunch of, "exhausting, argy-bargy testosterone-heavy men." It's not a woman's style.

But the point isn't why fewer women join. The point is that becoming a member of a group can help to meet at least three important needs that many non-joiners (men and women) may have overlooked. Consider whether joining an organization might not only enable good deeds, but also satisfy some needs for you, and live well between your ears.

Are you a good leader?

"If your actions inspire others to dream more, learn more,
do more and become more, you are a leader."

–John Quincy Adams

How do you lead your business, your committee, or your family? How effective are the leaders you know? Are they delegators, dictators, autocratic, democratic, or a mixed bag?

I spoke to an executive assistant for a construction company recently who is upset and quitting her job. She can't afford to, but she can't take it anymore. She's good at her job, makes over $60,000, and is fed up. The problem: The wrong leadership style at the wrong time. The owner, a go-getter, bottom-line-oriented task master, doesn't talk, he orders. He doesn't listen, he doesn't have time.

It all came to a head when an auto-deposit didn't make it to the bank, resulting in an overdraft. His response: "How could you not know? Dammit, what am I paying you for?"

I know the lady well. She is swamped. She runs the place. She handles more than her share and catches all kinds of screw-ups before they happen. "I'm his right-hand man. We've got 27 freakin' employees here; I handle all their problems. I've always got his back, and he knows it. He's so unpredictable. It's never about the people; it's always about the money," she said.

He's going to lose a great employee because of his leadership style.

When it comes to leadership, research from the sixties and seventies by psychologist Fred Fiedler is relevant. He identified two types of leaders—task specialists and relationship specialists—both found in today's research, although often under a different name. He also discovered the best style of leadership was heavily dependent upon the situation.

Whether you are a task or relationship leader depends on how you view your least preferred co-worker. Fiedler developed a test of leadership style called the "Least Preferred Co-worker Scale." You can Google it. The test is free and can be completed quickly.

The underlying assumption of his LPC test is that, if you can see the good in your least preferred co-worker, you will lead like a relationship specialist. Conversely, if you have a negative view of the person with whom you least enjoyed working, Fiedler says you will lead like a task specialist.

Research on the subject assigns the following characteristics to each type of leader: Task specialists are autocratic, dictatorial, distant, punitive, dominating, and controlling. Relationship specialists are democratic, collaborative, rewarding, delegators, hands-on, and transformational, meaning they strive to develop group members' full potential.

In 1995, Eagly, Karau, and Makhijami confirmed the above descriptions. They also found that women were more likely to be relationship specialists, while men tended to be task specialists. "So what?" you say. "Does that make them better leaders?"

Not necessarily, but according to Eagly and colleagues, in a rapidly changing, complicated, and high stress environment, they have a natural advantage. "Bull crap," say the men. "I told you so," say the women.

Because contemporary society is more challenging than ever, the research on leadership points to a greater need for leaders who are less autocratic and more collaborative. This is why female leaders may have the edge. Society's socialization of women, and their nurturing role, makes them more relationship-oriented from day one. Perhaps their time to lead is now.

According to a recent United Nations report, women occupy less than 20 percent of leadership positions but represent 48 percent of the work force. However, if society is more complex, and if relationship specialists are the most effective, we can expect to see more women leaders in the future. Similarly, we can expect to see more business seminars designed to help both sexes develop a more relationship-oriented style.

We shouldn't over emphasize the gender distinction. The simple fact is that life is more complicated. To be an effective leader today, whether you are a man or woman, requires a complex set of behaviors. This was confirmed in 2010, when Larry Norton reported in the Consulting Psychology Journal: Practice and Research, that, "leaders are more effective if they can flex their leadership style to match shifting problems, changing priorities, and different situations."

When is it better to be one or the other? In general, when the job is straightforward or when danger lies ahead, a task specialist is most effective. When you're in emergency mode and all hell breaks loose, organizations benefit from an autocratic, get-it-done approach; the time for discussion and soothing hurt feelings comes later.

Relationship specialists are best when tasks are complex. When the group you lead is diverse or composed of bright, skilled people the same thing applies. Similarly, if you lead a committee or a group of volunteers, you will be more effective if you are a relationship specialist. My personal experience is consistent with these conclusions.

From 1988 to 2008 I was a branch manager for two large financial service companies. Too often, I got wrapped up in the task and neglected the relationship concerns. Most commonly, I failed to communicate expectations or failed to compliment a job well done. The result was always the same: production and morale declined. I learned from my mistakes but they occurred more than once. Apparently, I'm a slow learner. During this time, those who were my leaders used both styles, but on balance, were more relationship than task oriented, and all were men.

The conclusion: You don't have to be a woman to be an effective leader. As Norton and Fiedler point out, the best leaders shift styles depending on the situation. Don't fight the complexities of your business, committee or family. Instead, check your LPC score, hone your relationship skills, and live well between your ears.

Control:
Whose list is on whose fridge?

"You have power over your mind - not outside events.
Realize this, and you will find strength."

– Marcus Aurelius, Meditations

DO YOU WALK ON EGGSHELLS TO AVOID SOMEONE'S TANTRUM? DO YOU fear unwarranted criticism from your boss or partner? Does their need to take charge and give direction exceed your willingness to listen and comply?

Each example illustrates the same thing: controlling behaviour. For the controller it's about them always promoting their own agenda. They seem oblivious to the social cues for privacy, courtesy, when to shut up, when to respect your autonomy, and when to take their to-do list off your fridge.

When you live or work with a controller, you soon tire of being bullied and manipulated by guilt, obligation, or coercive demands. Your responses to the controller lack personal endorsement, because they are not heartfelt and they don't come voluntarily. Decades of research have shown that being on the receiving end of a controlling personality produces stress, robs you of freedom and independence, reduces desire, and can even make you sick.

Conversely, Ryan and Deci (2002) report that individuals whose motivation is self-determined rather than coerced, display enhanced persistence, effort, performance, vitality, self-esteem and well-being. We like to discover on our own; we don't like to be told.

But hold on. What if you're the control freak? If the next paragraph sounds familiar, maybe your list is on their fridge.

Do you find that the harder you try to convince, the less anyone listens? Are you devoted to your family, but they don't appreciate it? Do people around you complain that you always interrupt? And, do you wonder why others disagree with or ignore you? Controllers fight an up-hill battle. Good people avoid them or conspire against them.

Psychological research on coaching indicates that controlling people, no matter how hard they try, will experience difficulty until they replace their controlling behaviour with encouragement for self-direction and autonomy in others. Coercive control does not promote motivation from within; it promotes frustration and resentment which stand in the way of success.

After all, didn't the psychologist, Abraham Maslow, say years ago that when social controls are loosened, people strive for self-actualization—to reach their full potential? Yes, he did, and the implication is clear: When we control ourselves instead of others, we are better bosses, parents, and friends, and the world has a rosier hue.

In 2010, Kimberley Bartholomew and colleagues, studying coaching styles at the University of Birmingham, described six types of controlling behaviour. For starters, control through the use of tangible rewards, such as gold stars, medals, and other symbols of recognition, is destructive when they are given for mimicking what the coach wants. But, when the prize is awarded for achievement of personal goals, it builds self-motivation.

The authors also draw a contrast between manipulative feedback such as, "good work, you did exactly as I asked", and informational feedback such as, "good work, the way you managed our campaign made a big difference." The former rewards obedience, whether or not it helped the overall effort, while the latter provides helpful information, and the recipient feels proud rather than obedient.

Control is excessive when the controller gets more satisfaction from proving their authority than from achieving a positive outcome. It leads to a permanently swelled ego exemplified by more "I" than "we" statements. Intimidation, the fourth type of control, is characterized by verbal abuse, yelling and threats of punishment designed to belittle. Such behaviours produce depression, a reduced sense of competence and social withdrawal.

An example of the fifth type of control is when the boss, teacher, or parent says, "you did well young man, but Mary got an A." It's a left-handed compliment that says you did alright, but it wasn't enough. It draws attention to shortcomings rather than success resulting in discouragement, not motivation. Conditional regard, the sixth and final type of control they identify, is the opposite of unconditional regard. It is when the leader makes his or her love or respect for you conditional upon you being a certain way, rather than just being.

It is hard to believe that the feelings on either side of control can be so different. The person controlled can hardly imagine a more dysfunctional and frustrating social environment, while the controller appears totally unaware of the problems they create. So, resolve to control yourself and not others. Encourage people to keep their own list on their own fridge, and live well between your ears.

WHAT ARE YOU REALLY SAYING?

"Deafness has left me acutely aware of both the duplicity that language is capable of and the many expressions the body cannot hide."

–Terry Galloway

ALL GOOD INVESTIGATORS, COMMUNICATORS, AND POKER PLAYERS have at least one thing in common: They've learned to read faces. It helps them solve crime, shape opinion, and win money.

Whether you're greeting a customer, hosting a party, briefing your staff, or simply having a conversation with an employee, spouse, or friend, the message on your face means as much as the words from your mouth. Psychologists have shown that accurate communication can be up to ninety percent dependent upon non-verbal cues—body language and facial expression—while as little as ten percent of the message is from the actual words.

Imagine being in total isolation and shown the words: I want you. The message is confusing until you hear and see the speaker. Is it a cop, your lover, your friend, or your enemy? Is the voice soft, loud, tender, or hesitating? Most importantly, would it help to see the speaker's eyes, mouth, and expression on their face? Of course it would. The example illustrates two things: (1) non-verbal signals are vital to clear communication, and (2) texting or email is great for staying in touch, but no substitute for a face to face meeting.

Do some conversations make you uneasy? Have you had a gut feeling you don't understand? And finally, can you tell when the look on your face does not match your words.

If you answered yes, even once, I recommend two books: *Blink* written in 2005 by Malcolm Gladwell, and *Unmasking the Face* by Paul Ekman and Wallace Friesen. The first is entertaining, but less instructive. The second is a how-to-read-faces manual written by world renowned experts. With illustrated pictures of faces, it explains what your face tells others, and what it tries to hide.

The authors identified forty-three distinct muscle movements our face can make. They catalogued them to form several hundred facial-muscle combinations and the message displayed by each. The shocker is that these face messages reveal the truth, and we send them out every second without much awareness. Once your face says something, it's out there and there is no way to take it back. We can always apologize for hurtful or inaccurate words, but we never say, "I'm sorry my face just lied to you." We'd know it as an insincere apology since usually the face does not lie.

Most face messages can be read. The common ones are surprise, fear, disgust, anger, happiness, sadness, and deceit. We read them when the signals appear. For example, surprise registers as raised, curved eyebrows, wide-open eyes, and a dropped jaw with relaxed lips. If you don't see this reaction when you tell your youngest associate she won employee of the year, it probably means she already knew. Someone told her. And, if you see the reaction too late, a fraction of a second after you announced the news, it probably means that she wants you to believe she really is surprised. In either case, her face didn't properly match the occasion, she likely feels a bit awkward, and her gushing "thank you" lacks authenticity.

The good news here is because you read her face, you created a teaching moment. You can tell her that the look on her face made you suspect she already knew. Tell her it is okay; that you understand. Most importantly, you can explain that she shouldn't feel compelled to make it look like a surprise just for your benefit; that all it did was cloud the issue which, in the long run, cripples clear communication.

We've been learning to pick up on facial displays since babyhood, but we're still not good at it. Untrained people are accurate about fifty percent of the time. Stroke victims and the deaf are more accurate; their reduced ability to carry on a conversation makes them sensitive to subtle changes in people's faces. Likewise, people from abusive homes, or who work in dangerous careers, or who occupy war zones, are often better face readers because it is critical that they sense what's coming next—before it is too late.

Most of us don't manage our faces well. Messages or feelings often flow from our face despite efforts to control them. In their chapter on facial deceit, Ekman and Friesen say our body-language and face reflect our true emotions which often contradict our words. Because we get so much practice talking, it is much easier to communicate—and mislead— with our words than with our face. The boss or politician can read from a prepared statement, the spouse can rehearse the explanation to their partner, and the sixteen year-old can practice explaining how the front fender dented itself. They can rehearse the words, but their face gives them away.

What might reveal deceit? It usually has to do with timing. Suppose you ask an interviewee if he's ever been charged with a felony. Before he can neutralize his face, and in the split second it took him to answer "no", his upper eyelids rise, the lower ones tense up, and his lips tighten and draw back. Did you catch it? It was a fear response. Fear of getting caught in a lie. The fear message flashed on his face before he could neutralize it. You can't describe all you saw, but your gut says he's lying.

But this is not about deceit. It is about honest communication. When your customers, spouse, or friends notice discrepancies between what you say and how you look, they drift away because something—they may not know what— is not right. Make sure your words and face always say the same thing, and live well between your ears.

COMMUNICATION VS. CONFRONTATION

"The void created by the failure to communicate is soon filled
with poison, drivel and misrepresentation."

– C.N. Parkinson

PARKINSON, A FAMOUS BRITISH NAVEL HISTORIAN, WHO DIED AT 83 IN
1993, wrote over 60 books on administration and bureaucracy. He is
most famous for Parkinson's Law: "Work expands so as to fill the time
available for its completion." But it's his view on the importance of communication that is relevant here.

Has the notion of not communicating with an enemy outlived its
usefulness? Not talking to enemies became popular after 9/11. "Don't
negotiate with terrorists" was a strategy that made sense in the immediate aftermath of the horror in New York. It was an attack—not a threat
to attack—and it warranted measured retaliation against the perpetrators
rather than discussion.

Since that fateful day, more people fear those who look different, wear
different clothes, have different customs, or speak a different language.
Such fears propel us in the wrong direction; they make us more isolated,
paranoid, and overtly hostile. Such fears propel us towards attack rather

than conversation. As the fear mounts, there's talk of greater Nationalism and Patriotism, and strangers are eyed suspiciously. Are people on the right track; is there any justification for such behaviour? Perhaps, but not much.

In 1998 Krauss and Morsella reported that, in the absence of a genuine desire to resolve conflict, communication is as likely to intensify the parties' disagreement as it is to moderate it. According to them, when there is no shared desire for agreement between the parties, communication does not eliminate or reduce conflict; it can even make matters worse. This suggests that communication with terrorists, or those who take hostages, may not be the best plan. Okay, we can agree on that.

But, in general, it makes sense to say that the vast majority of people everywhere prefer to live in peace, and in those cases, communication trumps no communication. Take the current debate about Iran, nuclear preparedness, and the Israeli/Western alliance. What's going on there? Israel, its' allies, and Iran prefer peace over war—let alone nuclear war—at least based upon what they say. If they truly do have common ground and shared values, then social scientists and political observers agree that communication is preferred. It would uncover those shared values and lead to alternatives that are more productive than fighting and war.

It isn't often that communication actually makes things worse. When it appears as though it might, it still makes sense to send in some special envoys, or schedule secret talks, or make use of a mediator to determine if there is a common desire for peace and understanding. If there is, then communication should follow. If there isn't, then hold off until it is clear that there are shared values, and at least, a common desire to make things better.

But—and it's a big but—you've got more than a few vocal politicians on both ends of the political spectrum, particularly on the right, who repeatedly call for no talks with enemies. They are worried about America looking soft and losing its leadership role.

Open your eyes! Ever since you were in grade school you've known that the leaders weren't the fighters. The fighters were trouble makers and playground bullies—not leaders. Leaders bring calmness to the table; war mongers—the fear-motivated, ready-shoot-aim guys—wouldn't know calmness, let alone leadership, if it jumped up and bit them on the ass. The leaders are the ones who, when all else fails, are among the first to act, defend themselves, and pound the crap out of the bullies. But that comes after all else fails.

The scared, the confused, the ones without communication skills— they are the ones who swing without asking why; who don't grasp the social realities of their environment. They are the bullies who yell the loudest when they know the least. The USA, Western Allies, or anyone else who wants to assume a position of leadership, must encourage talks with everyone. They need to be the bouncer at the night club; the one who chats to everyone, has muscles in his poop, but only acts to stop fights—not start them. That's how you earn respect.

It was Theodore Roosevelt who's given credit for the words, "speak softly and carry a big stick." That should characterize a leader's action rather than, "don't speak and swing your big stick." In the same vein, another former US President, Harry S. Truman, said, "We shall never be able to remove suspicion and fear as potential causes of war until communication is permitted to flow, free and open, across international boundaries." Some of us need to get a grip.

The same is true in your home-life. If you never agree on anything, then throw in the towel. But when you know there is common ground, communication will enhance the relationship. If you want to maintain peace in the family, acknowledge that the other isn't the enemy and talk your way to harmony. Put yourself in the other's shoes, discuss what's important, acknowledge their point of view, let them know you under-stand how they feel, and listen more than you talk.

Whether you're a politician, ordinary Joe, or an entire country, take Parkinson's advice: favour communication over confrontation, and live well between your ears.

SHOEBOXES AND VALENTINES

"The problem with human attraction is not knowing
if it will be returned."

– Becca Fitzpatrick, Hush, Hush

AS A KID IN GRADE FOUR OR FIVE, VALENTINE'S DAY WAS RIGHT UP there with Christmas and Halloween. At the school I attended we each decorated a shoe box with crepe paper and hearts, cut a slot and printed our name on the front, and stacked them up like a post office in the classroom. During the week we stuffed cards into slots, making sure the right card went in the right box.

The afternoon of the big day was party and cake time. We grabbed our shoe box, tore it open, and looked inside. I couldn't wait to find out who had given me a card. It meant they liked me! Cards with handwritten messages were always best; more thought was involved. If it came from a girl, I studied the words to find any extra indication of attraction.

As I look back, what was special was that I was in their thoughts. My name was on their lists, they selected my card, wrote something to me, found my shoe box, and stuck it in the slot. From there it was a short mental hop to conclude that they cared—Yippee!

Suppose your child got 100 valentines from her friends. How would she feel? Would she feel 100 times better than if she received only one? I don't know. But it's hard to get too many I-care-about-you messages. We all know people who haven't heard a caring message from us in a while, and it doesn't have to be a valentine. A kind word, helpful gesture, or acknowledgement of their worth is like another card in their shoe box.

From whom do we want these caring messages? What fuels our attraction to spouses and friends? Research on attraction and love offers some clues. Our need for love and belongingness is the third of seven needs found in Abraham Maslow's theory of motivation. We need to know we belong someplace, and one of the places we really want to belong is in someone's heart. Almost as strong as our need for food and safety, this third need, when unmet, creates an emptiness telling us something is wrong, but we're not sure what. Filling the empty space with over-eating or non-stop working is a poor substitute for love. Again, more cards in the shoe box might be the answer.

Studies show that birds of a feather really do flock together. We are more likely to become friends when we share similar values on major things like religion, politics, hobbies or life style. Over the long haul these similarities strengthen the bond. As relationships progress, opposites come into play, such as when husbands and wives find that strength in one complements a weakness in the other. For example, a left-brain logical spouse may help their right-brain partner—the creative, loosey-goosey one—manage the finances and logistical needs of the family.

As you think about those who haven't heard from you in a while, think also about reminding them of what you have in common. Let them know that you still vote for so-and-so, or that you often think of the road trip you shared. If they had strengths that complemented your weaknesses, remind them that you miss their advice, their annoying obsession, or whatever it was that filled a hole in you.

Don't worry about whether you should or shouldn't contact them, or about explaining why they haven't heard from you in a dog's age. Instead, remember those "yippee" moments. Find an opportunity to show someone you care—to add to their shoe box—and live well between your ears.

IT'S MY NAME!

"Tigers die and leave their skins;
people die and leave their names."

–Japanese Proverb

WHAT'S IN A NAME? NOT MUCH—UNLESS IT'S YOURS. DALE CARNEGIE, author of *How to Win Friends and Influence People* said, "A person's name is to him or her the sweetest and most important sound in any language." When asked to introduce or describe ourselves we usually start by saying, "My name is_____." Our name is deeply rooted in our identity.

Hearing it does something special in our brain. In 2006, Carmody and Lewis obtained MRI readings from male adults and found there was significantly more activity in the left middle cortex when they heard their own name than there was when they heard the name of someone else. This particular brain activity is similar to patterns found when we make judgements about ourselves and our personal qualities. It suggests a psychological connection between hearing our name and feelings of self-worth.

In 2009, three psychologists in Israel concluded that names may carry unconscious personal significance. They studied the relationship between a child's first name and attention deficit hyperactivity disorder

(ADHD) and found significant and unexpected results. There were fewer syllables in the first names of kids with the disorder. They also found that the names of kids with ADHD are not as common as those found in the general population. These results suggest that our name, at least for certain people, makes unique connections in the brain in an area affecting behaviour and personality.

Research by Joubert (1990) found that women who like their first name are less lonely and have fewer siblings than those who don't like their first name. If that's not confusing enough, they also found that first-born women liked their first name better than did women who were later-born.

Go figure. The research says there is some kind of relationship. Our name is a sweet and important sound that affects our behaviour, brain activity, and personality, but so far, we can't explain why.

Think of this: if your name is Anne and your husband or boyfriend said to you, either, "I love you" or "I love you Anne" do they create the exact same feeling? I doubt it. My guess is, you like the sound of the second one better. Of course, if your name is not Anne, you have a different problem!

Similarly, "Good morning Bob" versus just "Good morning" probably gets Bob's day off to a slightly better start—not much perhaps— but it reflects a slightly warmer and friendlier tone towards your neighbour, Bob. It makes a difference and it's an easy thing to do, so why not do it?

For the past two years my friend has taken her daughter to the orthodontist. While she has her braces tweaked, Mom goes to a small clothing boutique. The owner has never remembered her name. "It just infuriates me," says my friend. "I didn't expect her to remember my name at the beginning. But I've been there at least eight times, spent money on every visit, and of course, my name comes up on the till when I slide my card. You'd at least think she'd remember my face and say something to acknowledge my return to her store. But there is not an ounce of recognition—nothing—so I quit going, even though I love her stuff."

Experiences such as these, and the research results mentioned above, confirm that hearing our name has more than just passing significance. It activates many connections in our brain. Referring to people by name seems to magnify the message. Carnegie was right. Try it. See if it gets you better service, repeat business, warmer interactions, or just puts a smile on someone's face, and live well between your ears.

Who do you like, and why?

"It is not so much our friends' help that helps us,
as the confidence of their help."

– Epicurus

"A friend is one who knows you and loves you just the same."

–Elbert Hubbard

Good friendship has strong ties. research indicates there are at least nine ties that strengthen friendships. Think of your good friends. How many of the following ties exist between you and them?

The first and strongest tie between friends is similarity. Ledbetter, Griffin, and Sparks (2007) took two measurements between 45 pairs of friends—first in 1983 and again in 2002. They found that friends who had the most similar beliefs, values, and attitudes in 1983 had the strongest friendships 19 years later. It means that people who have been friends for years are those who see eye to eye on issues like religion, politics, family, and other strongly held lifestyle beliefs. Similarly, Chen and

Kendrick (2002) found that once you discover someone has dissimilar values and beliefs, you tend to stay away from them.

A second strong tie stems from close proximity. It is likely that at some point you worked with or lived close to your good friend, and you still may. Because of widespread use of the internet, text messages, and other mobile devices, physical proximity is less critical today than in years past. But, regardless of how contact is made, more frequent contact strengthens friendship.

Reciprocity is a third tie that binds. When we believe that someone likes us, we are more likely to like them. Think about how you react to people who appear friendly compared with those who do not; you probably send out a warmer message, both verbally and non-verbally. In return, the other person, sensing your smile, the twinkle in your eye, and your open body language, will reciprocate. It makes sense that if you want someone to be friendly towards you, you should at least let them know that you like them.

Fourth, friendship flourishes when attractiveness is in the mix. Right or wrong, physical attractiveness often ignites the initial flame of friendship. For years, psychological research has shown that physically attractive people, particularly in Western society, are judged to be more competent, smarter, and more desirable as friends.

Social-identity support, the fifth tie, means that your friend understands how it feels to be a member of a certain group with which you strongly identify. For example, if your religion is an important component of how you define yourself, a best friend might say, "You are such a good religious person." Or, if being a musician is a defining characteristic for you, a best friend is someone who understands how important it is and may say, "It is so cool that you were asked to play with the Symphony."

Carolyn Wiesz and her colleague Lisa Wood (2005) found that such social-identity support is a very strong factor contributing to long term friendship. They studied 50 men and 50 women. Those who were supportive of their friends' participation in such groups were significantly more likely to be judged as best friends after 4 years.

In 2004, Debra Oswald, in a research article on friendship, provided support for the remaining four ties in the bond of friendship: self-disclosure, supportiveness, interaction, and positivity. Friendships grow when two people are willing to disclose things about themselves. The more intimate and private the disclosures, the stronger the friendship becomes. Supportiveness means being a good listener and offering support in times of need and uncertainty.

Oswald makes the point that contact and interaction foster friendship. While physical closeness is not as critical now that we have the internet, there still needs to be some person-to-person interaction to maintain strong friendships. Finally, the ninth tie of friendship is positivity. We like to be around people who are positive. No one wants to be a sounding board for you when all you do is complain. Even the staunchest of friends become distant when they are repeatedly called upon to suffer through your latest tales of woe.

Ralph Waldo Emerson said: the only way to have a friend is to be one. So nurture the few that you have, strengthen the ties to acquaintances who you want as friends, and live well between your ears.

FEWER WALLS LEAD TO
BETTER FRIENDSHIPS

"Do not save your loving speeches
For your friends till they are dead;
Do not write them on their tombstones,
Speak them rather now instead."

– Anna Cummins

A MAJOR STUDY OF 6,928 PEOPLE OVER 17 YEARS IN CALIFORNIA'S Alameda County confirms that you stay healthier when you have good friends. This, and other studies, found that people with a strong network of friends have more resistance to the common cold, better self-worth, less stress, a greater ability to cope with illness, and live longer than those without strong friendships. That's good to know but, the problem is, not everyone has good friends.

Are you someone's best friend? If you have differences of opinion on major issues, or have secrets about yourself that you don't disclose, you are probably not best friends with anybody. For example, if you're gay, suffer severe depression, had an abortion, or adopted out a child at age 17, consider whether sharing such information with the right friend—might make you best friends.

"Bull crap" you say, "I don't have to see the world the same way as others, or confess my deepest secrets to have good friends." Okay— but think it through—if they recoil at your revelation, how strong was your friendship in the first place? On the other hand, they might say, "Oh my God, me too", which would make your friendship stronger.

How do people become best friends, and why is it difficult for some to make close friendships? Decades of psychological research on attraction and friendship confirm that people become good friends because they have similar values, attitudes, likes, dislikes, status, and even appearance. When shared similarities have high emotional content, the bond is strongest.

For example, similar views about religion, politics, and the mysteries of the universe, tie two people tighter than do similar views about hockey teams, beer, or where to take a vacation. Even though we seem to have things in common with a new acquaintance, if we don't see eye to eye on the big issues, we will probably remain an acquaintance and not a friend.

The answer to the second question, why is it more difficult for some to make and keep close friends, is that we erect walls to hide behind. It causes friendships to either unwind or never get off the ground. The most obvious walls are lies, secrets that no longer need to be secret, distrust, or events in our past we want to conceal. Some of our efforts to erect walls are more subtle. For example, we may try to disguise anxiety, fear, or depression with body language, such as leaning back, crossing our arms, or looking away whenever such things come up in conversation. Similarly, deception shows in our face when our eyes harden, or we try to neutralize our expression.

These non-verbal signals tell our would-be best friends that something is not right; a wall has gone up and we're hiding something. It creates discomfort that neither the deceiver nor the deceived wants to feel with their friend. A few such walls may not impede your garden-variety friendships, but since they prevent knowing the deeper more significant similarities, the possibility of a great friendship is doomed.

When you tell the truth, offer honest opinions, share inner thoughts, and reveal true feelings, the walls disappear. It's what it means to wear your heart on your sleeve, or become an open book. But, when you raise your walls, keep your heart's contents hidden, or rip out some pages of your "this-is-me" book, it's impossible for others to know you well, and it throws a monkey-wrench into friendship.

Taking down walls is risky business because it makes us vulnerable; what we once hid is now in the open for others to see. But, if you want the best of friendships, dismantling the walls you have built might be worth the risk. You can always slow the pace by discussing similarities on a tit-for-tat basis — you reveal a little and they reveal a little. Good friendships progress one shared similarity and one dismantled wall at a time, until you discover whether it is good, bad, or otherwise. If it's good, you will have made a friend, perhaps even a best friend. In any case, fewer walls reveal more similarities and yield better friends, and better friends help you enjoy life and stay healthy, so you can live well between your ears for a long time.

Friends

"Wishing to be friends is quick work,
but friendship is a slow-ripening fruit."

– Aristotle (BC 384-322)

CLOSE FRIENDS ARE ESSENTIAL TO OUR PHYSICAL AND PSYCHOLOGI-cal well-being. Larson, Mannell and Zuzanek (1986) found that older adults enjoyed greater openness, reciprocity, and positive feedback from participating with friends as opposed to family. Good friends made them happier campers.

An article published by the British Psychological Society in 2012, reviewed the beneficial effects of friendship. It concluded that the presence of good friends makes negative experiences less stressful. Similarly, Rosengren, Wilhelmsen & Orth-gomer (2003), following a six-year study of 736 Swedish men, reported that absence of strong friendships is exceeded only by smoking as a major risk factor to health. Other research confirms that strong friendships reduce the incidence of common colds and create personal optimism.

If friendship is so vital, it behooves us to know what makes a good friend. We all know friendship is a two-way street, characterized by mutual trust, respect, support, and understanding. When both people know their friendship is solid, it becomes a low maintenance source of unending pleasure. A best friend is like your dog: loyal, with no explanation necessary. You can count on them to be in your corner, and on your team.

How do we become best friends? At the core of any best friendship are shared values on such topics as religion, politics, sex, family, and marriage. For example, suppose you vote Conservative and your neighbour is a Liberal; you're against same sex marriage, he's okay with it; you're a Methodist, he's Jewish; you eat whatever you want, he eats nuts and twigs. Without seeing eye-to-eye on at least some of these things, you may remain acquaintances, but you won't be best friends.

As we transition from acquaintanceship to friendship, we disclose bits and pieces of how we feel. We do so to discover whether we have similar values and beliefs. Debra Oswold (2003) said that four basic behaviours are required to maintain the bond of friendship: self-disclosure, supportiveness, interaction, and being positive. Oswold says that once the friendship is established, the interaction does not have to be face to face, as long as it is sufficiently frequent, whether by phone, email, or text. According to Beverley Fehr (1996) from the University of Winnipeg, we go from acquaintance to best friends when we disclose more about ourselves in more detail.

The research suggests women's friendships can be more fragile than men's. Famous author, Anne Morrow Lindbergh, said, "Men kick friendship around like a football, but it doesn't seem to crack. Women treat it like glass and it goes to pieces." In a 1982 publication, Paul Wright, after studying the dynamics of friendship for men and women, said that men's friendships are shoulder-to-shoulder, while women's are face-to-face.

He means that men are less emotional; they talk about present-day activities more than feelings. Women, on the other hand, are more emotional; they talk about feelings more than activities. The implication is that men do things with their friends and women talk about things with their friends. Lindberg's football versus glass analogy has a ring of truth. Perhaps the emotional basis of women's friendships contributes to their instability, or maybe women disclose too much too soon, while men go a little slower.

It isn't clear, but the conclusion for men and women is still the same: build friendships based on disclosure. Don't confuse your hundreds of Facebook friends with real, face-to-face friendships built from the ground up. Only a small percentage of people say their online social networks have led to an increase in face-to-face contacts (Wellman et al, 2001; Waite et al, 2011). However, Putnam (2000) argued convincingly that TV and the internet have resulted in less social involvement and more isolation over the past 50 years which is consistent with the increase in illness, depression, anxiety, and stress over the same period. Perhaps what we're missing are a few more old-fashioned best friends. Go ahead and develop one or two, and live well between your ears.

Could it be their
Best Gift Ever?

"Christmas is the season for kindling the fire of hospitality in the hall, the genial flame of charity in the heart."

– Washington Irving

"It came without ribbons, it came without tags, it came without packages, boxes, or bags. Christmas can't be bought from a store—maybe Christmas means a little bit more."

–Dr. Seuss

IF YOU'RE LIKE MANY OF US, YOU'VE ARRIVED AT ANOTHER CHRISTMAS season only to spend money you don't have on gifts that aren't needed to meet expectations that are misplaced.

What does that mean—misplaced expectations? For me it means too much emphasis on gift giving and getting, and not enough on loving and caring. It got me thinking about doing something different. It has been a long time since I've felt child-like-Christmassy. I'm not Ebenezer Scrooge, but I've been sliding in that direction. This year might be different.

I have five grandkids. Not one of them needs another talking doll, or box of Legos. In fact, I don't think they need anything material at all. Another gift from grandpa is a favorite for a few minutes, but the shine wears off and it's forgotten in a week. The retailers have benefited more from my gift giving than the kids ever have. I wondered what I could do for them that might mean more and have a lasting benefit.

Child sponsorship! I've thought of it in the past, but never took the trouble to do the research and follow through. In years past, I've spent between $300 and $500 on gifts for kids. The national average spent on gifts alone this Christmas is projected to be $613.

Plan Canada enables you to sponsor one child for $444. Save the Children lets you do it for $336 per child, per year. You're not committed to it forever, so if money tightens up you can bow out gracefully. The whole thing seemed like a good idea with plenty of pluses. The sponsored child benefits, my grandkids get to feel what it's like to give, it replaces the commercialism of Christmas with something more like a good deed, and it lasts for months, maybe years, during which time pictures are shared, letters exchanged, and life is learned.

I decided to sponsor one child for each of my two sets of grandkids—three in Chicago and two in Colorado. All correspondence between the agency, the child, and my kids will be direct and won't involve me in any way, other than to pay for it. The first package they receive will include a picture of the girl they are sponsoring, her age, name, information about her family, her likes and dislikes, and I don't know what else. The kids will love it. Hopefully, the process helps them feel like good Samaritans. After all, they really are giving up their Christmas gift to help someone else have a better life.

I'm writing this in early November and right now I'm not sure how I'll explain the whole concept. It needs to be more tactful than a note in a card that reads, "Dear grandchild. This Christmas I'm giving you nothing. Instead, I've spent the money I would have used for your gifts on someone you don't know, will never see, and may not even exist. Merry Christmas, Love, Grandpa."

I doubt if they'll be head-over-heels excited. But who knows, it might end up being their best gift ever. I'll let you know how it goes. You might want to do it. In any case, my hope is it helps them—and two little girls in Africa—live well between their ears.

Broken hearts and love

"You always hurt the one you love, the one you shouldn't
hurt at all. You always take the sweetest rose and crush
it till the petals fall. You always break the kindest heart
with a hasty word you can't recall. So if I broke your
heart last night, it's because I love you most of all."

The lyrics were written by Allan Roberts and the music by
Doris Fisher in the 40's. The Mills brothers, Connie Francis, and more
recently, Michael Bublé has assured its place in the history of great songs,
more because of its universal truth than anything else.

Words or deeds are especially hurtful when the recipient loves us, and
trusts that we'd never hurt them. When we say or do things to shatter that
trust, the hurt runs deep.

Hurt is rarely felt by people who don't love us; they simply don't care
that much, and the relationship has less emotion buried inside. But your
kids, parents, pets, and good friends—the ones who trust you to love
them—are the ones we hurt. Those relationships brim with emotion.
When they get even a bit fragile, like the sweetest rose, the petals
crush easily.

How do we hurt the ones we love? There are many ways: neglect, criticism, damn them with faint praise, unfair comparison, lack of loyalty and

support, sexual infidelity, emotional infidelity (when we confide more in another than we do in our loved one), disrespect, dishonesty, withdrawal, and of course physical harm. Let's leave physical harm aside; it's a whole other topic and the song seems less directed at that.

Why do we hurt those we love? Neglect, due to self-absorption, is one reason. It's when we're so centred on our own lives we don't have the time or desire to tend to others. Even when we mean well, and are not self-centred, we often keep our distance from those we love because it is too much work to get involved. This happens in families, for instance, when you're reluctant to say something as innocent as, "I'm worried about you." You fear it could unleash an outpouring of all the things that are wrong with their life and create an obligation for you, someone who loves them, to jump in to help—a jump that takes more time and energy than you can afford.

Why is it easier to criticise than praise? Usually, it's because the things we don't like attract our attention, while the routine things go unnoticed. For example, you rarely compliment your daughter-in-law for the every-day support she provides to your son and grand-kids, but when she scolds (or fails to scold) one of the little beggars, you question her child-rearing.

Think about the times you felt hurt and the times you've hurt others. What's been the common element? Usually it is poor communication. A sizeable chunk of humanity seems unwilling or incapable of having a meaningful conversation about topics near and dear to their hearts—the ones that really matter (big or small). Why is that? Are they reserving those topics for their death-bed! They can discuss the weather or stupid politicians for hours, but not topics with emotional content that might heal a broken heart.

When we don't communicate, and when we shove emotional topics under the rug, we lay the ground work for hurt. Good communication makes hurt feelings less likely. And text messages don't count. Without face to face conversation we can't absorb the meaning that is accurately conveyed by body language, tone, and facial expressions. Texting is great for staying in touch, but no substitute for feeling your touch. The 14 little letters—How r u? Gr8 I hope—that beep into the mobile device of parents who miss you, a lonely daughter, or a depressed friend, is a cold hearted excuse for a warm hug and hearing the words, "I love you."

The biggest hurts are those we inflict on those who love us. Perhaps the lyrics should say you always hurt the one who loves you. So, as we head from one Valentine's Day to the next, extend a rose without crushing its petals, guard against heart breaking hasty words you won't recall, communicate your feelings to those you love, and live well between your ears.

Humour

"Through humor, you can soften some of the worst blows that life delivers. And once you find laughter, no matter how painful your situation might be, you can survive it."

– Bill Cosby

AN EMPLOYEE TEXTS HIS BOSS, "WON'T BE IN. FEEL TERRIBLE." THE boss texts his advice, "When I feel bad I make love to my wife." Two hours later the employee texts again, "Feel better. You have a nice house."

If you laughed out loud, the joke had some beneficial side effects. The research says that laughter reduces stress, increases pain tolerance, increases the response of tumor- and disease-killing cells such as Gamma-interferon and T-cells, defends against respiratory infections, releases endorphins which make us feel good, and improves alertness, creativity, and memory.

A study conducted at Johns Hopkins University Medical School even found that humor during instruction led to increased test scores. Similarly, a 2005 study at the University of Maryland Medical Center, showed a positive relationship between laughter and healthier blood vessels and blood flow. It raises good cholesterol and lowers inflammation in our heart. But, it takes actual laughter, not just positive mood, to generate all of these benefits. So what makes us laugh?

Rod Martin (2007), from the University of Western Ontario, says five things promote laughter. (1) It occurs more readily when we are with people rather than when we are alone; it is a social phenomenon, arising from things people do or say. (2) We laugh at incongruity; when things that don't belong together are paired. For example, when your prim and proper aunt farts at the dinner table. Similarly, one-liners, like this one from Dave Barry, "Never take a sleeping pill and a laxative on the same night", illustrate how incongruity can make us laugh. (3) Positive emotion makes us receptive to the humour in a situation. Martin says, "Mirth is what makes humour so enjoyable and causes us to want to experience it. It's like a drug." (4) Laughter is contagious; we often laugh or giggle once someone else starts. As a kid in church, whenever my buddy got so much as a smile on his face, I got the giggles, then he did, then we couldn't stop, and the more we tried, the worse it got. (5) Surprisingly, jokes only account for only about 20 percent of our laughter. Martin says that most of humour we encounter on a day-to-day basis comes from our interactions with others, whether it's a witty comment or a funny story. From a psychological perspective, these more spontaneous and social forms of humour are more important than jokes.

Marshall Brain, founder of the website *How Stuff Works*, says laughter also serves as a stress reducer. When in difficult or dangerous situations, we laugh involuntarily to reduce stress and let us function with a clear head. It accounts for the morbid humour that occurs in war and other life and death situations.

Robert Provine (2000), a neuroscientist from the University of Maryland, discovered interesting differences between men and women. Women laugh 126 percent more than men, but more men than women cause laughter. Internet dating sites reveal that more women than men want their ideal match to make them laugh, while more men than women offer their good sense of humour as an asset.

Similarly, researchers in Germany studied spontaneous conversations between mixed-sex pairs of young German adults meeting for the first time and found that the more a woman laughed aloud during these encounters, the greater her self-reported interest in the man she was talking to. In the same vein, men were more interested in women who laughed heartily in their presence.

Humour follows a winding route in the brain. It starts at the primitive base of the brain and moves up into the left hemisphere where we analyze the words or events. It then moves to the right hemisphere, where we may or may not "get it" depending upon how bright we are. From there, it moves to the vision and motor areas to finally provoke an out-loud laugh. All this takes four-tenths of a second.

Considering its many benefits, we don't know much about laughter. We do know that we feel fantastic when we laugh, and that we need more of it to live well between our ears.

Alone vs. Lonely

"The most terrible poverty is loneliness and the
feeling of being unloved."

– Mother Teresa

According to the June, 2012 *Euromonitor International* report,
27 percent of Canadian adults live alone. We rank 6th in the world and
the trend is up. Countries with a higher percentage of one-person house-
holds are Sweden (47), Britain (34), Japan (31), Italy (29), and the
USA (28).

But living alone does not, by itself, create loneliness. Lonely feelings
settle into our psyche when we are isolated from others and have weak
social networks. It is possible to live alone and be perfectly content, just
as it is possible for you to live with someone and feel incredibly lonely.
Because we are one of the most social creatures on earth, prolonged soli-
tude is not normal, and it takes a toll on our physical and mental health.

A 2008, Statistics Canada report by Mireille Vezina addresses factors
that cause loneliness. Lonely people have less "social capital" meaning
they do not have strong social networks. We add to our social capital
with family, friends, frequent contact with others, and people we can rely
on in times of need.

Her report lists low education level, low income, rent rather than own, unemployment, no community involvement, and being male that make it difficult to develop strong social networks. These characteristics describe people who relocate more often, have fewer close friends, or are less socially involved. Regardless of the reason, pity the person who falls into many of those categories.

The research indicates that absence of strong social networks is the main cause of loneliness. Of course, if you live alone you are at greater risk of being lonely, but as Vezina points out, there are "an increasingly large number of people who live alone who do not report being lonely. In fact many of them like the freedom of being alone." Whether or not you live by yourself, the consequences of loneliness are powerful, wide-ranging, and debilitating.

In the June, 2012 *Forbes Magazine*, Larry Husten reviewed a report published in the Archives of Internal Medicine that throws a spotlight on the grim effects of loneliness and living alone on health. Over 1600 people answered a questionnaire about loneliness, and then were monitored for 6 years. Forty-three percent reported feeling lonely. Six years later, when the researchers compared the ones who felt lonely with those who didn't, the lonely group had 9 percent more deaths, 12 percent greater decline in the activities of daily living, 9 percent greater drop in over-all mobility, and 13 percent had more difficulty climbing. And, there's more bad news for the lonely.

In 2007, Louise Hawkley, a Psychologist at the Chicago Center for Cognitive and Social Neuroscience, summarized a thorough review she and her colleagues conducted on the effects of loneliness by saying: "a chronic stressor such as loneliness can cause low-grade peripheral inflammation which, in turn, has been linked to inflammatory diseases such as diabetes, cardiovascular disease (e.g., atherosclerosis), and autoimmune disorders (e.g., rheumatoid arthritis, lupus). Whether chronic stress works causally or synergistically with underlying disease mechanisms remains unresolved. Nevertheless, the outcomes of these processes can be influenced by the stress and depression associated with loneliness. Indeed, the centrality of social relationships to well-being implies that loneliness may extract a great cost on human health, the mechanisms for which have only begun to be explored." Their article paints a bleak outlook for the lonely.

Social isolation means we have less interaction with other people, and when we live alone the problem is magnified. It leads to less positive feedback from others, fewer opportunities to meet and exceed expectations, and little or no opportunity to compare ourselves with our peers. Each of these factors contribute to low self-esteem, lack of confidence, increased anxiety, more depression, and a host of other things that are bad for us. The message is clear: Loneliness sucks.

If you feel lonely, strive to strengthen your social networks. Call your friends, join a group (other than Facebook), get out of the house, phone those people you haven't spoken to in years, become social again, and live well between your ears.

THIN SKIN

"When science finally locates the center of the universe,
some people will be surprised to learn they're not it."

– Bernard Bailey (1916-1996), American comic book artist

THIN-SKINNED PEOPLE ANNOY ME; NOT A LOT, BUT APPARENTLY IT'S enough to write about. I want to tell them to get a grip, and not make a mountain out of a mole hill. Webster defines thin-skinned as unduly susceptible to criticism or insult. Unduly is an understatement. People who I see as thin-skinned react with some version of "poor me" or hurt feelings, not because of insulting or critical remarks, but because of ordinary statements.

A difference of opinion makes them think you don't like them. If you ask for an explanation, they get defensive. It's as though you said they were wrong, when all you really wanted was clarification. They act offended if you change the topic. Like a child, whose brain has not yet developed to allow a sense of empathy, they can't see things from another person's perspective. They are self-centred.

Psychology Today editor, Lybi Ma, gave them this advice: "Here's an important rule for life: It's not all about you. To develop a thick skin you must first remember that you are not the center of the universe." The thin-skinned are insecure; they feel inadequate and are uncertain about how they are seen by others. They feel as though you are not giving them enough attention, and they are upset when you don't respond to their text quickly, or if your email messages seem curt. They have this round-eyed, needy-puppy-look that says please pet me. The fact is, as long as they act like that, no one will pet them. They need to get over it. The more they brood, the less they'll be liked.

Here's how someone who is thin-skinned describes herself: "I'm a bit emotionally labile, very easily upset, readily stressed and overwhelmed, preoccupied by what people think of me, hyper-vigilant of other peoples' reactions, prone to ruminating on situations, convinced most (if not all) acquaintances hate me until proven otherwise etc. On very dark days I wonder if my personality or temperament is just broken. I know my sensitivity makes me very difficult to deal with, and ultimately I'd like to not be a chore to be around or work with." Really! Does that not sound like it's all about her?

When the thin-skinned feel hurt by someone, do they want understanding, empathy, an apology, or what? Who knows? No matter how you handle them, they manage to feel hurt. I think, in some sort of passive-aggressive way, many of us are inclined to give them a little dig, just because they are so damn annoying. They certainly don't want someone to tell them to get over it, although that's what you want to tell them. Their thin-skinned nature is a product of wanting everything to be about them.

It's worse when their hurt feelings are expressed as anger. Anger responses from the thin-skinned eventually lead to a "walking on egg shells" environment. You're afraid to say or do anything that might upset them and set off an angry rant. So, you just try to avoid or ignore them. They don't like that either.

To my surprise I found that thin-skin has been given an official name. Clinical Psychologist, Elaine Aron (1996), says these are Highly Sensitive People (HSP). They pick up on subtle cues from other people that the rest of us miss. She says they are born that way and make up 15 to 20 percent of the population. She also cites research which shows that they take longer to make decisions and they pay closer attention to detail.

I question whether thin-skinned should have its own acronym and be treated as a personality disorder any more than the bad behaviour of a spoiled child. I think we run the risk of legitimizing a preoccupation with one's self by giving it its own label. A better response might be to communicate to the person how much more attractive they would be if they didn't insert themselves and their issues into every facet of daily life. Let's not give the thin-skinned an official label and a genetic excuse. Tell them you'd like them more if they kept themselves out of the centre of everything, and help them and you to live well between your ears.

LISTENING: THE IMPORTANT HALF
OF GOOD COMMUNICATION

"Most people do not listen with the intent to understand;
they listen with the intent to reply."

– Stephen R. Covey

HAVE YOUR CHILDREN, SPOUSE, OR FRIENDS BECOME MORE DISTANT?
Do you wonder why your son is not interested in the family business, or
why you don't know your daughter as well as you used to? Do they keep
things from you, or fail to discuss matters of importance? Has everybody
tuned you out? If this sounds like you, it is possible that your friends and
family have figured out that you don't listen, except to find a reason to
talk. The scoop on listening is that most of us are not very good at it.

In 1999, statistics from the US Department of Labour revealed that
46 percent of people who quit their jobs did so because they felt they
were not listened to and were unappreciated. According to research on
communication, we only comprehend 25 to 50 percent of what we hear
because we are too busy talking and interrupting to actually listen. We
drift along—only half listening—because we don't care, we think we've
heard it before, or we are more interested in pursuing our own agenda.
Conversely, the effective listener saves their personal need to be heard

for another day, and instead, concentrates on what the speaker means or feels in an effort to fully understand them.

As kids, we were told we had two ears and one mouth for a reason. Yet, for most of us, the advice fell on deaf ears, and we still talk more than we listen. If you are not a good listener, you're no fun to be around. People have heard what you have to say— too many times—and all they really want is to be heard, acknowledged, and understood. They want to know that you care, before they care what you know, and to prove it, you have to listen more than talk.

When communication suffers, friends and family fade away, and life is less rewarding than in the past. There are many reasons why friends and family become distant, but if not listening is one of them, the good news is the problem is fixable.

Good listeners have characteristics that poor listeners don't have. They display humility, patience, awareness, sincerity, and empathy. W.F. Doverspike, writing for the Georgia Psychological Association, identified some additional traits of good listeners. They ask questions for clarification; it signals to the speaker that you are listening. He says you should turn off your own worries, consider taking notes, react to the ideas and not the speaker, and not argue mentally or jump to conclusions. It is impossible to listen carefully when your thoughts are on what you want to say next, and the speaker senses that you are not really listening. You demonstrate that you care, and encourage the speaker to continue, when you make opening-up statements (tell me more; what else) rather than closing-off statements (I get it; that's enough).

Clifford Lazarus added a few more characteristics of good listeners in his 2011 article on effective communication. An important one is to face the speaker and make eye contact. As everyone knows, nothing says "I'm done listening" quite like having your spouse or best friend turn their back on you while you are speaking. Lazarus also suggests that we nod, smile, or make other affirming gestures to convey we are paying attention. And, when the topic turns to detailed or complicated content, it is helpful to paraphrase what you heard, so both you and the sender are sure you got the right message.

But listening is only one half of effective communication; the other half is how well we send our messages. The next column is about speaking to be understood. In the meantime, listen carefully, and live well between your ears.

Effective Speaking

"Intelligence, knowledge or experience are important
and might get you a job, but strong communication
skills are what will get you promoted."

– Mireille Guiliano, author of French Women Don't Get Fat

THE PREVIOUS COLUMN DEALT WITH EFFECTIVE LISTENING, THE important half of good communication. Today is about the other half: effective speaking.

Speaking skills are not as critical if your message is simple. For example, you don't have to be the world's greatest orator to say "I'm not interested, please leave" when the missionaries show up at your door. But not all messages are that simple, and as they become more complicated— when they start to deal with feelings, relationships, and all the important stuff—good speaking skills are critical.

In a July, 2011 article in *Psychology Today*, Clifford Lazarus offered four guidelines for effective speaking. The first is to establish and maintain eye contact to gain the attention of your audience. Of course, if you are a politician running for council, speaking in a large room full of people, it is difficult to maintain eye contact with everyone. It is also possible that your droning on will put them to sleep, in which case eye contact is irrelevant.

The second guideline offered by Lazarus is to make sure your words, tone, and body language all say the same thing. If you want your audience to see you as a kind, capable person who, as their new councillor, will do all you can, you want to be sure you are sending a message that matches your intention. For example, you could arch your back, look to the heavens with arms raised, and wail out, "I need your support". Or, you could tone down your evangelical rant, lean forward, look directly at the audience, extend your arms to them, and say the same words in a clear, calm voice. In the first instance, your delivery taints your message; it paints you as a zealot pleading for help from the gods. The second conveys sincere, sane mannerisms consistent with a request for support from actual humans.

His third recommendation is to say what you mean and mean what you say. Be direct and honest and don't dance around the issue or play games. This seems obvious, but it's one we probably fall short of the most. How often have you listened to someone, and you know in your gut, they are not telling the truth. If they don't feel it, they can't sell it. When your face and body send a different message than your words, when you aren't saying what you mean, the incongruity is obvious, and we don't believe you.

Lazarus's fourth guideline is to ask for feedback to ensure your message is accurately received. Don't assume that everyone understands you. First off, you may not be as clear as you think, and secondly, the listener's mind may wander and cause them to miss part of your message. When you encourage your audience to ask questions or to speak up if they don't understand, you signal that they are free to join the conversation. It helps keep them engaged. It allows them to ask for clarification when your over-familiarity with your message causes you to under-explain your thoughts.

Of course, if you don't use proper grammar, sentence structure, and effective words in the first place, it doesn't matter if you follow these guidelines. If your listener(s) can't understand your version of the English language, eye-contact is irrelevant. Poor communication is arguably worse than no communication. As Mark Twain said, "it is better to remain silent and be thought a fool than to speak and remove all doubt." So make sure your speech doesn't remove all doubt, be a thoughtful speaker, follow the guidelines so you are not misunderstood, and live well between your ears.

FATHER'S DAY

"Dad taught me everything I know.
Unfortunately, he didn't teach me everything he knows."

– Al Unser

IT'S THE PRE-DAWN HOURS OF FATHER'S DAY, 2013, AND I'M DEEP IN thought. I have two sons. They live far away. I see them rarely—once or twice per year. I want my phone to ring—any time before mid-night. They've missed some father's days—no card, no call—and it hurts. In fact, I haven't received a card from either one in years, but I still describe our relationship as close. They don't know how it hurts; they might someday.

We know fathers are role models for sons, and mothers for daughters, but beyond that I didn't find a great deal of data on the topic of father-son relationships. Melanie Mallers (2010), speaking at the 118th American Psychological Association Conference, said that sons with fond child-hood memories of their fathers are better able to cope with stress. Based on a study of over 900 adult men and women she said, "Fathers do play a unique and important role in the mental health of their children much later in life… Sons with happy childhood memories were more likely to be emotionally stable when faced with typical daily stresses." The finding wasn't as common with women. I handle stress well and believe I'm relatively stable; I must have had a good relationship with my Dad. But, did I thank him for it?

I was around both parents until I left home at eighteen. After that, not so much. I never got to know my Dad as I would have liked. I would have, if I had lived closer, but that wasn't the case. I played hockey and baseball; they didn't come to my games. Sports I did with my sons, I never did with my Dad; not one puck, Frisbee, or baseball. There were few hugs or "I love you" words or acts, but I know it was a loving home. They did attend and were proud when I received my graduate school degrees; they reinforced in me what they valued themselves. They weren't big sports fans, but they did believe in higher education; they had those priorities right.

The older I become, the more I realize how much my Dad shaped who I was and who I became. He was way ahead of his time when it came to things like eating nutritious food and having an appreciation for the off-beat stuff, and for that influence I am grateful. He was a tolerant man, always able to see things from the other guy's perspective. I got that from him, and I am grateful. He taught me to appreciate music. We sat side-by-side most evenings for one entire winter and built a Heath-Kit Stereo from scratch so we could listen to music on a good sound system. He showed me how to use a wood lathe, table saw, and all the carpentry tools. He showed me how to solder and fix things around the house. He was a thinker and a talker, and those characteristics certainly found their way to me. My values and my acceptance—indeed, my endorsement of choosing adventure vs. status quo—definitely came from my Dad.

But, as I list all these things for which I am grateful, I realize a problem: I never told my Dad. I took him for granted. Other than a card or a call on Father's Day, I did little to let him know how much he meant to me, and I certainly didn't create a culture in my own family that said be grateful to your parents. Because of my neglect, Dad died without feeling enough thanks from the son he loved. Neither he, nor anyone else (including, of course, my sons), saw or heard me thank him for surrounding me with those important and influential attributes that came so naturally to him. Shame on me!

Yes, I've done tons of things with, and for, my boys. Yes, I've hugged them and told them I love them. But we reap what we sow, and they never saw or heard me thank my father. Shame on me! So today, thank those you take for granted, and live well between your ears.

THE REUNION

"Middle age is when your classmates are so gray and
wrinkled and bald they don't recognize you."

–Bennett Cerf

HAVE YOU BEEN TO A CLASS REUNION LATELY? I ATTENDED ONE IN JULY.
I liked it. It's a bit like ancient Rome. The graduates are the gladiators. The
last time we saw each other—before going to battle in a different coli-
seum—was the day we graduated. All these years later there's a gladiator
reunion. We get to see who fought successfully, who was wounded, who
didn't make it, who became a hero, who won the hand of the fair maiden,
and who returned with the most loot.

We watch each other arrive and murmur, "Well I'll be damned" or,
"holy crap!" or, "I told you so." We realize that what we thought would
become of Jane was the furthest thing from the truth. We assumed she
wouldn't make it, but she's VP of a multinational. We believed John
would achieve prominence and wealth, but he's on his third wife, can't
retire, and finds a number of occasions to pop another beer.

The men are interested in how their friends made out financially;
the women attend more to how they look. We ask questions and make
comparisons, but in the end, learn more about us than we do about them.

288

As bits and pieces of history come together, we measure how we dealt with our own life issues compared to the firmest baseline available—the people with whom we grew up. We are reminded of many things: how wrong we can be, how bald we can get, how different we were, how lives evolve, and how the skin on our neck failed to note it was time to quit growing.

Reunions are also characterized by authenticity and a stripping away of facades. We remember Jack as fun-loving Jackie, and there's something magic and incredible about the realization that everyone at his company calls him Mr. so and so and is somewhat afraid of him. But throughout the reunion he's just Jackie—talks like him, laughs like him, and has the same values at his core—but you know when he returns to his business, the 47 years of experience kick in and he's in charge. Some employees have known him a long time, but they didn't grow up with him so they don't know him like we do.

Age takes on new meaning when you look at your wrinkled classmates. Damn, these people look old. Then, as it always does, it hits you—you look old too—maybe older. They all looked older and different when I got there on Friday (several I wouldn't recognize on the street). By Sunday, they didn't look as old or as different; I saw them as I remembered them at 18.

As we sat on lawn chairs in the local park, listening to the oldies station, each face reflected a calm and sincere sense of caring and thankfulness. It washed through and around us in the sunny afternoon while we joked, ate, drank, and caught up on small portions of our past—and it was good. No other group of people has such a unique and honest window into you. Some of them knew your most important secrets, things no one else knew. As kids, we discovered each other as our personalities formed. We have a shared history as though we're different bowls from the same clay. It goes unsaid because we can't describe it—but we feel it.

According to national averages, only 20-30 percent of graduates show up at reunions. We had 81 percent at ours—13 of 16—after 47 years. Two had other commitments, and Diane had moved on to her next life. Granted, I suspect such a small class creates a stronger sense of community which tugged at our decision to return, but none-the-less, the percentage is impressive.

We're the same gladiators and we'll be back again, a few years older with a bit more skin; happy to re-connect but—we're starting to realize—not permanently in need of as many chairs. So, if you have a class or family reunion coming up, don't miss it. Go as you are, without pretences, and let the flood of memories, love, and inevitability bathe you in kindness, and live well between your ears.

VI
CHANGE AND TECHNOLOGY

MANY OF OUR BIGGEST CHALLENGES STEM FROM THE EXPONENTIAL growth in technology. The experts agree that digital capability and storage is doubling every two years. It impacts us in every way imaginable. Some try to fight it (a futile effort), while others struggle to integrate it into their lives with varying degrees of success. No matter where you look, what was normal just a couple of years ago, is now different, sometimes radically different.

Our world is changing faster than we can adjust. The effects are as exciting as they are challenging. The digital revolution has created so much potential for unprecedented growth and development in every field that we can't totally wrap our minds around it. This section focuses on psychological issues related to our adjustment.

DEVIANCE CAN BE GOOD

"If you have extremes of haves and have-nots where the gap
keeps growing, the have-nots group together and create social
disorder, as they can't see a way out of their situation."

– Ross Kemp, British actor, author, and journalist.

DEVIANT, WAY-OUT-THERE BEHAVIOUR IS THE NEW NORMAL. IS THERE
no limit to the unusual? When I was a kid deviance was much less
deviant, cursing on TV or radio was never heard, blood and guts were
at a minimum, no one was actually shot or blown up on TV, politicians'
sexual exploits were not commonplace, people were slow to call each
other liars, and a fashion statement was not two inches of butt crack. TV
series and movies did not show people morphing or shape-shifting into
wild animals, news broadcasts did not show corpse after corpse lying in
the streets, and demonstrations against authority were not as common.
In fact, just about everything was a less extreme version of what it is today.
The boundaries of normalcy have been pushed back and it upsets many.

Extreme is becoming more so. The bizarre is almost common. What
used to entertain us is now boring. What was once great is now ordinary.
The world is becoming smaller and weirder, and we might as well get
used to it.

A model of deviance proposed years ago by Jessor & Jessor (1977) predicts more of the same, and it's not all bad. They said three factors contribute to deviant behavior.

First, they draw attention to the gap between what we want and what we have or can afford. It is growing. For example, people want greater achievement, more affection, or more money, toys, happiness, and justice, to name a few. The greater the gap, the more motivated we are to close it.

The second factor contributing to deviance is alienation. It creates a general sense of meaninglessness, helplessness, and social isolation. Jessor & Jessor say alienation makes people less concerned about other's reaction to their behavior. Out of desperation they are more likely to engage in extreme behavior to provide meaning and close the gap.

Third, is a willingness to tolerate deviance, especially when we believe it is required to accomplish some end and is unlikely to result in punishment. It makes us more willing to engage in deviant behavior to get what we want. If you watch TV, and pay attention to what is going on, you'd have to be blind not to see a growing tolerance, if not outright acceptance, of a wider range of deviant behaviour.

If Jessor & Jessor are right, deviance will become more common and more extreme. The three factors they used to explain deviance are more prevalent than ever. As the middle class shrinks it causes a greater gap for more people between what they want and what they have. And, as the gap between the haves and the have-nots widens, the sense of isolation, alienation, and helplessness grows. More people are becoming more tolerant of deviant methods to correct inequity because they don't see any other way.

There are two sides to deviance. It is negative when we become desensitized to behaviour such as bullying and violence against minorities, family members, the elderly, animals, and of course, the environment. It is positive when we become tolerant of deviant behaviour that brings positive social outcomes.

For example, at the beginning, only a few people protested racial inequality in the 60's. People who spoke out against the social norm that called for white-only schools, diners, and water fountains were brave and unpopular deviants. Eventually, they prevailed. As more people got involved in such protests, social change took place. Similarly, today we see more gutsy deviants (often celebrities) willing to raise their voice against social inequality, environmental destruction, the ignorance caused by rejection of science in favour of myth, and political carelessness, waste, and outright criminality.

Let's take a closer look at being deviant. What can you do to close the gap between the way things are and the way they should be? Don't feel alienated if you stray from what's popular. Support constructive deviance and live well between your ears.

WHAT HAS HAPPENED TO
DISCIPLINE?

"Independence isn't doing your own thing; it's doing the right thing on your own."

– Kim John Payne, Australian Educator

A COUPLE OF MONTHS AGO I STOPPED TO VISIT A FRIEND. WE HAD lunch. Her daughter and grandson were there. It was God-awful. It's doubtful I've ever seen such misbehaviour or such ineffective discipline. For the two hours I was there the kid—age four —yelled, demanded, was defiant, played loud, would not listen, and interrupted everything. The mother had no control. She was embarrassed, as was Grandma.

Little kids are less well-mannered today. Have you noticed it? They throw food, scream for sweets, kick up a stink at bedtime, strike out at their sister for little reason, and turn and walk away when you try to correct them. And the worst part is these behaviours persist. They're a regular occurrence; it's a zoo, controlled by the animals.

What has changed? It's not the kids. Kids have always misbehaved. The parents have changed. They no longer discipline their kids. They are afraid to tell their little urchin they are bad when they are bad. Behaviour has consequences, and discipline is all about managing those consequences. The parents are so confused by all the self-styled experts, that discipline has become a strategy of 'give them what they want' rather than 'give them what they need'. As a result, many little angels are out of control, discipline has gone the way of the dinosaurs, and parents are fatigued to the breaking point. Parenthood has become something to endure, not enjoy.

Granted, not all kids are like this, and not all parents are ineffective. But, in general, kids are less disciplined than in past generations; in many homes the kids rule the roost. Parents are concerned that actual discipline will ruffle little Johnnie's feathers or damage his self-esteem. Most often, they don't deal correctly with bad behaviour, and even worse, the good behaviour goes unnoticed and unrewarded because it is—well—good.

That's exactly the opposite of what needs to happen. Good behaviour needs to be noticed and praised, whereas bad behaviour needs to be ignored or punished. "What" you say, "ignore the bad behaviour?" Well, not totally. You have to do something first, and then ignore it. You first have to isolate the misbehaving kid, and then ignore him. Behaviour therapists in the sixties called it time-out, and when done effectively, nothing eliminates bad behaviour more reliably in toddlers and young children.

It is really time out from reinforcement, and it works like this: the kid screams (or does something he's not supposed to do) and you ask him to stop. If he doesn't stop, pick him up immediately and deposit him where there are no people, and no entertainment—a vacant room, closet, or a place where they can't amuse themselves—and close the door, leaving him by himself. Let him know what he did is unacceptable, and that you disapprove. Tell him he can come out when he's quiet or ready to behave, and then ignore him until he's quiet for 20 seconds, at which time you convey your approval, and bring him out to rejoin the others. Twenty seconds is an arbitrary duration, but don't make it much longer. He might yell and fuss for several minutes before he quiets down. Just ignore it until he stays quiet for the designated time. It will work if applied consistently.

It doesn't work if parents make the mistake of using time-out as a break for themselves; leave the kid in there too long, and then continue to scold him after he's out. Behaviour is determined by its consequences more than anything. If you follow good behaviour with attention, praise, or benefits, it will persist. In the case of time-out, the good behaviour is complete absence of misbehaviour for 20 seconds, the consequence of which is to return to your good graces.

From a discipline standpoint, the best results are obtained when you notice good behaviour and follow it with attention to the child. You may praise or thank him for behaving well, include him in the conversation, and treat him like a welcome person. The point is: if you follow any behaviour with attention and positive consequences, it will increase. Parents need to reclaim their responsibility for disciplining so we can all live well between our ears.

IS IT TIME TO VOTE LIKE AN INDEPENDENT?

"Hyper-partisanship makes you stupid, and you start playing to
the cheap seats."

– John Avlon, American journalist and political commentator.

THE US ELECTION CAMPAIGN IS HITTING ITS PEAK. THE POLLS CONFIRM
that lies are rewarded, and truth takes a back seat to rumour. Political lies
and fuzzy half-truths mislead us as we pick our way through mounds
of BS to separate fact from fiction. South of the border, the lies are too
plentiful to list. But, give us a break, Obama is not an Iranian sympathizer,
and Romney's business experience is an asset not a liability. Don't spend
millions of dollars to tell us otherwise.

A high percentage of voters don't care about the lies, they just want
their party to win. It's called partisanship; you are biased in favour of
your party no matter what. According to a January, 2012 Gallup poll,
60 percent of the electorate feel compelled to vote along partisan lines.
It's when they view themselves as Liberal, Conservative, NDP, Green,
Republican, or Democrat, and blindly vote for their party in spite of lies
and fuzziness.

For partisans, their politics is like their nationality—Canadian, American, or Mexican—it defines who they are. They believe that the party ideology is consistent with their values, so that's how they vote. Besides, they think their party's lies are the truth. But not everyone is so easily swayed.

Politicians on both sides of the border should realize that no matter how much they stretch the truth or spout their party gospel, the 40 percent of the electorate who are non-partisan will recognize a plate of crap no matter how they serve it up. The research on the subject suggests we should strive to be more non-partisan.

In the Canadian Journal of Behavioural Science, a study by Pancer, Brown, Gregor, and Claxton-Oldfield (1992) showed that non-partisan people are perceived as having greater integrity. In 1995, Leigh Thompson found non-partisan folks to be more even handed in their judgements of others, and better able to detect possible areas of agreement between arguing groups. In 2012, Van Boven, Judd, and Sherman found that highly partisan people assumed that others were just as biased in their views, thus contributing to greater polarization between groups, with even less being accomplished. There are additional reasons to be less like a party puppet.

Today's economic problems make it more important that we research each party's position on the issues rather than vote blindly. If each politician, or the party they represent, were as great as they claim, the gap between the 'haves' and 'have-nots' would not be growing so quickly. Yet, according to a 2010 report by Business Insider, "in 1950 the ratio of the average executive's paycheck to the average worker's paycheck was about 30 to 1. Since the year 2000, that ratio has exploded to between 300 and 500 to 1." It's not hard to see that the percentage on the 'have-not' end of the stick is increasing.

No country functions well when too many of its people are on the 'have not' side of the ledger, struggling to meet their basic needs, and seeing a decline in their standard of living. The keys to a sustained high standard of living for everyone are top-rate infrastructure and education, quality affordable food, fair pay and availability of jobs, reasonable financial security for the elderly, decent medical care, military to protect our borders and do our share as peace-keepers, fewer regulations (except for those required to protect the population), and a host of other things that aren't possible without prosperity across all groups. In the coming years, these keys to a high standard of living will be provided by oneself, the government, the private sector, or a combination of the three.

The government can provide these benefits, or sub-contract them to the private sector. Either way, they have to be run efficiently and within a budget funded by us. We each have a huge stake in the outcome, so check your bank account to see whether you're a worker or an executive, question your political bias, be well enough informed to vote wisely for the long term, hold government to their promises, and live well between your ears.

Is the Universe unfolding as it should?

"We are just an advanced breed of monkeys on a minor planet of a very average star. But we can understand the Universe. That makes us something very special."

– Stephen Hawking

Do you marvel at the rate of change? Weather patterns, world economy, civil unrest, technological and scientific developments, and international balance of power are just a few of the things that are changing, and they are changing fast. Is it unsettling? For many people it is.

Ray Kurzweil, a renowned inventor, author, and futurist, said in 2003, "We're entering an age of acceleration. The models underlying society at every level, which are largely based on a linear model of change, are going to have to be redefined. Because of the explosive power of exponential growth, the 21st century will be equivalent to 20,000 years of progress at today's rate of progress."

It's not just your perception. There is real and massive change; the rate is faster than most of us can imagine, and the rate is increasing. Kurzweil focuses on the evolution of technology as the primary driver of change.

But, what if the driver of technology is something else we can't yet see or understand? Is there such a primary mover? Is it the Universe itself?

Just because we can't see or understand something, doesn't rule out its existence. For example, we all know there are millions of electronic pictures floating through the air. As humans, we just don't have the receptors to see them. Without showing them a television, we would have trouble explaining TV to people from the 17th century. They would be sceptical. Similarly, we don't have the technology to be able to identify a field of intelligence anywhere in the universe, and we are sceptical. But it doesn't mean there isn't such a field.

In his 2005 book, *A Briefer History of Time*, renowned physicist Stephen Hawking says, "Today we know that stars visible to the naked eye make up only a minute fraction of all the stars. We can see about five thousand stars, only about .0001 percent of all the stars in just our own galaxy, the Milky Way. The Milky Way itself is but one of more than a hundred billion galaxies that can be seen using modern telescopes—and each galaxy contains on average, some one hundred billion stars. If a star were a grain of salt, you could fit all the stars visible to the naked eye on a teaspoon, but all the stars in the universe would fill a ball more than eight miles wide."

The last sentence, written by one of the most highly regarded scientists of our time, is a most astounding piece of information. It certainly leaves room to believe in the existence of some form of intelligence within the universe which may be at the root of all change. The point is: (1) change is taking place at an unprecedented and increasing rate, and (2) we are part of the change and will never fully control it. Rather, it may be a field of all-knowing intelligence in the universe, or some other primary moving force pulling the strings.

For now, let's assume the universe is unfolding as it should; that whatever is in charge is a source of intelligence that exceeds anything we can imagine. All we can control is our reaction to it—our ability to adapt. There is no point in stewing or losing sleep over 'the way things are'. They just are. Our job is to take it with a smile and adjust as best we can.

But, it's stressful. Psychologists (eg. Rotter, 1966) have found that people who believe their life's outcomes are due more to luck, a higher power, or other people, experience more stress than those who believe they have personal control over their life. The former are the 'externals', the ones most likely to blame their troubles on the weather, the technological gadgets, the internet, the politicians, the economy, or maybe even the Chinese. These folks yearn for the 'old days,' but those days are gone.

Psychologist, Abraham Maslow's (1954) hierarchy of needs has a place in this discussion. The rapid rate of change has helped meet the world's lowest level needs for food and safety. However, the more advanced needs—those for love, self-esteem, knowledge, orderliness, and self-actualization—are more elusive for those who are confused by the rate of change. But, shouldn't the increase in technology help us adapt to all the change, and live more contented lives?

The Techies say yes. Kurzweil implies we need full awareness of the exponential rate of change. He says we cannot live our life, and make predictions from one day to the next, based on the way things were a few years ago because things aren't sufficiently similar to how they were a few years ago.

We have always had to take control of ourselves and adapt. In the face of so much change, it is critical that we get good at it. Accept the unfolding of the universe and strive to control yourself. Welcome the unknown and revel in life's complexities. Our contentment—and society's progress—depends on how well we take direction from the universe and adapt to its changes. Stay open to the notion that the force that connects everything occupies a space in the universe just like the TV signals, and one day, equipped with the necessary receptors, you'll have access to that space. Believe, and live well between your ears.

Recipe for Freedom

"Everything that is really great and inspiring is created by the individual who can labor in freedom."

– Albert Einstein

WHAT'S COOKING WITH THE HISTORIC CITIZEN UPRISINGS IN TUNISIA, Egypt, Libya, and Syria? Many things I'm sure, but three ingredients stand out: first, an oppressive geo-political lock on the gate of freedom and opportunity; second, the arrival of technology, the key to unlock the gate; third, a psychological factor, the motivation to swing the gate wide open. The first two are external, but the third lies within us.

First, decades of oppression by the rich and powerful over the poor and weak create a pressure cooker of geographic, economic, and political stew. It's a mixture of negative emotion, fear, and distractions that block each citizen's drive to fulfill their potential and their dreams. The majority of the people are poor, without resources, without political voice, and until recently, not fully aware of what they were missing. During the mid-80s my work took me to Saudi Arabia and Egypt several times. I usually travelled alone, stayed three or four weeks, and met with businessmen in the region.

Back then, like now, the media was controlled by the state. Soldiers and police were ever-present and unpredictable. Due to the nature of my work and the restrictive environment, I frequently felt a low level of fear. The local people expressed a similar feeling, fed by secrecy and a smattering of impending doom. But they hunkered down and adapted to it. They didn't complain to anyone, except their most trusted friends, for fear of being ratted out to the authorities. But now, twenty-six years later, the pressure cooker lid has been lifted and the entire region smells freedom.

The arrival of affordable technology in general, and Facebook and Twitter in particular, is the second external factor contributing to the uprising. People can communicate, form groups, share information, make friends, and organize gatherings right under the nose of the authorities who are ignorant of the technology, underestimate it, or can't control it.

These two factors—a history of oppression and the arrival of Social Media—set the stage for the third driving force, the psychological one, the one that has always been there; that deep-seated desire of every member of the human race to be all we can be. This desire is universal, but seldom realized. Skin colour, religion, life style, diet, politics, family history—nothing—stops this powerful, deep-seated force.

What is this force? Religions see it as a God-centered life while Philosophers speak about the search for truth. Many psychologists believe it is the need to maximize our human potential. For example, Maslow said self-actualization was our ultimate need. Karen Horney had a similar view. Erich Fromm referred to a sense of oneness with the world. Carl Rogers called it a force of life that can't be stopped. It's a powerful force, not just for humans but for all living things, explaining why a weed finds a way to grow through the sidewalk, and animals adapt to survive in the frozen north, or on the ocean floor.

When freedom is suppressed and fear sneaks in, whether in a relationship between two people, or in an entire country, life is less fulfilling to say the least. But history is filled with oppression of the poor and weak by the rich and strong, so what's different now? Two things are different: social networks and search engines, the best known being Facebook and Google. Neither one existed prior to the internet. They're widely available, dummy proof, and provide limitless communication and information to educate and empower. Together they throw open the door of possibilities, and re-ignite our desire to take a chance and go for it.

Geo-political oppression, the internet, and our inherent desire for self-fulfillment show no sign of going away. The forty-five year old hippie slogan, "power to the people" is getting new legs. So get ready for change, recognize it as mostly good, and live well between your ears.

Here come the women!

"If you want something said, ask a man;
if you want something done, ask a woman."

– Margaret Thatcher

"A woman is like a tea bag - you can't tell how strong she is
until you put her in hot water."

– Eleanor Roosevelt

MARCH IS WOMEN'S MONTH. WHAT ABOUT MEN'S MONTH? SOME would argue it's been men's month for centuries. Throughout history men and women developed different skills and values appropriate for their roles: men to provide food and safety, women to give birth and nurture families. Right or wrong, these historical roles have resulted in more men than women in leadership positions.

Women have been on the short end of the leadership stick for quite a while. In places like Afghanistan where education, political voice, and freedom are still denied, women certainly need a month, if not several generations, just to experience the good life, let alone leadership.

Canadian women in Alberta, Saskatchewan, and Manitoba couldn't vote until 1916, followed by Ontario and BC (1917), Nova Scotia (1918), New Brunswick and the Yukon (1919), Prince Edward Island (1922), Newfoundland and Labrador (1925), Quebec (1940), and the North West Territories in 1951. But much has changed.

In the last few decades, men and women's roles have blurred. More women occupy positions once held only by men and vice versa. In fact, on March 14, British Columbia's Christy Clark became Canada's first female premier.

There are other signs of women taking the lead. In September, 2010 the Wall Street Journal reported that 53 percent of women graduate from university vs. 38 percent of men. Among recent business graduates, the earning power of single women is 8 percent greater than for comparable men. But, the average income for women is still 20 percent less than for men doing the same jobs. While women now occupy 50 percent of the jobs in management, only 17 percent of top management positions are held by women (Dencker, 2008). Still, these numbers reflect greater equality today than twenty years ago, and the gap continues to close.

Why is the gap closing? Is it driven by the immorality of inequality, or do female leaders bring more of what society needs to the table? Are we coming to a point in history where we need understanding and nurturance more than muscle?

A massive program of research on leadership, begun in the 60's by psychologist Fred Fiedler, sheds some light on why women are destined for more positions of leadership. Among other things, he found that people with a social-emotional style of leadership were most effective when the goals and challenges were complex. But, when the goals were clear and straight forward, a task-specialist—drill-sergeant type of leader—was most effective.

More recent research indicates that social-emotional leaders have several characteristics found more commonly in women. In 2008, Schmitt and his colleagues studied personality differences in 17,637 men and women from 55 different countries. They found that women were rated slightly more anxious, temperamental, emotional, and vulnerable than men. While these aren't characteristics associated with leaders, others are. For example, they were rated harder working, more organized, and more persevering than were the men. The women were also described as soft hearted, trusting, generous, lenient, affectionate, talkative, and passionate.

Similar results were obtained in a study of 77,528 people from 70 countries. Psychologists, Schwartz and Rubel (2005), confirmed that men in almost all cultures place a higher value on authority, wealth, controlling others, social power, success, ambition, and admiration for one's abilities. Women, on the other hand, place a higher value on social justice, equality, wisdom, world peace, protecting the environment, and being helpful, caring, loyal, and supportive.

These two studies indicate that women, more than men, resemble Fiedler's description of social-emotional leaders. The research indicates that women are more effective leaders, especially in a complex world. If the research on leadership is correct, and if you believe today's challenges are more complex than ever, then women bring more to the table. So, get ready—here come the women—and live well between your ears.

IS PROGRESS ON YOUR CHRISTMAS LIST?

"Progress is the mother of problems."

– G. K. Chesterton

CAN WE STAND ANY MORE PROGRESS? IT FEELS MORE LIKE REGRESS. Canada's national debt increases at $1000 per second. On October 11, 2011 our national debt was over $569 billion, or $17,169 per citizen. In the USA, the national debt stood at over 14 trillion, or $47838 per citizen. Most European countries are worse, Greece in particular. It takes acrobatic accounting to see this as progress. If we ran our personal lives in a similar fashion, we'd be unhappy and broke. So Santa, please bring governments a calculator and a live-within-your-budget kit.

Speaking of happiness, progress has not made us happier. Over fifty years of goods and gadgets has left us with lives full of stuff but feeling a little empty. Happiness is declining. A 2005 British survey found 36 percent of people reported they were "very happy" compared to 52 percent in 1957. Progress makes life easier maybe, but not happier.

This year's political upheavals in Tunisia, Egypt, Libya, and Syria, reflect lack of happiness too. The Occupy Wall street movement spreading around the globe suggests not everyone sees progress the same way.

The path to riches for the wealthy is a superhighway traveled in limos and private jets. The path for regular folks is a winding trail, traveled in aging vehicles or on foot. It has been that way for decades in developing countries, but now developed countries are feeling it too. A big box of "closing the gap" would be nice, Santa.

Progress ushered in another problem. In June of 2011, the International Energy Agency (IEA) reported the world used 88 million barrels of oil per day. They estimate the 88 million will increase, year over year, by 2.8 million barrels per day. 'Peak oil' refers to that point in time when the world's supply of oil plateaus and begins to decline relative to the demand. Some say we've already reached that point. Others say it may be a couple of decades down the road.

We can't agree on how long it will take, but we know the global demand for fossil fuel will someday exceed the supply. As supply becomes scarce, the cost of energy to operate ships, trains, planes, cars, trucks, power plants, and factories necessary to feed our life-style will increase substantially. Unless we develop alternate sources to replace oil and gas, the problem won't go away, and it won't be a happy time. So Santa, add alternate energy to my list.

Other pesky problems, such as world water shortage and climate change have accompanied progress. The World Health Organization says that one billion of the seven billion people in the world lack access to potable water. To make matters worse, 70 percent of fresh water is used for irrigation. The current fight over rural vs. urban water-rights is child's play compared to what it will be if we don't find solutions.

In May, 2010, two hundred and fifty-five scientists from the National Academy of Sciences signed an open letter in *Science* magazine confirming the reality of global warming. They emphatically agree that the vast majority of scientific data calls for long term action to deal with the reality of climate change before it irreparably changes many of the life supporting eco-systems of the planet. I'm not sure Santa has room in his sleigh for all we need.

Let's summarize the reasons to re-think progress. National debt clocks say we can't afford it. Current research says happiness is declining. There is growing inequality between rich and poor. Shortage of fossil fuel will increase the cost of transportation, agricultural production, and hydrocarbon based products (think tires and everything made of plastic), and lead to fierce competition between nations for a dwindling resource (think war). And finally, as if we need more bad news, the reports of water shortage and global warming do not bode well for the future. But good news is on the way.

The age-old saying, "if it ain't broke, don't fix it" has shaped public policy and protected the status quo for a long time. The good news is there is a world-wide, technology-driven movement afoot; people are finally saying, "it is broke, we must fix it." And they're being heard.

David Kirkpatrick, one of the world's top technology journalists and founder and CEO of *Techonomy Media*, convincingly maintains that technology is coming to the rescue. He refers to graphic illustrations at gapminder.org which show, "technology driven progress is rapidly reducing the global economic divide" and goes on to say, "change from now on is likely to be bottom up—driven by people empowered by iPhones and Android devices, and Facebook, Apple, Amazon, and Google."

Referring to the political changes mentioned above, he claims, "people are not going to accept the old answers. They no longer feel powerless and they are taking action." He's right; we are seeing that.

Addressing the economic disparity he says, "technology-empowered billions in the developing world will not be satisfied languishing in second-class status." Not just internet technology, but also energy tech, biotech, civil engineering, and science based progress generally, leads Kirkpatrick to feel very optimistic about the future. He says, "the fastest growing resource in the world is computing power and storage" and that "countries where this is understood are those investing in technological R&D and education, especially science, math, and engineering."

Finally, Kirkpatrick makes a tremendously reassuring claim when he says, "those of us who are technological optimists also see plenty of ways that technology can help enormously with our other grave challenges— climate change, cultural misunderstanding, food shortages, inadequate housing, antiquated transportation, and reliance on unsustainable energy sources." I hope he's right.

There's one last thing in our favour. Psychologists have long known that fear is a powerful motivator, and it's most effective when it's right in our face. It's like getting religion as you lie on your death bed, or slowing down after you see the cop, or eating like a rabbit after your first heart attack. Perhaps fear is the motivator and technology is the cure—the tool to escape the fear. In any case, time frames are shrinking, the game-changers are lined up against us, and it's time to fish, not cut bait.

So Santa, I don't need that other stuff. All I want for Christmas is for people everywhere to see the threats and feel the fear. From there let nature take its course. Hopefully, enough of us will do the right thing, and progress won't feel like regress. In the meantime, have a Merry Christmas, a great 2012, and continue to live well between your ears.

Losing control to
Mother Nature

"The 'control of nature' is a phrase conceived in arrogance, born
of the Neanderthal age of biology and philosophy, when it was
supposed that nature exists for the convenience of man."

– Rachel Carson, American biologist, writer, and
ecologist. Considered the founder of the contemporary environmental movement.

Have you been paying attention to the world's weather? It is
becoming more extreme; anywhere from mildly disturbing when you see
an overseas weather report, to absolutely terrifying if it's washing down
your street, ripping your house off its foundation, or overturning your car.

No one can ever fully prepare for a crisis. Yes, you can have sand bags
ready, provisions set aside, a storm cellar built, and emergency plans in
place, but it's still difficult to prepare for the psychological disruption
that a crisis delivers. At such times, at least a couple of predictable things
happen which upset the fragile sense of equilibrium that keeps our lives
on track.

When faced with an emergency, we know our body pumps chemicals
into our blood stream to energize our fight or flight response. We go on

high alert ready for anything; ready to attack or retreat. It happens immediately, and it's a good thing; it gets us focused. But, there are at least two other challenges to face: First, we have to deal with immediate threats to our ability to control outcomes, and second, we must make sure we utilize good coping methods to maintain a steady state of mind—clear, focused, and on your game.

When it comes to big natural events like tornadoes and floods, we lose control to Mother Nature; we're forced to play catch-up, and she's a tough opponent. The reality is, she's always in control, but we've learned to adapt to her during normal times. For example, when she attacks with the type of danger that we've seen before—like snow storms—we aren't as upset because we're used to it. It's because it falls within what the famous psychologist, Harry Helson (1964), called our adaptation level. When it's something we've handled before, adapting is easier. We can deal with it because, to us, it's normal. But, and it's a big but, what's normal for one is not necessarily normal for the other.

Younger, less experienced, or more safety conscious people, have less extreme adaptation levels. Their internal comfort zone is narrower and more conservative. As a result, some challenges or disasters fall outside their range of easy adaptation and are more difficult to deal with. They simply haven't experienced and incorporated as many extremes into their world view. On the other hand, experienced emergency workers, such as police and fire fighters, have broader, more extreme adaptation levels, which make it less stressful for them to deal with disaster.

As the severity of the situation increases beyond what we are comfortable with—outside our adaptation level—we start to lose our sense of control. We become anxious, we don't like our choices, or we feel we have no choice, and we begin to feel helpless. Nothing is much worse than being in a situation where you, those you love, or your property, is at risk and you believe you can't control the outcome.

Coping with catastrophe is largely about regaining your sense of control. Research has shown that any action you can take to directly influence the outcome in a positive way, either pre-emptively or after the fact, will help regain or maintain your sense of control and keep you relatively free of anxiety and its debilitating effects. For example, when you fill sandbags, protect your property, dig trenches, and help those most at risk, you restore a sense of control which serves as a good coping mechanism.

Another coping strategy is to talk with others about the issues you face, the feelings you have, and the possible outcomes. When you acknowledge the possibility of the worst, prepare for it mentally, and discuss courses of action with others in the same boat (perhaps literally), you reduce stress and anxiety. It helps us make better decisions and feel less helpless.

Research on disasters reveals other successful coping strategies: relax, meditate if you can, keep a diary or journal of the events and your feelings, get adequate rest, remind yourself to breathe deeply, eat well, focus on the future, and look for the silver lining. All these remedies help lessen the sense of loss and regain balance.

The reality is that nothing written, said, or done, can undo the loss or misery caused by floods, fires, or other catastrophic events. Use whatever coping mechanisms help regain your sense of control, and live well between your ears.

IS IT A JUST WORLD FOR YOU?

"If the machine of government is of such a nature that
it requires you to be the agent of injustice to another, then,
I say, break the law."

– Henry David Thoreau

THERE HAS BEEN A CHANGE IN HOW JACK FEELS ABOUT A LOT OF things. Issues that were once black or white for him are now shades of grey. He's always been a hard-ass, but now, not so much. He won't admit to getting softer. He still hates the liberals, but he's become less enchanted with Conservatives also.

He used to trust more. While he did not always agree with them, he trusted most elected officials. He didn't really believe they would screw him. But now he is not so sure. He used to be more trusting of the church and its teaching. He used to trust his bank, the makers of food and bug spray, credit card companies, the police, the legal system, and the authorities in general. He still believes in these institutions, and supports them in an argument if some weirdo goes on the attack, but in his heart, he's not sure the other guy doesn't have a point.

He used to distrust the geeks and academics. They always found fault with authority, went against tradition, and argued in favour of things he was against, like rehabilitation, the green movement, global warming, and equal rights and pay for women, blacks, and gays. To him, they were on the stupid side of social issues, but he now sees some merit in their views. He believed big was better, that success came to those who deserved it, and that people were poor because they didn't work hard, or they lived a bad life.

He used to believe the world was just, but now he is not so sure. Some of his long-held beliefs are on a collision course with his conscience. Are you like Jack, or are you sticking to your guns? If you are sticking to your guns, is it because you haven't yet figured out that your blind belief in a just world—the thing that's been your moral beacon for all these years—is actually causing uneasiness about who you really are, and what you really believe.

The 'just world hypothesis' is the belief that what happens to people is what they deserve. It was first put forward by a Canadian psychologist, Melvin Lerner (1966), and has received tons of research support. It states there is a universal psychological desire to believe that events proceed rationally, and not by chance. Such an attitude explains why people have a tendency to blame victims for their plight. Raped women looked too sexy, homeless hobos drank everything away, the Wall Street protestors are just lazy, and somehow, patients are responsible for their own suffering: they ate wrong, smoked too much, lived a hard life, or any number of other rational explanations which lays responsibility at the feet of the victim. In some cases it is true—but not always.

Do unto others as you would have them do unto you. It is a central belief in 21 major religions. You would think it would have a more powerful influence on all the believers: the 2 billion Christians, 1.5 billion Muslims, 980 million Hindus, 500 Million Buddhists, 800 million believers in folk religions such as Taoism and Confucianism, 50 million Shintoists, 25 million Sikhs, 15 million Judaists, 10 million people of the Jainism and Baha'i faith, and 13 million other religious denominations. That is a large number of people—most of the world population—who, if they practiced the one rule that they are supposed to observe, would be more empathetic towards victims, and consequently, less likely to believe the world is always just.

The research also tells us that if you believe the world is just, you feel less empathy for victims; you are less likely to help them. It gives you an excuse for not treating others as you would like to be treated. It causes you to firmly believe that what goes around comes around, that karma is real, we reap what we sow, and all kinds of folklore wisdom.

Make no mistake: folklore wisdom serves a useful purpose in our moral development. Throughout childhood it is important to develop a belief in a just world. It helps us learn that hard work is necessary for success, behaviour has consequences, and if you work hard and stay out of trouble you can be anything you want. We were taught to delay gratification; that persistence paid off. We learned that even Santa kept a list of who is naughty and who is nice, and that the big gifts went to those who obeyed authority and were good. So, it is no surprise that we grow up believing in a just world. The problem arises when we don't grow out of it.

The downside to this belief emerges when we continue to believe in the fairy tale. We fail to realize that those in control might be wrong. They may not always have our best interests at heart. We overlook the fact that corporate push for profit might result in us consuming something harmful. They might even mislead us. We do not stop to think that the child born in a card board shack in poorest India didn't do it on purpose—to herself.

The belief that authority figures are always right, or should be obeyed, led to the rise of Hitler's Germany; it enables dictators to stay in power, and sometimes even prevents us from "doing unto others as we would have them do unto us" because we believe that, somehow, they must be getting what they deserve. But change is on the way.

Our immediate access to information from everywhere allows us to see injustices. Jack, and all those like him, unless they are deaf, blind, and live in a hole, are realizing that not everything is as it should be. The folklore wisdom that helps us grow to responsible adulthood goes too far when it leads to unquestioning belief in authority. Maybe it's time to notice injustice when it is staring you in the face, follow the golden rule, and live well between your ears.

CHANGE SOMETHING!

"However confused the scene of our life appears, however torn
we may be who now do face that scene, it can be faced,
and we can go on to be whole."

– Muriel Rukeyser, American poet and political activist

ARE YOU ANXIOUS AND DEPRESSED BECAUSE YOU ARE NOT HAPPY WITH your life? The problem may be cognitive dissonance, and the solution may be obvious. Change something! Cognitive dissonance was first introduced by Leon Festinger (1954) to explain why people are motivated to change behaviour, beliefs, or both. Up to the present day, this popular explanation has been cited thousands of times in psychological literature.

The American Psychological Association dictionary defines cognitive dissonance as, "an unpleasant psychological state resulting from inconsistency between two or more elements [beliefs, thoughts, or behaviours] in a cognitive system. It involves a state of heightened arousal and has characteristics similar to physiological drives such as hunger. Thus, cognitive dissonance creates a motivational drive to change something—a behaviour, attitude, or thought—to reduce the dissonance it creates."

Dissonance causes emotional upheaval and angst because one set of thoughts and behaviours are dissonant with, or contradict, another set of thoughts and behaviors. An extreme example is, *I am pregnant* (thought number one) and *I'm seventeen, a good person with a great future, and want nothing to do with motherhood* (thought number two). Those two thoughts are at odds with one another; they're dissonant. She has two options to reduce the dissonance and create consonance. The first is to have an abortion, and the second is to change her view of being a mother. She must either have the abortion or adopt a mind-set that says, *I'll get through this, bear this child, work hard, and still accomplish all I want.*

A similar example is a person faced with two conflicting views about his job. The first thought is *I'm stuck in this rut*; the second, opposing, thought is *I have to get out of this job quickly because it drives me crazy and doesn't pay enough.* These two thoughts are inconsistent, they create dissonance, and the situation is not sustainable. To reduce the dissonance the man has two choices: (1) take action and change jobs, or (2) change his belief about his situation.

Cognitive dissonance creates an uncomfortable feeling, varying in severity depending upon how desperate you are or how close the deadline. In the first example, the girl's deadline for action is a few months away at best. In the second, the man's deadline is when he can no longer stand the job or pay his bills. The feeling is a combination of anxiety and depression.

The girl is anxious because a decision is needed soon. She's depressed because she can't seem to take action. The guy is anxious because he is running out of money and nearing the end of his rope. He is depressed because he can't bring himself to quit the crappy job. They both know that if something doesn't change, they won't like their life.

But, it's what happens next that is the larger problem. Instead of making a decision and taking action, too many of us do nothing. Suppose the pregnant girl does nothing; she doesn't want to think about abortion or what comes next, and she buries her head in her blankets. A few weeks or months of this, and her sub-conscious starts to play a role, because something has to reduce the dissonance. Her thoughts about who she is slowly begin to change. Sub-consciously, she gradually comes to believe that this is who she is—someone who got pregnant at seventeen and might not finish school. She begins to see herself less positively, with few options and a dim future. After a while, being pregnant doesn't seem so bad. She starts to think *I'll have the baby, eventually get married—or not— and settle for a much less optimistic life.* Because she could not bring herself to change voluntarily, the dissonance reduction took place automatically and at a steep cost. It caused her to have a negative view of her future and a damaged self-concept.

What about the guy who is going broke in a job that doesn't suit him, but he can't begin to look for a new one? He is dissatisfied and may be headed for financial ruin. Rather than reducing the dissonance by embarking on a job hunt, suppose he does nothing. Before long his dissonance is reduced, not because he took action, but because he took none, and instead allowed himself to succumb to the belief that he isn't worthy of more. He starts to think *maybe this is just the way my life will be,* and his self-concept goes down-hill. Because he failed to take action, his freedom from dissonance came at a steep cost: a victim mentality and a damaged self-concept

There is only one acceptable alternative to these dismal scenarios: something has to change. The misery has to be reduced either by taking action, changing beliefs, or a combination of both.

The first of two possible changes for the girl is to have the abortion. This could be the wrong choice because the irreversible action may create greater dissonance in the future if she has conflicting moral or religious views. Second, she could decide to keep the child or put it up for adoption and commit to finish school, work on the side, enlist family support, go to college, get a good job, and basically kick ass and take names. Option two reduces the dissonance but means much more work. She must pick her poison: do nothing and condemn herself to living a life half full, or work her tail off, feel better, and give herself a fighting chance to have it all.

It is the same story for the guy. If harder work isn't going to make him more money at his current job, he has to retrain, get a better job, or suffer the alternative: live with parents, live with friends, go on welfare, or miserably scrimp by.

The difficult choices are usually the ones that lead to greater peace of mind—making the world feel right. In our heart we know which belief or behaviour needs to change; we just have to do it. If we don't take action, dissonance will be reduced inevitably when we lower standards and accept mediocrity. This creates its own problems because it diminishes our self-concept and makes us feel less worthy.

So, when cognitive dissonance causes anxiety and depression, don't just accept your fate, change the beliefs or behaviours you know you have to change, and live well between your ears.

ARE YOU MISLED BY BLIND CONFORMITY?

"The opposite of bravery is not cowardice but conformity."

– Dr. Robert Anthony

"Be who you are and say what you feel, because those who mind don't matter and those who matter don't mind."

– Dr. Seuss

WHY DO YOU DO WHAT YOU DO? IS IT BECAUSE YOU MIMIC YOUR parents, give in to faint recollections of what a teacher, friend, pastor, or politician told you to do, or do you follow your own principled course? Are you able to take risks and depart from the norm, or are you so stuck in the conventions of your social group that departure from them never occurs to you. Maybe you fear you'll be judged as different, unique, or worse.

Conformity is a powerful force. It causes you to change your opinions, judgements, or actions so that they match (a) the opinions, judgements, or actions of other people, or (b) the normal rules of a social group or situation. Pressure to conform can lead you to publicly agree with a group, but privately disagree, and not accept its position as your own—at least, not until you are free of the group's influence. For example, you bad-mouth the tree-huggers and global-warming folks in order to blend in with your buddies, while you secretly cross your fingers and hope that something slows environmental destruction. Are you a liar if you conform to the group rather than support what's in your heart?

Research on conformity blossomed after WWII, when psychologists attempted to understand what made thousands of Nazis follow Hitler's orders and send millions of Jews to the gas chambers. The simplest explanation is fear. They feared demotion or feared for their lives if they disobeyed. They conformed because they wanted to be liked; to be safe; to be part of the group.

You might suspect that certain people conform more than others because of different personality types. True, people who are more internally controlled tend to conform less, but conformity is a function of social roles and group-endorsed rules, more than personality. Membership in a social group, where you feel bound by its rules, can lead you to do or say things that don't reflect how you really feel or who you really are.

Three classic studies illustrate the extent to which group norms and authority figures control our behaviour, often to our detriment. Phillip Zimbardo's (2007) Stanford Prison experiment showed us that ordinary people, when given a role of authority (prison guard), rapidly conformed to their group norm and denied their prisoners food, water, and sleep. With even the slightest provocation, the guards were quick to strip the prisoners naked, or place them in solitary confinement for minor infractions. These results demonstrate that in the right situation, and given a social role of authority, even you, as peaceful and kind as you are, could adopt a cruel persona and exercise mean-spirited power over the powerless.

Similarly, Stanley Milgram (1965, 1974) found that people were willing to administer near lethal electric shocks, up to 450 volts—despite screaming and begging from the recipient—if an authority figure urged them on, or if they believed their peers also administered such levels of shock. In actual fact, the shock was not being received—the recipients were only acting—but the experimental subjects were led to believe it was all real.

Before the experiment, Milgram asked 40 psychiatrists to estimate the percentage of people willing to administer the highest shocks. They estimated that most would quit before they shocked them with150 volts. They also estimated that only 4 percent would administer 350 volts, and that .1 percent would go all the way to 450 volts. The disturbing conclusion is how wrong the experts were. The majority of participants obeyed the authority figure fully. Not one participant quit before 300 volts, and 65 percent delivered the full 450 volts. The people doing the shocking protested and expressed concern for the recipients, but still, they continued to deliver the shocks when the authority figure urged them on.

The third classic experiment on conformity was first conducted by Solomon Asch in 1956. He placed individuals in groups of people who were thought to be fellow participants but, in fact, were accomplices of the experimenter. The individuals, who were not confederates of the experiment, were given the task of choosing one of three sample lines that matched a target line in length—a simple and obvious choice. The individuals always matched correctly when left on their own, but when several other people picked the wrong answer, a full 25 percent of those tested changed their choice and defied all logic by siding with the majority, despite the fact that it was obvious their choice was incorrect.

What makes conformity such a troublesome phenomenon is that it can make you, (a) behave in a cruel and mean-spirited fashion, (b) knowingly hurt someone because the authority-figure assures you it's okay, and (c) contradict what you know is correct.

How much of what you do is influenced by something, someone, or a group, rather than your own conscience? How easily misled are you? These three studies have stood the test of time in psychological research. The results remind us, especially when we are overwhelmed with information, to question the group, question the source, and question the voices of authority. They could easily be wrong. Rather than following your automatic tendency to conform, replace it with reasoned thought—consistent with your principles—and live well between your ears.

THE MIDDLE CLASS AND YOU

"There's class warfare, all right, but it's my class, the rich class,
that's making war, and we're winning."

– Warren Buffet

THERE'S MUCH TALK ABOUT THE MIDDLE CLASS. ARE YOU STILL PART
of it? It is the largest class of people in North America. But there's a
problem. Each year, more of us are sliding backwards but don't want to
admit it. In fact, of those asked to describe their economic status, as many
as 90 percent define themselves as middle class. But, it's more wishful
thinking than fact. In North America, much of the middle class is being
replaced by a burgeoning lower class. People, who once were the "haves"
of the middle class, have slid toward the "have-nots". If we keep sliding,
we'll become those stereotypical Southerners the comedians make fun
of. You know who I mean: they have fewer teeth, live in a trailer, eat squir-
rel, and think it is okay to marry their cousin.

A study conducted at Stanford University, and reported in the
November 15, 2011 edition of the New York Times, revealed that from
1970 to 2007, the middle class became 21 percent smaller. Over those
four decades, the rich and the poor grew in size, while the middle shrank.
In 1970, only 15 percent of families were classified as either affluent or

poor, and today that number has doubled. As the gap between rich and poor has grown, many who once believed they were middle, upper-middle, or even upper class, have had to confront the fact that they are not as well-to-do as they once were.

A report by Iglika Ivanova, in the July, 2011 *Progressive Economics Forum*, based on data from 2009, says the annual income of people who are either lower-middle, middle, or upper-middle ranges from $40,000 to $125,000, and represents 59.7 percent of the families in Canada.

But, regardless of income earned, does it still make sense to call yourself middle class if you can't pay your bills, send your kids to college, or look forward to a comfortable retirement? According to Ivanova, 21.1 percent of families, considered poor or near poor, have annual incomes less than $40,000, while 19.2 percent are well off and have over $125,000 in yearly income.

As the vast middle class loses ground, it might be worth asking, "Where are you in this jumble of numbers?" In past decades, we had fewer people in our immediate peer group with whom to compare ourselves, and we were happier; we didn't know what we were missing. Besides, we all had the same stuff back then—a car, a radio, a place to live, and a few treats. But today, thanks to the digital age, we see thousands of rich people and gazillions of gadgets that provide a daily reminder of ways we fall short and things we do without.

Many folks try to compensate for this status decline with new cars, more trips, and more toys. It might work for a short time. They might fool their neighbours, but they soon bump up against reality, and gradually—almost imperceptibly—start to think and act like they are poor. Most of us say we aren't status seekers, and that none of this bothers us. But the research says otherwise.

In a 2009 *Scientific American* article, Adam Waytz, a postdoctoral researcher in Psychology at Harvard University, maintained that for many of us, a decline in status is a big deal; it bothers us more than we let on. We notice differences and draw comparisons between our lives and the lives of countless athletes, movie stars, inventors, CEOs, and God knows who else. If we repeatedly feel like we're on the short end of the stick, resentment starts to build, self-esteem drops, and we begin a slow slide down the social status ladder.

Referring to research on social class by P. J. Henry in 2009, Waytz said, "low-status people are much more sensitive to being socially rejected and are more inclined to monitor their environment for threats. Because of this vigilance toward protecting their sense of self-worth, low-status individuals are quicker to respond violently to personal threats and insults." In short, as we see ourselves losing status, we become bitchier, angrier, and more discontent with our lot.

In large national surveys, Henry found that people of low-socioeconomic status display more psychological defensiveness; they believe they are taken advantage of, and trust people less. He analyzed data from 92 countries and found that greater status disparities predicted greater levels of violence.

Psychologists Anderson and Kilduff (2009) say that people can regain their status and minimize negative psychological effects if they suppress their anger and resentment, and instead, find ways to bring value to their community. For example, if they volunteer at community events and are generous with their help, their value and status within their community will be retained. However, the aggressive and violent tendencies of low-status individuals that Henry observed are the opposite of what is required to regain the lost sense of status.

As the gap between rich and poor grows larger, it is inevitable that many will feel they are losing ground. But, according to Waytz, without more income, struggling to retain our sense of status is futile. Barring major economic change, the middle class will continue to shrink, with a larger percentage of people getting poorer, while the rich get richer. According to Waytz and others, while volunteering and behaving generously will not make you richer, it is the best way to deal with the problem. It takes the sting out of falling behind, and helps you live well between your ears.

IT AIN'T LIKE IT USED TO BE

"He who rejects change is the architect of decay. The only human institution which rejects progress is the cemetery."

– Harold Wilson

"The only difference between a rut and a grave is their dimensions."

– Ellen Glasgow, American novelist (1873-1945)

MANY WOULD AGREE THAT RECENT, RAPID CHANGE HAS MADE THE world a more chaotic place. For some, the chaos takes away the structure and predictability they need in their lives, leaving them bewildered and scratching their head. We all like structure. Some need it more than others. If you crave structure in your life, you may do more than scratch your head in its absence; you may get downright upset and anxious.

In 1989, Thompson, Naccarato, and Parker developed a test to measure our personal need for structure, the PNS (Personal Need for Structure) scale. Made up of 12 items, you are asked to choose whether you (1) strongly agree, (2) moderately agree, (3) slightly agree, (4) slightly disagree, (5) moderately disagree, or (6) strongly disagree with each item. For example, four of the twelve statements comprising the PNS scale are: (a) It upsets me to go into a situation without knowing what I can expect from it, (b) I become uncomfortable when the rules in a situation are not clear, (c) I like to have a place for everything and everything in its place, and (d) I hate to be with people who are unpredictable. As you can see, rating yourself as 1, means you strongly agree with a statement, whereas 6 indicates strong disagreement. Or you may be somewhere in between.

According to the authors, "The Personal Need for Structure Scale estimates the extent to which people are motivated to structure their world in a simple and unambiguous way." After rating your agreement or disagreement with the four sample questions (a through d above), your score could range from 4 to 24, with low scores (4-12) indicating a greater need for structure and predictability in your life. Higher scores (from 13-24) indicate that you do not need as much structure and predictability. Simply stated, if you agree more than disagree with these statements, you lean towards needing structure in your life. If you disagree more than agree with the four sample questions, it means you are not bothered as much by the lack of structure and predictability. You should note that rating yourself on only four of the twelve items makes the results invalid. The sample questions are presented here only to give you an idea of how the scale works.

Exactly what is this 'structure' thing? It is the extent to which life is experienced as orderly and predictable. Some people require more order and predictability in their lives, and for them, a fast-paced, ever-changing world is less structured and more stressful. We know what to expect when life has structure, and when it doesn't, we don't.

For an extreme example of the difference, consider two different trips to the grocery store. You could drive through your comfortable, predictable neighbourhood if you live in North America, or you could dart and scramble through the rubble in war-torn Syria. There's a difference. You know what to expect on your street, but you haven't a clue in the war zone. The first is structured and feels safe; the second is not structured and feels anything but safe.

However, even the peaceful trip through the neighbourhood begins to lose structure when, for example, your sensibilities are assaulted by suspicious looking characters in the street, a half-naked woman on a billboard, or the thought of your daughter's recently acquired nose ring. Such departures from expectation—from the way things used to be—is more upsetting to the person who needs greater order and predictability in their lives. And, according to the experts (e.g. Kurzweil, 2006; Saylor, 2012) we're just getting started.

The more your life deviates from what you are accustomed to, the more diminished is your sense of structure and predictability. When we only have a few adjustments to make, our lives are structured and simple. But as change hits us from all angles, our senses are overwhelmed—we sense it as a loss of structure—and our reactions range from frustration, to intolerance, to anxiety, and possibly, to anger.

Neuberg and Newsom (1993) reported that people can reduce the impact of loss of structure by two different courses of action. First, they can stay at home, erect high fences, wear head phones in the street, close the door to their room or office, and boycott technology. Their second choice is to add structure to their lives with strict daily routines and by simplifying how they choose to see the world.

To do the latter means you organize your world in broad strokes and strive to stick with what you know, rather than struggle with the new and unknown. In short, you try to look at the world in a simple light at a time when nothing is simple. Attempting to find simplicity when it doesn't exist means you start to believe that people and things are either good or bad—you reject shades of grey; you become intolerant and resentful of ideas, people, and things that are different. This desire for structure and predictability generates its own problems.

As the developers of the PNS scale put it, the people with greater need for structure have to "make sense of things around them more quickly or completely than do other people." It is a difficult task; as we adapt to the first change, two more pop up. But if we choose to retreat from the world, shun technology, or attempt to over-simplify what is already complex, we cut ourselves off from the richness of life. A more rewarding course of action is to tackle the world bravely, get on board with complexity and change, and live well between your ears.

THE FAVOURED ONES

"Like the 'little emperors' of one-child China, too many Boomers were taught early that the world was made (or saved) for their comfort and enjoyment. They behaved accordingly, with a self-indulgence that was wholly rational, given their situation."

– Eric Liu, American born author, educator and former Clinton speech writer

HAVE YOU LED A SPECIAL LIFE? IF YOU'RE BETWEEN 49 AND 67 YOU have. You won't all agree, because some of you have endured hardship and don't believe you've been favoured. But, in many respects, you have.

The Baby Boomers, born between 1946 and 1964, have had it their way forever. They have been the largest single demographic since birth. They represent 28 percent of the population; close to 10 million in Canada, and just over 100 million when US numbers are included. Whatever they need or want is invented for them. Today's teenagers, and twenty, thirty, or forty-something's, as well as those over 70, must be sick of the fact that they've always been treated like also-rans.

Catered to their entire lives, whatever the Boomers need or want arrives at the right time. New schools were built to accommodate them. Sports fields, playgrounds, and a wide selection of toys came when they were kids. As teens, they were the largest buying segment of the population and marketers clambered to sell them stuff. As they raised families, you couldn't count the number of Dr. Spock-type books that hit the market, and self-help advice has continued to keep pace with their unique little issues at every stage of their life.

Raised in prosperous times, they were given much and had many choices—certainly more than their parents and grand-parents. Even their music remains popular today, and their favourite musicians, now in their 60's and 70's, still pack large venues.

As the Boomers' sex life slipped in to neutral, science came to the rescue with Viagra and Cialis. But as they age, marketers have found other products for them such as Hurry Canes, Depends, walk-in bath-tubs, feminine leakage products, and shoe horns with a three-foot handle so they don't have to bend over. They have a choice of monitored wrist bands, necklaces, or remote gadgets that signal a dispatcher if they fall, get sick, or God-knows what else.

The onset of wrinkles brought hundreds of skin creams, and those with weak legs and poor balance can buy stair lifts to carry them up and down. We would never have seen these things had it not been for the Boomers, but now the conveniences are here to stay. As they get aches and pains, the drug companies design more pain killers, analgesics, and icy-hot wraps than ever before. We've seen advances in heart surgery, and most other medical procedures, that might otherwise have lagged. And, we're just getting started. The proliferation of products and services directed at this demographic will mushroom.

More assisted living, home care, and personal care services will be tailored to their needs. It's happening now and the first baby boomer just turned 65 in 2011. In North America, ten thousand Baby Boomers hit retirement age every day, and that will continue for the next 18 years.

This retirement bubble will be with us for the next two to four decades. Each passing year will bring a need for more specialized care, and like always, they'll get what they need. And, most of them have the money to pay for it.

According to a report in Wikipedia, the Boomers account for over 80 percent of personal financial assets, and more than half of all consumer spending. They buy 77 percent of all prescription drugs, 61 percent of over-the-counter drugs, and 80 percent of all leisure travel. Think about it! If you want to invest in a sure thing, buy stock in firms that offer special housing or health care for the Boomers, and live well between your ears.

A NATION OF LAWS

"Good people do not need laws to tell them to act responsibly,
while bad people will find a way around the laws."

– Plato

THE POWER PEOPLE IN THE WORLD—POLITICIANS, CORPORATE giants, and individuals who have amassed considerable wealth—understand best what it means to be a nation of laws. Is this why they are rich? Does this belief open the door a crack to unethical and greedy behaviour? Adhering to the nation of laws doctrine leads us to accept anything, as long as it's legal. But, if we adhere to a nation of morals doctrine instead, and accept that anything is okay as long as it's moral, would we be better off?

Consider these two possibilities: It's March, and your neighbour allowed ice to build up on his step after a freezing rain. As you approach his house, you slip on the ice and break your back. Or, what if his dog "played" with your two-year old and gave him a nasty bite on the leg. Would you sue your friend for negligence, or chalk it up to an unfortunate accident?

If you are governed more by laws than morals, your preferred course of action may be to sue. Alternatively, you may view these as unfortunate accidents, something that could happen to anyone, and say, "it's just bad luck."

Business tycoons, Donald Trump for example, seem to live more by the letter of the law than by moral conviction. They, and successful people like them, believe that being a nation of laws, and adhering to a system of laws, is what makes nations great. True, but when you decide to live solely in accordance with the law, is it possible that you behave differently than if you lived in accordance with a strong moral standard? At least up to a point, people like Warren Buffet and Bill Gates, who have pledged most of their billions to philanthropy, appear to be governed as much by morality as legality.

The phrase, "as long as it's legal" leaves plenty of room for the in-between stuff—between what is barely legal and totally moral. For example, it is illegal to steal, but legal to charge more than the job is worth. Similarly, it is legal for banks to charge 20-30 percent interest on credit balances or cash advances, but it hardly seems moral. Hopefully, the majority of us adhere to a moral code; one that leads us to treat others the way we would like to be treated.

Most large corporations have teams of lawyers whose purpose is to make sure their company policies go up to, but do not cross, the legal line. There are many examples: the law allows pollution up to a legal limit; banks and bankers, complicit in financial harm to many ordinary citizens, did not act illegally, only recklessly; companies that manufacture food and drugs adhere to legal criteria, while at the same time, employ lawyers and lobbyists to look for loopholes to maximize profit and minimize expense. I don't blame them. After all, we are a nation of laws, and corporations act within those laws until they make a mistake. Most individuals do not use the law like this, but a few do—they're often less well liked—and they are richer, not poorer.

The point is this whole 'nation of laws' thing is not perfect, but it is better than the alternative which would involve dictators and an oppressive culture. But, just because we are a nation of laws does not make every legal act morally right. When pushing the law to the limit causes people, corporations, and governments to cross a moral line, it might be time to step back and do what is legal and moral—not just legal—so we can continue to live well between our ears.

DON'T BE DROWNED BY CHANGE

"Life is a series of natural and spontaneous changes. Don't resist them; that only creates sorrow. Let reality be reality. Let things flow naturally forward in whatever way they like."

– Lao Tzu, Chinese philosopher of the 6th century BC.

DO YOU FEEL UNDER ATTACK BY TODAY'S PACE? DOES STUFF HAPPEN SO fast it makes you anxious or depressed? Everyone comments on it. Hi-tech growth has changed our lives at a rate not before experienced, and it's speeding up. Those who study the impact of technology say the rate of advancement in this twenty-first century will be one thousand times greater than in the last century (Kurzweil, 2006).

In the past, if new information, inventions, and distant events affected us at all, they did so slowly, like the drip-drip from a leaky faucet. Today, it blasts us like a fire hose. According to Moore's law, the rate of digital chip capacity doubles every two years. It doesn't sound like much when you just say it. But it's causing incredible acceleration of technology due to the exponential growth in speed of transmission and concomitant reduction in size. If your money grew the same way, you'd be one grinning son-of-a-gun.

Imagine: start with $1000 in a shoe box and it doubles every two years. In ten years, you'd have $32,000 in a cubic centimeter. In ten more, you'd have over a million dollars in a box the size of a speck of dust. The digital world enjoys exactly that rate of growth, and it will inundate us with thousands of unimaginable inventions, annoyances, and services over the next two decades. Whether the inventions are good or bad is not the point. The point is they come at us like a hurricane. You can choose to work with the changes to make your world better, or you can fight them and make your world worse.

For better or worse, there is a connection between how we think and how well we handle change. Some people get anxious, irritable, frustrated, or just plain pissed off; others take it in stride. Research shows that our ability to deal with rapid change and maintain composure depends on how, more than what, we think. Complex thinkers handle the onslaught of information better than less complex (simple) thinkers. They differ in several ways.

Simple thinkers value certainty, logic, and control. When problems are complicated, they often revert to slogans such as: "When in doubt, punt", "If it ain't broke, don't fix it" or, with respect to international problems, "details, details, let's just nuke 'em'." Each reflects a preference for simple—often inaccurate— explanations, rather than those which are complicated, but often closer to the truth. For example, a simpler Sir Isaac Newton would have said the apple fell from the tree because it was heavy, rather than wrestle with the concept of gravitational pull. To treat a complicated issue as if it is simple is to wander down a dangerous path.

Puccio (2006) says simple thinkers resist novel ideas, and are less tolerant of ambiguity, so they jump to conclusions. They are also less tolerant of complexity, and are overwhelmed by large amounts of information. It's a growing dilemma; they thrive on simplicity but are drowning in complexity.

According to Streufert and Swezey (1986), complex thinkers are not stressed-out by disorderliness or complexity. For example, if a complex thinker buys a fancy electronic gadget, he's not opposed to cracking the owner's manual if he has trouble. If the simple thinker has trouble, he'll turn the switch off and on, shake the thing, poke every button—and if he still can't make it work—throw it in the corner, or take it back to the store—the manual is just too complicated.

Streufert and Swezey also found that less complex thinkers are "more stable in their attitudes and prone to polarize on an issue." Holding firm to their opinion is one way they cope with diversity and uncertainty; it helps them feel secure. In contrast, "highly complex persons change attitude more easily; presumably because they consider a greater variety of information resulting in more moderate attitudes."

In the midst of an ambiguous, uncertain, and rapidly changing world, the message from the research is clear. If you don't become a more complex thinker and swim with, rather than against, the rushing river of change, you will drown. Embrace new technology and the change it brings. To lower your stress level, adjust rather than resist, and live well between your ears.

THE VANISHING SIMPLE LIFE

"The only way to make sense out of change is to plunge into it,
move with it, and join the dance."

– Alan Watts, British philosopher and speaker (1915-1973)

I'VE BEEN ON A ROLL WRITING ABOUT CHANGE LATELY. I'M SORRY. I
can't help it. It's a frequent topic of conversation; it's fascinating because
it changes our lives as we speak. It is also upsetting for some. History
has seen nothing like it. Sure there's been change; but not this fast. As
Michael Saylor points out in his best-selling 2012 book, *The Mobile Wave:
How mobile intelligence will change everything*, the agricultural revolution
took thousands of years to transform barren land, inhabited by a few
nomads, into towns, cities, and an infrastructure that feeds, clothes, and
powers almost seven billion people. The industrial revolution took a few
hundred years, and by extrapolation, the information revolution will only
take tens of years.

Saylor is an expert on the topic. He is an American entrepreneur,
the co-founder, CEO, and chairman of the board of MicroStrategy
Incorporated, a global provider of business intelligence, mobile software,
and cloud-based services. He is a software guru. He says that ninety
percent of the world has access to a mobile network—more people than

have access to clean water—and it is reasonable to expect that, by 2018, we will see a massive upsurge in innovation relating to mobile applications. By 2025, we will see almost universal use of mobile computers as the primary means of navigating all aspects of modern society: work, play, travel, shopping, preventative medicine, education, and you name it.

If you don't get on board soon, you will be left in the proverbial dust. Most of us don't fully understand the labels on our food, let alone know how to get full function out of our TV remote or smart phone. We are heavily dependent on things we know little about, and all our electronic gadgets are designed to be replaced, not repaired, once they beep their last beep.

Even normal behaviour has become less normal. For example, you thought you were upset when your daughter got her nose pierced by her new boyfriend Brad, the body artist she met online. Just wait a few years, till your grand-daughter shows up with a laser-implanted chip in her brain; she won't only talk online to Ahmed in Yemen, she'll feel his touch. Oh, for the days when it was just Brad and a nose ring.

It wasn't long ago when you could fix your own car, a text was a book, a tweet was a sound, and you sent hand written letters from the post office. It was when bad stuff happened someplace else, doors weren't locked, the phone hung on the wall and was only good for talking, and no one wore home-made bombs or killed kids at school. The simpler life was slow, safe, predictable, and local; but it's gone.

The internet, and globalization it feeds, have shrunk both distance and time. People and things get to the other side of the world overnight, and information gets there in a second.

What's on the horizon? A chip in your windshield once obscured your vision, but one will soon guide your car, while you monkey with your latest gadget. You used to worry about curing your ills, but in a few decades you'll be injected at birth with biological micro-robots (nanobots) that will scan your DNA and identify and manage disease so you never suffer from it.

The bottom line is that when we open our mind, welcome the new and different, and relax our grip on the past, we live well between our ears.

Uncle Sam's favourite niece

"Canada has great natural resources, and its people have the spirit
and ability to develop them."

– Charles E. Wilson, former CEO of General Electric

I'M SURE THE NEW WORLD ORDER AND ONE WORLD GOVERNMENT ARE
topics that crop up from time to time among heads of state or Bilderberg
Group members. Such chatter, together with the reality of China's ascendance and the United States' determination to stay on top, leads me to
ponder how long it will be before Canada's 10 provinces and 3 territories
swell the 50 United States to 63.

To retain their top spot in the world, the USA will need more oil, gas,
nickel, copper, uranium, timber, clean water, and who-knows-what-else
that lies between the 49th parallel and the North Pole.

Is Uncle Sam worried? Nope. If push comes to shove, and he can't
negotiate what he needs from Canada, he'll just conquer us and take it.
Why wouldn't he? If his choice is to take over Canada, or succumb to
threats to National security, we've seen what he'll do. Books and blogs
will refer to US/Canada history as BM and AM—before merger and after.

After-all, we've been best friends since 1812, when the United States
pushed to occupy colonial Canada and was driven back. But they won't

be driven back again. Canada's planes, ships, and brave (but few) fighting men and women are no match for the firepower of Uncle Sam on a mission.

How will it happen? Will there be a fight? It's doubtful. The process has already started. The Free Trade Agreement (FTA) of 1987, and what it morphed in to, the 1984 North American Free Trade Association (NAFTA), places fewer restrictions on international trade between the countries. In 2000, 84.2 percent of Canada's total exports went to the USA. By 2011, it had dropped to 72.6 percent—still larger than pre-NAFTA. Given our porous border, free trade, and neighbourliness, we're like a 51st State already.

According to Wikipedia, there are 17 treaties between the US and Canada. Mostly, they cover trade and water issues, but at least one sets the precedence for treating Canada like a State. Under the terms of the 1976 Shakwak Agreement, the USA approved funds for Canadian Contractors to rebuild the Alaska Highway, just like they would if we were a State. And, the family ties will get closer.

One thing is certain, as Canada gets chummier with China, and Uncle Sam sees his claim on bountiful Canadian assets grow weaker, he will negotiate tighter ties to Canada's natural resources. Of course, the tie is tightest when those resources become US resources, by negotiation, boycott of Canadian exports, or—failing those solutions—force.

In a 2011-2012 report, the Department of Foreign Affairs and International Trade Canada said it, "will reinforce Canada's relationship with the United States, our most important economic and security partner, through support for a joint vision for perimeter security and initiatives to maintain market access for Canadian companies and attract U.S. direct investment into Canada." The point is we are heavily dependent on each other already, and in many respects, both countries would benefit from a merger (probably them more than us).

Today, Canada is like a college girl under the guardianship of her uncle next door; free to do whatever with whomever she wants. But she should beware. If she gets too frisky, and threatens to give her virgin resources to the bad guys, Uncle Sam will say, "Enough is enough," playtime will be over and her world will change.

No matter what transpires, as sure as night follows day, the two countries will, someday, become one, simply because the USA has to assure it has easy access to abundant resources. It will happen gradually, through secret back channels, person-to-person alliances, and open negotiation of new and modified treaties, up to the time when Statehood is imminent. At that point, Canadian resistance, great or small, will be met with an avalanche of US dollars to do two things: (1) fund a media campaign to sell Mr. and Mrs. Canuck on the short- and long-term benefits of official adoption, and (2) guarantee the election of the Canadian Party that can deliver the merger.

Put it this way, if you were a US Senator or Congress person, with your eye on the empire-saving resources of the friendly Canadians, how would you vote? All they have to do is decide and it will be a done deal. It won't be up to Canada.

Besides, there's nothing to say that Russia, China, or the European Union don't also have their eye on our resources. Then what? With whom would you rather share our bounty? If it isn't the USA, get ready for a fight you can't win. Wait and watch—and live well between your ears.

References

Ahn, W.Y., Rass, O., Fridberg, D.J., Bishara, A.J., Forsyth, J.K., Breier, A., Busemeyer , J.R., Hetrick, W.P., Bolbecker, A.R., & O'Donnell, B.F. (2011). Temporal discounting of rewards in patients with bipolar disorder and schizophrenia. *Journal of Abnormal Psychology. 120,* 911-21. Retrieved in October, 2013 from http://www.ncbi.nlm.nih. gov/pubmed/21875166

Allwood, Carl M, & Salo, Ilkka. (2012). Decision-making styles and stress. *International Journal of Stress Management, 19*(1), 34-47. Retrieved in November, 2013 from psycARTICLES database.

Anderson, C. & Kilduff, G. J. (2009). The pursuit of status in social groups. *A Journal of the Association for Psychological Science, 18,*295-298. Retrieved March 2013 from http://web-docs.stern.nyu.edu/ management/Kilduff/Anderson&Kilduff%202009.pdf

Aron, E. N. (1966). *The highly sensitive person: How to thrive when the world overwhelms you.* New York, NY: Broadway Books.

Asch, S.E. (1956). Studies of independence and conformity: A minority of one against a unanimous majority. *Psychological Monographs, 70,*

Baird B., Smallwood J., Mrazek M. D., Kam J., Franklin M. S., Schooler J. W. (2012). Mind-wandering facilitates creative incubation. *Psychological Science. 23,* 117-1122. Retrieved November, 2013 from http://www.ncbi.nlm.nih.gov/pubmed/22941876

Bakker, A.B., & Heuven, E. (2006). Emotional dissonance, burnout, and in-role performance among nurses and police officers. *International Journal of Stress Management. 13*, 423–440

Balch, Philip; Ross, A. William (1975). Predicting success in weight reduction as a function of locus of control: A unidimensional and multidimensional approach. *Journal of Consulting and Clinical Psychology, 43,* 119

Bandura, *A. Social learning theory.* (1977). Englewood Cliffs, NJ., Prentice-Hall

Bargh, J.A. & Morsella, E. (2010) Unconscious behavioral guidance systems. Retrieved from http://www.yale.edu/acmelab/articles/ BarghMorsella_UBGS_final.pdf

Bartholomew, K. J., Ntoumanis, N. & Ntoumanis, C.T. (2010) The controlling interpersonal style in a coaching context: development and initial validation of psychometric scale. *Journal of Sport & Exercise Psychology, 32,* 193-216. Retrieved April 2013 from http://www.selfdeterminationtheory.org/SDT/documents/2010_ BartholomewNtoumanisThogersen-Ntoumani_JSEP.pdf

Basadur, M. (2011) Basadur applied creativity. Retrieved in April 2013 from http://basadur.wordpress.com/tag/basadur-profile/

Bem, S. (1974) The measurement of psychological androgyny. *Journal of Consulting and Clinical Psychology, 42,* 155-162. Retrieved November, 2012 from APA PsychNET direct.

Benight, Charles C., & Bandura, Albert (2004). Social cognitive theory of posttraumatic recovery: the role of perceived self-efficacy. *Behaviour Research and Therapy 42,* 1129–1148. Retrieved in July 2013 from http://www.uky.edu/~eushe2/Bandura/Bandura2004BRTb.pdf

Ben-Zur, Hasida. (2009). Coping styles and affect. *International Journal of Stress Management, 16,* 87-101.

Ben-Zur, Hasida & Zeidner, Moshe. (2012). Appraisals, coping and affective and behavioral reactions to academic stressors. *Psychology,*

3, 713-721. Retrieved in November, 2013 from http://dx.doi. org/10.4236/psych.2012.39108

Biswas-Diener, Robert. (2012). *The courage quotient: How science can make you braver.* Hoboken, NJ: John Wiley & Sons.

Blazer, D. G., Kessler, R.C., & McGonagle, K.A. (1994). The prevalence and distribution of major depression in a national community sample: the National Comorbidity Survey. *American Journal of Psychiatry, 151,* 979-986. Retrieved in August, 2013 from http://ajp. psychiatryonline.org/article.aspx?articleID=170440

Brotherton, R. (2012) The psychology of conspiracy theories. Online blog retrieved 2012 from http://conspiracypsychology.com/

Brown, H. D. (1994). Affective variables in second language acquisition. *Language Learning, 23,* 231-244.

Budner (1962) Tolerance of ambiguity scale. Retrieved in May 2013 from http://www.google.ca/url?sa=t&rct=j&q=&esrc=s&source=web& cd=2&cad=rja&uact=8&ved=0CDwQFjAB&url=http%3A%2F% 2Fpeople.westminstercollege.edu%2Ffaculty%2Fmkoerner%2F00_ courses%2Fmtech_616_spr_05%2Ftolerance_of_ambiguity_ scale.doc&ei=n8c4U5G6PMeJrAGopIDoCA&usg=AFQjCNHRY 6pGyh-sd2r8iMYy4PYn0K9KMA&sig2=7uhLNIOSFTZxpsxvL9 v9Wg&bvm=bv.63808443,d.aWM

Burton, Neel (2012). *Hide and seek – The psychology of self-deception.* United Kingdom: Acheron Press

Byrne, R. (2006). *The Secret.* Hillsboro Oregon, Beyond Words publishing.

Callan, M.J., Shead, N.W., & Olson, J.M. (2011) Personal relative deprivation, delay discounting, and gambling. *Journal of Personality and Social Psychology, 101,* 955-73. Retrieved in October, 2013 from http://www.ncbi.nlm.nih.gov/pubmed/21875231

Carmody, D. P. & Lewis, M. (2006). Brain activation when hearing one's own and others' names. *Brain Research, 1116,* 153-158. Retrieved in August, 2012 from http://www.ncbi.nlm.nih.gov/pmc/articles/PMC1647299/

Chelminski, I., Ferraro, F. R., Petros, T. V., & Plaud, J. J. (1999). An analysis of the "eveningness–morningness"dimension in "depressive" college students. *Journal of Affective Disorders, 52*, 19–29. Retrieved from http://www.tc.umn.edu/~cdeyoung/Pubs/DeYoung_2007_circadian_metatraits_PAID.pdf

Chen & Kendrick (2002). The neural correlates of ethnic and gender similarity and dissimilarity with avatars in online shopping environments. Retrieved at online draft from http://misrc.umn.edu/workshops/2010/fall/JMR_Gender%20Differences%20in%20Similarity%20with%20Anthrompomorphic%20Recommendation%20Agents_draft.pdf

Coan, Richard (1973) Toward a psychological interpretation of psychology. *Journal of the History of Behavioural Sciences, 9*, 313-327. Retrieved in November, 2012 from http://onlinelibrary.wiley.com/doi/10.1002/1520-6696%28197310%299:4%3C313::AID-JHBS2300090405%3E3.0.CO;2-M/abstract

Collins, D., (2009) Chronotype influences diurnal variations in the excitability of the human motor cortex and the ability to generate torque during a maximum voluntary contraction. *Journal of Biological Rhythms 24*, 211-224. Retrieved in February, 2013 from http://jbr.sagepub.com/content/24/3/211

Costa, Paul Jr. & McCrae, R. (1992) Five factor model of personality. Retrieved in December, 2012 from http://www.psych-it.com.au/Psychlopedia/article.asp?id=80

Dane, E., Baer, M., Pratt, M.G., & Oldham, G.R. (2011). Rational versus intuitive problem solving: How thinking "off the beaten path" can stimulate creativity. *Psychology of Aesthetics: Creativity and the Arts. 5*, 3-12. Retrieved in February, 2013 from http://www.academia.edu/802921/

Rational_versus_intuitive_problem_solving_How_thinking_off_
the_beaten_path_can_stimulate_creativity

Dencker, John (2008). Study: Women Make Management Strides When
Firms Downsize, Restructure. ASA Press Releases. Retrieved June
2012 from http://www.asanet.org/press/20080612.cfm

DeNeve, K.M. & Cooper, H. (1998). The happy personality: a meta-
analysis of 137 personality traits and subjective well-being.
Psychological Bulletin, 124: 197-229. Retrieved in November, 2013
from http://www.subjectpool.com/ed_teach/y5_ID/personality/
wellbeing/1998_Deneve_cooper_psych_bull.pdf

Diener, E., Fraser, S., Beaman, A., & Kelem, R. (1976). Effects of deindi-
viduation variables on stealing among Halloween trick-or-treaters.
Journal of Personality and Social Psychology, 33 178-183. Retrieved in
August, 2013 from http://psych-your-mind.blogspot.ca/2011/10/
what-do-halloween-and-social-psychology.html

Docherty, B. (2007) The Time Is Now: A Historical Argument for a
Cluster Munitions Convention. *Harvard Human Rights Journal, Vol.
20,* 53

Dollard, J., Doob, L.W., Miller, N., Mower, O.H., & Sears, R.R. (1939).
Frustration and aggression. New Haven, CT: Yale University Press.

Doverspike, W. F. (2005d). Listening and Learning. *Georgia Psychologist,
59,* 5

Eagly, A. H., Karau, S. J.,& Makhijani, M.J. (1995) Gender and the effectiveness of leaders: A meta-analysis. *Psychological Bulletin,117,* 125-
145. Retrieved in May 2013 from http://teaching.fec.anu.edu.au/
BUSN2007/Eagly%20et%20al_1995.pdf

Ekman, P. & Friesen, W.V. (1975). *Unmasking the face: A guide to recognizing emotions from facial expressions.* Englewood Cliffs, NJ: Prentice-
Hall Inc.

Eliot, John. (2004) Overachievement: *The new model for exceptional
achievement.* New York, NY: Penguin Group

Esmond, J. & Dunlop, P. (2004) Developing the volunteer motivation inventory to assess the underlying motivational drives of volunteers in western Australia. Retrieved in Feb 2012 from http://volunteer. ca/content/clan-wa-inc-developing-volunteer-motivation-inventory-assess-underlying-motivational-drives

Ewart, C.K., Elder, G.J., Smyth, J.M., Sliwinski, M.J., Jorgensen, R.S. (2011). Do agonistic motives matter more than anger? Three studies of cardiovascular risk in adolescents. *Health Psychology, 30,* 510-24. Retrieved in May, 2013 from http://www.ncbi.nlm.nih. gov/pubmed/21534673

Fehr, Beverley. (2006). *Friendship processes.* Thousand Oaks, CA: Sage Publications, Inc.

Feinmann, Jane (2010). The 'toxic fat' that can strangle your organs and how to shed it. Retrieved in November, 2013 from http://www. dailymail.co.uk/health/article-1258185/The-toxic-fat-strangle-organs-shed-it.html

Festinger, L. (1954). A theory of social comparison processes. *Human Relations.7,* 136-172

Fetterman, A. K. & Robinson, M.D. (2013) Do you use your head or follow your heart? Self-location predicts personality, emotion, decision making and performance. *Journal of Personality and Social Psychology, 105,* 316-334. Retrieved in November, 2013 from http://www.academia.edu/3543823/Do_you_use_your_head_or_follow_your_heart_Self-location_predicts_personality_emotion_decision_making_and_performance

Fiedler, Fred E. (1971) Validation and extension of the contingency model of leadership effectiveness: A review of empirical findings. *Psychological Bulletin, 76,* 128-148. In L.S. Wrightsman (Ed), Social Psychology in the Seventies. 1972, 499-506. Monterey, CA: Brooks/ Cole Publishing Co.

Florida, R. (2002). *The rise of the creative class... and how it's transforming work, leisure, community, & everyday life.* New York, NY: Basic Books.

Gibson, A. & Foster, C. (2007). The role of self talk in the awareness of physiological state and physical performance. *Sports Medicine 37*, 1029-1044. Retreived November 2012 from https://apps.sgu.edu/ UNN/Gazette.nsf/GazetteFullStory?openForm...

Gladwell, Malcom. (2005). *Blink: The power of thinking without thinking.* New York, NY: Little, Brown, and Company.

Gleibs, I.H, Morton, T.A, Rabinovich, A., Haslam, S.A. & Helliwell, J.F (2013) Unpacking the hedonic paradox: A dynamic analysis of the relationships between financial capital, social capital and life satisfaction. *The British journal of social psychology.* 52, 25-43. Retrieved in November, 2013 from http://onlinelibrary.wiley.com/ enhanced/doi/10.1111/j.2044-8309.2011.02035.x/

Goodfellow, D.H. (1980). Relationships between field independence-dependence and student and faculty performance in a baccalaureate nursing program (Doctoral dissertation, Vanderbilt University), Dissertation Abstracts International, 41, 3951. Retrieved in May 2013 from http://www.personal.psu.edu/staff/t/x/txm4/paper1. html

Greenberg, Melanie (2012). Nine essential qualities of mindfulness. Retrieved in November 2012 from http://integral-options.blogspot. ca/2012/03/melanie-greenberg-phd-nine-essential.html

Greyson, B. (2010). Science and post-mortem survival. Retrieved online from http://msv-nhne.org/ dr-bruce-greyson-science-postmortem-survival/

Griskevicius, V., Tybur, J. M., Delton, A. W., & Robertson, T. E. (2011). The influence of mortality and socioeconomic status on risk and delayed rewards: A life history theory approach. *Journal of Personality and Social Psychology, 100,* 1015–1026. Retrieved in October, 2013 from http://web.mit.edu/joshack/www/Griskevicius_Life-history-spending.pdf

Hans, T.A. (2000). A meta-analysis of the effects of adventure programming on locus of control. *Journal of Contemporary Psychotherapy, 30,* 33-60

Hansen, J. (1980). Field dependent-independent cognitive styles and foreign language proficiency among college students in an introductory Spanish course (Doctoral dissertation, University of Colorado), Dissertation Abstracts International, 41, 3460. Retrieved in May 2013 from http://www.personal.psu.edu/staff/t/x/txm4/paper1.html

Hansen C.J., Stevens L.C., & Coast J.R. (2001). Exercise duration and mood state: how much is enough to feel better? *Health Psychology, 20,* 267-75. Retrieved in May 2012 from http://www.ncbi.nlm.nih.gov/pubmed/11515738

Haslam, David (2010). Visceral Fat and the Weight Debate: Why we must act now. Retrieved in November, 2012 from http://www.alli.co.uk/Global/updates/Visceral_Fat_and_The_Weight_Debate.pdf

Hassmen, P. Koivula, N., & Uutela, A. (2000). Physical exercise and psychological well-being: a population study in Finland. *Preventative Medicine, 30,* 17-25. Retrieved in May 2013 from http://www.dswfitness.com/docs/ExRxforP.pdf

Hawking, Stephen (2005). *A briefer history of time.* New York, NY: Bantam Dell

Hawkley, L.C. & Cacioppo, John T. (2007). Aging and loneliness: Downhill quickly? *Current Directions in Psychological Science, 16,* 187-191. Retrieved in October, 2013 from http://psychology.uchicago.edu/people/faculty/cacioppo/jtcreprints/agingandloneliness.pdf

Hayes, Stephen (2005) *Get out of your mind and into your life: The new acceptance and commitment therapy.* Oakland, CA: New Harbinger Publications, Inc.

Heider, F. (1958). *The psychology of interpersonal relationships.* New York, NY: Wiley

Helson, H. (1964). *Adaptation level theory.* New York, NY: Harper & Rowe.

Henry, P.J. (2009). Low-Status Compensation: A Theory for Understanding the Role of Status in Cultures of Honor. *Journal of Personality and Social Psychology, 97,* 451-466. Retrieved in December, 2013 from http://nyuad.nyu.edu/academics/faculty/pj-henry/publications/2009HenryJPSP.pdf

Hill, Napoleon (1960). *Think and grow rich.* New York. Fawcett Crest.

Hirsh J.B, Guindon, A., Morisano, D., & Peterson, J.B (2010). Positive Mood Effects on Delay Discounting. *Emotion, 10,* 717-721. Retrieved in October, 2013 from http://individual.utoronto.ca/jacobhirsh/publications/Hirsh_Guindon_Morisano_Peterson.pdf

Hurrelbrinck, N. (2001). Stevenson studies children who remember past lives. Inside UVA online. Retrieved May 2013 from http://www.virginia.edu/insideuva/2001/03/stevenson.html

Infurna, F.J. Gerstorf, Denis; Zarit, Steven H.(2011). Examining dynamic links between perceived control and health: Longitudinal evidence for differential effects in midlife and old age. *Developmental Psychology, 47,* 9-18.

Jang, Y., Chiriboga, D. A., Kim, G., & Rhew, S. (2010). Perceived discrimination, sense of control, and depressive symptoms among Korean American older adults. *Asian American Journal of Psychology, 1,* 129-135. Retrieved in March 2013 from APA PsychNet Direct.

Jessor, R. & Jessor, S. (1977). *Problem behavior and psychosocial development: A longitudinal study of youth.* New York, NY: Academic Press. Retrieved in May 2012 from http://www.colorado.edu/ibs/jessor/pubs/1995_Jessor_VanDenBos_Vanderryn_etal_DEVPSYCH_ProblemBehaviorModeratorEffects.pdf

Jordania, Joseph. (2009). Intrapersonal communication. *American Journal of Primatology, 11,* 163-179

Joshi, P.D. & and Fast, N.J. (2013) Power and reduced temporal discounting. Psychological science. Retrieved in October, 2013 from http://www-bcf.usc.edu/~nathanaf/power_and_reduced_temporal_discounting.pdf

Joubert, C. E. (1990). Relationship of liking of first names to birth order and loneliness. *Psychological Reports, 66,* 1177-1178. Retrieved in May 2012 from http://www.ncbi.nlm.nih.gov/pubmed/2385707

Kelley, H. H. (1967). Attribution theory in social psychology. Nebraska Symposium on Motivation, 15, 192-238. Retrieved in September, 2012 from http://www.communicationcache.com/uploads/1/0/8/8/10887248/attribution_theory_and_research_-_1980.pdf

Keri, S. (2011). Genes for psychosis and creativity. *Psychological Science, 20,* 1070-1073. Retrieved Jan 2013 from http://cogsci.uwaterloo.ca/courses/Phil447.2009/keri.pdf

Killingsworth, M.A. & Gilbert, D.T. (2010). A wandering mind is an unhappy mind. *Science, 330,* 932. Retrieved April 2013 from http://www.wjh.harvard.edu/~dtg/KILLINGSWORTH%20&%20GILBERT%20%282010%29.pdf

King, D.W. (1983). Field-dependence/field-independence and achievement in music reading (Doctoral dissertation, University of Wisconsin), Dissertation Abstracts International, 44,1320. Retrieved in May 2013 from http://www.personal.psu.edu/staff/t/x/txm4/paper1.html

Kirschbaum, C., Klauer, T., Filipp, S. H., & Hellhammer, D.H. (1995). Sex-specific effects of social support on cortisol and subjective responses to acute psychological stress. *Psychosomatic Medicine, 57,* 23-31. Retrieved in April, 2013 from http://www.scientificjournals.org/Journals2011/articles/1510.pdf

Kraus, R.M. & Morsella, E. (1998) Communication and conflict. In the *Handbook of Conflict Resolution. Ch, 6,* 131-143. Retrieved in October, 2012 from https://lacfla.memberclicks.net/assets/documents/WOODY/krauss%20and%20morsella%20communication%20and%20conflictlacflawoody.pdf

Kubler-Ross, E. (1969). *On death and dying.* New York, NY: Scribner

Kurzweil, R. (2003). *The Ray Kurzweil Reader: A collection of essays.* Retrieved April 2013 from http://www.kurzweilai.net/pdf/RayKurzweilReader.pdf

Kurzweil, R. (2006). The future of human-machine intelligence. *The Futurist,* March-April. Retrieved February, 2013 from http://www.kurzweilai.net/reinventing-humanity-the-future-of-human-machine-intelligence

Lapierre, Sylvie; Dubé, Micheline; Bouffard, Léandre; Alain, Michel. (2007) Addressing suicidal ideations through the realization of meaningful personal goals. *Crisis: The Journal of Crisis Intervention and Suicide Prevention, 28,* 16-25. Retrieved December, 2012 from APA PsycNET direct

Larsen, R.J. & Buss, D.M. (2005) *Personality psychology* 4th edition. Retrieved in November, 2012 from www.gobookee.org/personality-psychology-4th-edition-larsen-and-buss/

Larson, R., Mannell, R., & Zuzanek, J. (1986). Daily well-being of older adults with friends and family. Psychology and Aging, 1, 117-126. Retrieved March, 2012 from psycARTICLES database http://psycnet.apa.org/psycinfo/1986-26913-001

Latané, B. & Darley, J.M. (1970). *The unresponsive bystander: Why doesn't he help?* New York, NY: Appleton-Century-Crofts.

Lazarus, Clifford N. (2011). *Simple keys to effective communication: How to be a great communicator.* Published in Think well by the Lazarus institute. Retrieved in December, 2011 from

http://www.psychologytoday.com/blog/think-well/201107/
simple-keys-effective-communication

Ledbetter, A. M. Griffin, E.M. & Sparks, G. G. (2007). Forecasting
"friends forever": A longitudinal investigation of sustained closeness between best friends. *Personal Relationships*. *14*, 343–350.
Retrieved in September, 2012 from http://onlinelibrary.wiley.com/
doi/10.1111/j.1475-6811.2007.00158.x/abstract

Lerner, M. J. (1966). The unjust consequences of the need to believe
in a just world. Paper presented at the meeting of the American
Psychological Association, New York, September, 1966.

Löckenhoff, C. E. (2011). Age, time, and decision making: from proc-
essing speed to global time horizons. *Annals of the New York Academy
of Sciences*, *1235*, 44-56. Retrieved in October, 2013 from http://
onlinelibrary.wiley.com/doi/10.1111/j.1749-6632.2011.06209.x/
full

Lu, C., & Suen, J. (1995). Assessment approaches and cognitive styles.
Journal of Educational Measurement, *32*, 1 - 17. Retrieved in May,
2013 from http://www.personal.psu.edu/staff/t/x/txm4/paper1.
html

Lyttle, D., Spencer, D., & Perry, R. (1976). Satisfaction and self-esteem in
patients attending a juvenile amputee clinic. *Inter-clinic Information
Bulletin*, *XV*, 1-8.

Mallers, M. H. (2010). Childhood Memories of Father Have Lasting
Impact on Men's Ability to Handle Stress. Symposium: Social
relationships and well-being – A life span. San Diego APA conference. Retrieved from http://www.apa.org/news/press/
releases/2010/08/childhood-memories.aspx

Martin, Rod (2007) *The psychology of humor: An integrative approach.*
Burlington, MA: Elsevier Press. Retrieved from https://archive.
org/details/psychologyofhumo00martrich

Maslow, A. (1954) *Motivation and personality.* New York, NY: Harper & Row.

Mason, M.F., Brown, K., Mar, R.A. & Smallwood, J. (2013). Driver of discontent or escape vehicle: The affective consequences of mind wandering. *Frontiers in Psychology,* 4,1-12. Retrieved in August, 2013 from http://www.ncbi.nlm.nih.gov/pmc/articles/PMC3722495/

Mason, M.F., Norton, M.I., Van Horn, J.D., Wegner, D.M., Grafton, S.T., & Macrae, C.N. (2007). Wandering minds: the default network and stimulus-independent thought. *Science,19,* 393-395

Meier, L., Semmer, N., Elfering, A., & Jacobshagen, N. (2008). The double meaning of control: Three way interactions between internal resources, job control, and stressors at work. *Journal of Occupational Health Psychology, 13,* 244-258

Milgram, S. (1965). Some conditions of obedience and disobedience to authority. *Human Relations. 18,* 56-76

Milgram, S. (1974). *Obedience to authority.* New York, NY: Harper & Rowe

Morisano, D., Hirsh, J.B., Peterson, J.B., Pihl, R.O., & Shore,B.M. (2010). Setting, Elaborating, and Reflecting on Personal Goals Improves Academic Performance. *Journal of Applied Psychology. 95,* 255-264. Retrieved in January 2012 from http://www.selfauthoring.com/JAPcomplete.pdf

Musser, Terry. (1996) Individual differences: How field dependence-independence affects learners. Retrieved in May 2013 from http://www.personal.psu.edu/staff/t/x/txm4/paper1.html

Neuberg, S. L.; Newsom, J. T. (1993) Personal need for structure: Individual differences in the desire for simpler structure. *Journal of Personality and Social Psychology,* 65, 113-131. Retrieved April, 2013 from APAPsycNET http://psycnet.apa.org/psycinfo/1993-41321-001

Nolen-Hoeksema, S., Wisco, B.E., & Lyubomirsky, S. (2008) Rethinking Rumination. *Perspectives on Psychological Science*, 3, 400-424 Retrieved in August, 2013 from http://pps.sagepub.com/content/3/5/400.short

Noone, J. H., Stephens, C. & Alpass, F. M. (2010) Do men and women still differ in their retirement planning? Testing a theoretical model of gendered pathways to retirement preparation, *Research on Aging*, 32, 715-738.

Norton, L. W. (2010). Flexible leadership: An integrative perspective. *Consulting Psychology Journal: Practice and Research, Vol 62*, 143-150. Retrieved July, 2012 from PsycARTICLES database http://psycnet.apa.org/journals/cpb/62/2/143/

Oltman, P.K., Goodenough, D.R., Witkin, H.A., Freedman, N., & Friedman, F. (1975).

Psychological differentiation as a factor in conflict resolution. Journal of *Personality and Social Psychology*, 32, 730 - 736. Retrieved in May, 2013 from http://www.personal.psu.edu/staff/t/x/txm4/paper1.html

Oswold, Debra. (2003) Friends for life. The Psychologist. 16, 544-545. Retrieved in October, 2012 from http://www.thepsychologist.org.uk/archive/archive_home.cfm/volumeID_16-editionID_99-ArticleID_616-getfile_getPDF/thepsychologist%5Coct03rib.pdf

Ozer, Muammer. (2008). Personal and task-related moderators of leader-member exchange among software developers. *Journal of Applied Psychology*, 93, 1174-1182. Retrieved in November, 2012 from APA PsycNET Direct.

Pancer, S. M., Brown, S. D., Gregor, P. & Claxton-Oldfield, S. P. (1992) Causal attributions and the perception of political figures. *Canadian Journal of Behavioural Science/Revue canadienne des sciences du comportement, Vol 24*(3), 371-381. Retrieved from APApsycNET. http://psycnet.apa.org/psycinfo/1993-13342-001

Provine, Robert R. (2000) *Laughter: A scientific investigation.* New York, NY: Penguin Books.

Puccio, G.J. (2006). Creativity 101: An introduction to some Basic Concepts and the Field of Creativity Studies. Paper prepared for the Indo-US workshop on Design Engineering, Bangalore, India, January, 2006. Retrieved May 2012 from http://tsf.njit.edu/2006/fall/puccio-creativity-101.pdf

Putnam, Robert. (2000). Social Capital: Measurement and Consequences. Retrieved from http://www1.oecd.org/edu/innovation-education/1825848.pdf

Reuter, M, Weber, B., Fiebach, C.J., Elger, C., Montag, C. (2009). The biological basis of anger: associations with the gene coding for DARPP-32 (PPP1R1B) and with amygdala volume. *Behavioural Brain Research, 202,* 179-183. Retrieved in July 2013 from http://www.ncbi.nlm.nih.gov/pubmed/19463699

Riolli, L. & Savicki, V. Coping effectiveness and coping diversity under traumatic stress. *International Journal of Stress Management, Vol 17*

Roberts, R. D., & Kyllonen, P. C. (1999). Morningness–eveningness and intelligence. Early to bed, early to rise will likely make you anything but wise! *Personality and Individual Differences, 27,* 1123–1133. Retrieved in April 2012 from http://personal.lse.ac.uk/kanazawa/pdfs/paid2009.pdf

Rosenbaum, M., & Ben-Ari Smira, K. (1986). Cognitive and personality factors in the delay of gratification of hemodialysis patients. *Journal of Personality and Social Psychology, 51,* 357–364. Retrieved in October, 2013 from http://www.psychologie.uzh.ch/fachrichtungen/psypath/ForschungTools/Schwerpunkte/6_Forst_Dro_Mck_MotEm_2011.pdf

Rosengren, A., Wilhelmsen, L. & Orth-Gomer, K. (2003). Coronary disease in relation to social support and social class in Swedish men: A 15 year follow-up in the study of men born in 1933. *European*

Heart Journal, 25, 56-63. Retrieved in May, 2013 from http://eur-heartj.oxfordjournals.org/content/25/1/56.full.pdf

Rosenthal, R. (1974). *On the social psychology of the self-fulfilling prophecy: Further evidence for Pygmalion effects and their mediating mechanisms.* New York, NY. MSS Modular Publications

Rosenthal, R. & Jacobson, L.F. (1968) *Pygmalion in the classroom: Teacher expectations and intellectual development.* New York, NY: Holt

Rotter, J. (1966). Generalized expectancies for internal versus external control of reinforcement. *Psychological Monographs. 80,* 1-28.

Ryan, R.M. & Deci, E. L. (2002). Overview of self-determination theory: An organismic dialectical perspective. In R. M. Ryan & E. L. Deci (Eds.), *Handbook of self-determination research.* Rochester, N.Y.: The University of Rochester Press. Retrieved from http://researchnotes.maksl.com/index.php?title=Ryan,_R._M.,_%26_Deci,_E._L._%282002%29._Overview_of_self-determination_theory:_An_organismic_dialectical_perspective._In_R._M._Ryan_%26_E._L._Deci_%28Eds.%29,_Handbook_of_self-determination_research._Rochester,_N.Y.:_The_University_of_Rochester_Press.

Salmon, P (2001). Effects of Physical Exercise on Anxiety, Depression and Sensitivity to Stress - A Unifying Theory. *Clinical Psychology Review, 21,* 33-61. Retrieved in March 2013 from https://ulib.derby.ac.uk/ecdu/courseres/dbs/currissu/salmon_p.pdf

Saylor, M. (2012) *The mobile wave: How mobile intelligence will change everything.* Boston, MA: Da Capo Press.

Schimelpfening, Nancy (2011). Depression and grief. Retrieved at About.com in May 2013 from http://depression.about.com/od/grief/a/griefdepression.htm

Schmitt, Neal (2008) The interaction of neuroticism and gender and its impact on self-efficacy and performance. *Human Performance,*

21:49–61. Retrieved May 2013 from http://iopsych.msu.edu/cbstudy/HP_2008_Schmitt.pdf

Schwartz, Shalom H.; Rubel, Tammy. (2005) Sex differences in value priorities: Cross-cultural and multi-method studies. *Journal of Personality and Social Psychology, 89,* 1010-1028. Retrieved June 2012 from APAPsycNET http://psycnet.apa.org/psycinfo/2005-16185-013

Scott, S., Carper, T. M., Middleton, M., Whitea, R.,Renka, K., & Grills-Taquechel, A. (2010). Relationships among locus of control, coping behaviors, and levels of worry following exposure to hurricanes. *Journal of Loss and Trauma: International Perspectives on Stress & Coping, 15.* Retrieved on August , 2013 from http://www.tandfon-line.com/doi/abs/10.1080/15325020902925985#.UznSklc87S4

Scott, E., Rumination And How It Affects Your Life (2013). Retrieved in October, 2013 from About.com http://stress.about.com/od/psychologicalconditions/a/rumination.htm

Seeman, M., & Evans, J. W. (1962). Alienation and learning in a hospital settings. *American Sociological Review, 27,* 772-783.

Seligman, M.E.P. (1975). *Helplessness: On depression, development, and death.* San Francisco, CA: Freeman.

Seligman, M.E., Steen, T.A., Park, N., & Peterson, C. (2005) Positive psychology progress: empirical validation of interventions. *American Psychologist, 60:* 410-21. Retrieved November, 2012 from http://happierhuman.com/positive-psychology-progress-2005-seligman-m-p-steen-t-a-park-n-peterson-c/

Seligman, M.E. (2005). *Flourish: A Visionary new understanding of happiness and well-being.* New York, NY: Free Press.

Selye, H. (1956). *The stress of life.* New York, NY, US: McGraw-Hill. Retrieved fromhttp://en.wikipedia.org/wiki/General_adaptation_syndrome#General_adaptation_syndrome

Smith, P. K., Wigboldus, D. H. J., & Dijksterhuis, A. (2008). Abstract thinking increases one's sense of power. *Journal of Experimental Social Psychology, 44*, 378-385. Retrieved in March 2012 from http://rady.ucsd.edu/faculty/directory/smith/

Smith, T.W., Uchino B.N., Berg C.A. & Florsheim P. (2012) Marital discord and coronary artery disease: a comparison of behaviorally defined discrete groups. *Journal of consulting clinical psychology, 80.* 87-92. Retrieved September, 2013 from http://www.ncbi.nlm.nih. gov/pubmed/22182260

Spencer, C. Doug (1978). Two types of role playing: Threats to internal and external validity. *American Psychologist, 33*, 265-268

Steel, P. (2007). The nature of procrastination: A meta-analytic and theoretical review of quintessential self-regulatory failure. Psychological Bulletin, 133, 65–94.Retrieved in August 2012 from http://studie-metro.au.dk/fileadmin/www.studiemetro.au.dk/Procrastination_2. pdf

Steel P. (2011). *The procrastination equation. How to stop putting things off and getting stuff done.* New York, NY: HarperCollins Publishers

Streufert, S.; Swezey, R.W. (1986). Complexity, managers, and organizations. New York, NY: Academic Press. Retrieved from http:// faculty.css.edu/dswenson/web/Cogcompx.htm

Tajfel, H., & Turner, J. C. (1979). An intergrative theory of intergroup conflict. In W. G. Austin & S. Worchel (Eds.), *The Social Psychology of Intergroup Relations* (pp. 33 – 47). Monterey, CA: Brooks/Cole. Retrieved in November, 2012 from http://dtserv3.compsy.uni-jena. de/__C12579E500316406.nsf/0/916B517AB58093DDC12579 E6002805C4/$FILE/Tajfel%20&%20Turner%201979.pdf

Thompson, L. (1995). They saw a negotiation: Partisanship and involvement. *Journal of Personality and Social Psychology, 68*, 839–853. Retrieved April 2013 from http://psych.colorado.edu/~vanboven/ VanBoven/Publications_files/van-boven-etal-2012-jpsp.pdf

Thompson, M. M., Naccarato, M. E. & Parker,K. E. "Assessing Cognitive Need: The Development of the Personal Need for Structure and the Personal fear of Invalidity Scales," Paper presented at the Annual meeting of the Canadian Psychological Association, Halifax, Nova Scotia (1989). Retrieved at http://highered.mcgraw-hill.com/ sites/0070876940/student_view0/chapter3/activity_3_5.html

Thompson, Sonya (2006) Adolescent Access to Sexually Explicit Media Content in Alberta: A Human Ecological Investigation. Retrieved March 2013 from http://www.eurekalert.org/pub_ releases/2007-02/uoa-oit022307.php

Van Boven, L, Judd, C. M. & Sherman, D.K. (2012). Political polarization projection: social projection of partisan attitude extremity and attitudinal processes. *Journal of Personality and Social Psychology, 103*, 84-100. Retrieved April 2013 from http://psych.colorado. edu/~vanboven/VanBoven/Publications_files/van-boven-etal-2012-jpsp.pdf

Vollmer, C. & Randler, C. (2012). Circadian preferences and personality values: Morning types prefer social values, evening types prefer individual values. *Personality and Individual Differences 52*, 738-743. Retrieved in May 2012 from http://www.scopus. com/record/display.url?eid=2-s2.0-84856968988&origin=in ward&txGid=D7648ED903D3A870AEA216BAD524735A. N5T5nM1aaTEF8rE6yKCR3A%3a7

Waite, S., Evans, J., Rogers, S. Simmons, B. & Spalding, N. (2011) Play-based Outdoor Learning: a Route to greater social cohesion? (Draft), Presented at AERA 2011: Inciting the Social Imagination, New Orleans, 8-12 conference. Retrieved online.

Wang, Q, Bowling N.A., Eschleman, K.J. (2010). A meta-analytic examination of work and general locus of control. *Journal of Applied Psychology. 95*,761-8. Retrieved from http://www.ncbi.nlm.nih.gov/ pubmed/20604595

Weiss, A., Bates, T.C., & Luciano, M. (2008). Happiness is a personal(ity) thing: The genetics of personality and well-being in a representative sample. *Psychological Science, 19*, 205-210. Retrieved from http://midus.wisc.edu/findings/pdfs/383.pdf

Weisz, C. & Wood, L. F. (2005). Social identity support and friendship outcomes: A longitudinal study predicting who will be friends and best friends 4 years later. *Journal of Social and Personal Relationships, 22*, 416-432. Retrieved in November, 2012 from http://spr.sagepub.com/content/22/3/416.short

Wellman, H.M., Cross, D. & Watson J. (2001) Meta-analysis of theory-of-mind development: the truth about false belief. *Child Development. 72*, 655-84. Retrieved in October 2012 from http://www.ncbi.nlm.nih.gov/pubmed/11405571

Wilson, Timothy (2002). *Strangers to Ourselves: Discovering the Adaptive Unconscious.* Cambridge: Belknap Press.

Witkin, H.A. & Asch, S.E. (1948b) . Studies in space orientation III. Perception of the upright in the absence of a visual field. *Journal of Experimental Psychology. 38*, 603-614.

Witkin, H.A. & Goodenough, D.R. (1981) *Cognitve styles, essence, and origins: Field dependence and field independence.* Madison, CT: International Universities Press

Wright, Paul. (1982). *A theory of self and personal relationships.* Chapters 1-3. University of North Dakota. Retrieved in October 2012 from http://paulhwright.com/paulhwright/Book.pdf

Ylvisaker, Mark. (2006). Tutorial: Concrete vs abstract thinking. LEARNet.org. Retrieved in March 2012 from http://www.projectlearnet.org/tutorials/concrete_vs_abstract_thinking.html

Zajonc, Robert B. (1965) Social facilitation. *Science 149*, 269-274 Retrieved in June 2012 from http://www2.psych.ubc.ca/~schaller/Psyc591Readings/Zajonc1965.pdf

Zimbardo, P.G. (2007). *The Lucifer effect: Understanding how good people turn evil.* New York, NY: Random House.

Zimbardo, P.G. & Boyd, J. (2008). *The time paradox: The new psychology of time.* New York, NY: Free Press.

Zimbardo, P. & Duncan, N. (2012). *The demise of guys: why boys are struggling and what we can do about it.* (Kindle edition). Retrieved January, 2013 from http://www.amazon.com/The-Demise-Guys-Struggling-About-ebook/dp/B00850HTHO#reader_B00850HTHO

CPSIA information can be obtained at www.ICGtesting.com
Printed in the USA
LVOW11s0826141114

413577LV00003B/11/P

9 781460 229224